Business Result

Intermediate | Student's Book

John Hughes & Jon Naunton

Interactive Workbook material
by Alastair Lane & Chris Speck

D1207980

OXFORD
UNIVERSITY PRESS

Contents

VIDEO : This section of the unit has a video clip linked to the topic.

Welcome to *Business Result Intermediate*. In this book you'll find:
| 16 units | Practice files | Information files | Audio scripts |
| Interactive Workbook on DVD-ROM |

We hope you find this introduction useful, and that you enjoy using the course.

What's in a unit?

Starting point
- an introduction to the unit topic
- discussion questions

Working with words
- includes reading and listening based on themes from business and the world of work
- teaches important new words and phrases that you can use immediately in your work
- practises the new vocabulary in a realistic final activity

Business communication skills
- presents key expressions for exchanging information, attending meetings, presenting information, and socializing
- helps you express yourself more clearly in real work situations
- lets you choose which phrases to use from the *Key expressions* list in every unit

Practically speaking
- teaches really useful everyday phrases for small talk, telephoning and short conversations
- helps you sound more natural when you speak English

Language at work
- reviews key grammar from *Business communication skills*
- helps you communicate more accurately in real work situations
- lets you check your knowledge of grammar and practise it in the classroom
- if you need more explanation, refer to the language reference section in the *Practice file*

Case study / Activity
- each unit ends with an authentic case study or activity
- find out about situations related to the unit topic that affect real companies and organizations
- take part in a longer work-related activity with lots of opportunities to practise the language from the unit

Fast-track option

If time on your course is limited, *Business Result* has a unique fast-track option to use in class. For each unit, combine the *Business communication skills* section and the *Case study* or *Activity*. This creates a practical, highly communicative shorter course, enabling you to get the maximum benefit from your Business English studies – fast.

What's in the Practice file?

The *Practice file* is like a mini-workbook in the back of the *Student's Book*. It allows you to think about and practise important words, expressions, and grammar. It has written exercises on the key language from each unit, plus a language reference section with more detailed grammar explanations.

Use the *Practice file*
- in class to check your understanding
- after class for extra practice.

Follow the links to the *Practice file* in each unit.

>> For more information and exercises, go to **Practice file** 3 on page 106.

What's the *Interactive Workbook* on DVD-ROM?

The *Interactive Workbook* gives you practical tools to use immediately in your work by helping you to practise the language and skills from the *Student's Book*, and make them personal to you and your own work situation. It also helps you review and test your own progress.

Exercises and Tests
- review and practise key language with interactive exercises
- check your progress with unit tests

Glossary
- check the meaning of around 600 words and phrases
- personalize the vocabulary to your needs

Phrasebank
- listen to all the key expressions from the *Student's Book*
- learn phrases for exchanging information, meetings, presenting, socializing, telephoning, and travel
- create your own personal phrasebook

Email
- learn useful phrases for writing the most common work-related emails
- copy model emails to your out-box, or create your own

Listen again
- listen again to the *Student's Book* audio recordings, or download to your MP3 player

Video
- Watch a video clip related to a section in the unit. Every unit has a video clip which recycles and extends the language of the unit.
- Complete the interactive exercises while you watch the video clips
- This icon **VIDEO** shows you the section of the unit that the video relates to. Watch the video after you have completed the work in the *Student's Book*.

When you see this link, you can go to the *Interactive Workbook* for more practice.

(i) >> Interactive Workbook >>

Case studies with the Expert View from Cranfield School of Management

Each of the case studies in *Business Result Intermediate* is accompanied by an Expert View from Cranfield School of Management, one of Europe's leading management schools. It is part of Cranfield University, renowned for its high quality postgraduate teaching and research and its strong links to industry and business. The School of Management was established in 1967, and offers a range of MBA, Executive MBA, Executive Education, and Doctoral programmes.

For more information, visit: **www.som.cranfield.ac.uk/som**.

Your panel of experts is made up of faculty from Cranfield, plus successful businesspeople who are recent MBA graduates from Cranfield.

Cranfield UNIVERSITY
School of Management

1 Dr Martin Clarke, Programme Director, General Management Programme Group (see page 11)

2 Chris van der Hoven, Lecturer in Innovation (see page 17)

3 Cora Lynn Heimer-Rathbone, Programme Director, Centre for Customized Executive Development (see page 29)

4 Lynette Ryals, Professor of Strategic Sales and Account Management (see page 35)

5 Dr Michael Dickmann, Senior Lecturer, Director MSc International HRM (see page 41)

6 Eyal Ben Cohen, Managing Director, Verifile Limited, MBA alumnus (see page 47)

7 Raj Mulvadi, Full-time MBA graduate (see pages 53 and 95)

8 Manish Singh, Full-time MBA graduate (see pages 53 and 95)

9 Simone Taylor, Full-time MBA graduate (see pages 53 and 95)

10 David York, Full-time MBA graduate (see pages 53 and 95)

11 Richard Wilding, Professor of Supply Chain Risk Management (see page 59)

12 Simon Knox, Professor of Brand Marketing (see page 65)

13 Keith Goffin, Professor of Innovation and New Product Development (see page 77)

14 Dr Bob Lillis, Lecturer in Service Operations Management (see page 83)

15 Graham Clark, Senior Lecturer in Operations Management (see page 89)

16 David Molian, Bettany Centre for Entrepreneurial Performance & Economics (see page 101)

1 | Working life

Learning objectives in this unit
- Talking about your work and responsibilities
- Introducing yourself and others
- Expressing interest in conversations
- Using the present simple and frequency adverbs to talk about your job and routine activities

Case study
- Speed networking

Starting point

1 Which things in this list are the most / least important for you in a job?
- money
- job satisfaction and professional development
- free time
- recognition
- job security
- career opportunities and opportunities for promotion
- variety
- training

2 When you were a child, what job did you dream about doing? Why?

Working with words | Describing work

1 Ed Lu is an astronaut who spent six months on the International Space Station. Read what he says about working there. List the positive and negative points of his job.

A job among the stars

Working on the ISS (International Space Station) is every astronaut's dream. Life on board may sound glamorous to some people, but conditions can be uncomfortable and we have a demanding schedule – we work ten-hour days and have one and a half days off – although when you live in your office, it's hard to separate on-duty and off-duty.

Our tasks are quite varied – we do a range of different scientific experiments – but we also have to perform routine maintenance and regular safety checks, like cleaning the air filter and inspecting our emergency equipment. We exercise twice a day – if you don't, your muscles just disappear in the weightless conditions.

Life is never dull, but you can feel lonely up here, away from friends and family. The work can also be stressful, so in my free time I relax by writing and answering emails. I also love taking photos of the views from up here. It's fun to watch stars as they rise through the atmosphere.

2 01, 02 ▷ **When Ingrid was a child she wanted to become a doctor. Mansour's ambition was to be a pilot. Listen and find out**
1 what they do now
2 what they like / dislike about their work.

3 How near are they to their childhood dreams?

4 Work with a partner. Match the words from the list to definitions 1–11.

fun   varied   challenging   routine   depressing   stressful
glamorous   worthwhile   rewarding   dull   demanding

1 a good thing to do: _____
2 boring: _____
3 needing all our effort and attention: _____
4 difficult in a satisfying way: _____
5 lively and enjoyable: _____
6 looks attractive from the outside: _____
7 predictable, the same every day: _____
8 makes us feel unhappy: _____
9 different, not always the same: _____
10 makes us feel worried or anxious: _____
11 makes us feel good: _____

▶▶ For more exercises, go to **Practice file 1** on page 102.

5 Work with a partner. Describe these jobs using words from **4**.

> **Example:** *Being a teacher is quite a challenging job because you have to teach large groups of people who have different abilities. It's also very rewarding.*

6 Work with a partner or in small groups. Describe your own job using words from **4**.

Socializing | Introductions and saying what you do

1 An NGO is a non-governmental organization. Amnesty International and the Fairtrade Foundation are two well-known NGOs. Can you think of any others?

2 03▷ The Culham Health Trust is an NGO based in New York. It has invited its key personnel, sponsors, and fundraisers to its headquarters to mark its 20th anniversary. Listen to these two conversations. Which is more formal? How do you know?

3 03▷ Listen again and write notes in this table.

	Job and responsibilities
Luc Akele	
Jo Johansson	
Walter Mayer	

4 Put phrases a–h below into categories 1–3. Then decide which are more formal and which are less formal.
  1 Introducing yourself: _____
  2 Introducing someone else: _____
  3 Responding to an introduction: _____

  a I want you to meet …
  b This is …
  c I'm delighted to meet you.
  d I'm very pleased to meet you too.
  e I don't think we've met. I'm …
  f Nice to meet you.
  g I would / I'd like to introduce you to …
  h My name's …

5 04▷ Listen and complete these sentences.
  1 Well, I _____ fund applications.
  2 Well, I'm _____ our sub-Saharan Africa operations.
  3 I _____ projects and make sure that the money is well spent.
  4 I'm _____ their medical donations programme.
  5 I _____ all the inter-governmental work.
  6 It _____ a lot of negotiation.

>> For more exercises, go to **Practice file 1** on page 102.

Tip | actually

Use *actually* to mean *in fact*, not *at the moment*, or *right now*. It's a polite way to correct or contradict someone.
  A Which part of the States are you from?
  *B **Actually**, I'm from Ontario, in Canada.*

6 Work with a partner. Choose a job from **A**, but don't tell your partner which one. Describe the job's responsibilities using words from **B** and phrases from **5**. Your partner must guess the job.

> *Example:* **A** *This person deals with customers and is responsible for responding to complaints.*
> **B** *Is he / she an after-sales assistant?*

A

sales rep

marketing director

administrator

website designer

finance controller

human resources manager

lab technician

team leader

after-sales assistant

B

budget

personnel

customers

paperwork

targets

travel

product development

projects

training

recruitment

publicity

complaints

money

machinery

7 Work in groups of three. Each person chooses a job from **6**.
1 Student A, introduce yourself to Student B, and then introduce Student C to Student B. Find out about each other's jobs and responsibilities.
2 Change roles and use your own jobs and responsibilities. Work together and find out as much as you can about each other.

> (i) » Interactive Workbook » **Email**

Practically speaking | How to express interest

1 Which of these phrases is *not* a direct response to something someone has just said?
1 Really?
2 A recruitment consultant?
3 That sounds …
4 So tell me, …
5 Oh right.

2 Complete this conversation with phrases from **1** above.
A I'm a recruitment consultant.
B 1_____
A Yes. I oversee recruitment for ten of our key accounts.
B 2_____ really demanding.
A It can be at times. 3_____ what exactly does your job involve?
B Well, I'm responsible for the department's spending.
A 4_____ Do you enjoy your job?
B I love it. It's great to be in a such a position of responsibility.
A 5_____ I think I'd find it stressful.

3 05▷ Listen and compare your answers from **2** above.

4 Work with a partner. Tell each other some information about your job. Respond with phrases from **2** and try to continue the conversation.

> *Example:* **A** *I work twelve hours a day.*
> **B** *Twelve hours a day? What do you do?*

Key expressions

Introducing yourself
Hello. / Hi. I'm …
Hello. / Hi. My name's …
I don't think we've met. I'm …

Introducing other people
This is …
I want you to meet …
I'd like to introduce you to …

Exchanging greetings
Nice to meet you.
I'm very pleased to meet you.
I'm delighted to meet you.

Saying what you do
I deal with …
I handle …
I oversee …
I'm in charge of (+ noun / *-ing*) …
I'm responsible for (+ noun / *-ing*) …
My job involves (+ noun / *-ing*) …

> (i) » Interactive Workbook
> » **Phrasebank**

Unit 1 | Working life

Tip | *right* and *really*

In the UK, *really* and *right* can mean the same thing. They can both show that you are interested in what someone is saying.
> **A** *I do a lot of work in China.*
> **B** *Right. / Really?*

In the US, *right* confirms that what someone has said is correct.
> **A** *So, you work twelve hours a day?*
> **B** *Right – four days a week.*

Language at work | Present simple review | Frequency adverbs

1 **Read this conversation. Why are the verbs in bold in the present simple?**

    Hitoshi Dr Mayer, this is Véronique Denvir. She **works** for Medicine on the Move. It's a small medical NGO.

    Dr Mayer Pleased to meet you, Ms Denvir. So, which countries does your organization deal with? Do you work in Nigeria?

    Véronique No, we mainly **focus** on Angola. We regularly **visit** villages and set up temporary clinics.

    Dr Mayer And who funds your projects?

    Véronique Mostly the general public, but we also get some government grants.

    Dr Mayer Oh, that's interesting. Can I ask who your medical supplier is?

2 **Which of the questions a–d below from 1**

  1 can only be answered *yes* or *no*? _____

  2 require information in the answer? _____

  3 is / are indirect? _____

  4 doesn't / don't use an auxiliary verb? _____ Why is this?

  a So, which countries does your organization deal with?

  b Do you work in Nigeria?

  c And who funds your projects?

  d Can I ask who your medical supplier is?

    » For more information and exercises, go to **Practice file 1** on page 103.

3 **Work with a partner. Ask and answer questions about your jobs. Think about the hours you work, the distance from home, your tasks / responsibilities, and your colleagues / partners.**

4 **Now work with a different partner. Ask your new partner questions about his / her first partner. Start each question with *Do you know …?***

    *Example: Do you know **where** Johann **works**?*

5 **Frequency adverbs say how often we do something. Complete this scale with frequency adverbs from the list.**

    ~~never~~   usually   rarely   sometimes   often   ~~always~~   occasionally

    0% ●————————————————————————————● 100%

    never 1 _____ 2 _____ 3 _____ 4 _____ 5 _____ _always_

    » For more information and exercises, go to **Practice file 1** on page 103.

6 **Match adverbs from 5 to the phrases in *italics* in 1–5.**

  1 I work late *once in a while*, if I have a lot of work to finish. _____

  2 My colleagues seem to be stressed *all the time*. _____

  3 *I hardly ever* use the phone – I prefer to use email. _____

  4 *From time to time* I go on a trip abroad if my boss can't go. _____

  5 We *don't often* meet socially – maybe two or three times a year. _____

7 **Work with a partner. Ask and answer questions about how often you do these things. Try to keep the conversation going as long as possible.**

- travel for work
- work at the weekend
- have meetings with your boss
- eat lunch at your desk
- deal with clients
- socialize with your colleagues

    Example: **A** ***How often do you*** *travel for work?*
                 B ***Once in a while****. Every few months, I guess.*

    ⓘ **»** Interactive Workbook **»** Exercises and Tests

Speed networking

Background

Need more good contacts?
Contact25 thinks it has the answer

Networking is increasingly important for individuals and companies who want to succeed in the world of international business. Contact25 organizes business-to-business speed networking events. At these events, participants have a series of mini-meetings with new contacts. The idea is that within a few minutes of talking to someone, they will know whether it is possible to do business with them. This makes it a very efficient form of business networking – by meeting lots of people, you have more chance of meeting ideal contacts for your business.

How does it work? Each meeting lasts

5 minutes. You have:
- 2 minutes to talk about your company / organization
- 2 minutes to talk about your partner's company / organization
- 30 seconds to score your partner, and note down future action
- 30 seconds to move on to the next meeting.

Speed networking is proving to be a good solution for many businesses who simply want to get results. Contact25 estimates that each attendee creates €5,000 worth of new business per event. So it seems that speed networking is simple, effective, and generates results.

The Expert View

Networking is important not only for generating business. In today's more complex and inter-related organizations, networking is also an essential management skill. Personal relationships are a source of information and power – the better the quality of your network, the more 'social capital' you have. Contacts outside your organization and industry give you an external perspective that enables innovation. A wide range of relationships inside your organization provides you with opportunities to build support and develop your ideas.

Dr Martin Clarke, Programme Director, General Management Programme Group
Cranfield School of Management

Unit 1 | Working life

Discussion

1 Why is networking important?

2 What are the advantages and disadvantages of speed networking?

3 Contact25 is thinking of going international. How could they make international speed networking possible?

Task

1 You are going to participate in a speed networking event. Be yourself or choose a profile from File 01 on page 135. Make a note of your name, what you do, the name of your company / organization, what it does, and your personal and professional reasons for attending the event.

2 Work in small groups. Follow the rules of speed networking. Try to make as many useful contacts as possible and make a good impression on the people you meet. For each meeting
- introduce yourself, say what you do, and who you represent
- explain what the company / organization you represent does and why you are at this event
- listen to your partner do the same as above and take notes
- give your partner a score from 1 to 3 based on the following three statements
   'I would never want to work with this person.' = 1 point
   'I might want to work with them but I need to find out more about them.' = 2 points
   'I'm definitely interested in working with this person and will follow this up immediately.' = 3 points
- note what you are going to do next with your contact.

3 Tell the group who your most useful contact was, and what follow-up action you will take.

Case study

11

2 | Projects

Learning objectives in this unit
- Talking about projects
- Updating and delegating tasks in a meeting
- Starting and ending phone calls
- Talking about your work and current activities using the present simple and continuous

Case study
- Planning a launch party

Starting point

1 What makes a project successful?

2 Do you prefer to lead a project or just be part of the project team? Why?

3 Do you like being involved in long-term projects?

Working with words | Projects

1 **Read this article and answer questions 1–4.**
   1 What is volunteerism?
   2 What sorts of things can employee volunteers do?
   3 Who benefits from volunteering and how?
   4 What has Samira Khan learnt from her project?

A commitment to volunteerism

What does volunteerism mean?
The clothing manufacturer, Timberland, is one of many large companies that are committed to volunteerism. The company encourages staff to spend up to 40 paid hours a year on community and social projects. The community benefits from the company's **resources**, staff gain new skills and **teamwork** improves.

The French food manufacturer, Danone, allows its employees to spend time in developing countries, working on projects in areas like conservation, teaching, caring, or building. In doing so, they can share their own **skills**, and at the same time, they gain new ideas and insights, and learn from the experiences of others.

A team from the banking group, HBOS, volunteered to help build an extension to a school in La Esperanza in Honduras. Linda Marshall, the project leader, said, 'I learnt that when new teams are forming, it is essential that **objectives** are agreed and everyone buys into them. This is a crucial factor to any project's success.'

What can volunteering do for you?
Software engineer, Samira Khan, is in charge of a volunteer project to redecorate a community centre for the elderly in Chicago. Managing a project is a new experience for her. She is learning how to organize a **schedule** so that they are able to complete the project before its **deadline**. She also has to deal with the **budget**, which is fairly limited, so she has to spend carefully. And every few days, she gets **updates** from her project team to check on progress and decide if they need more resources. She finds working on this project very rewarding and is pleased to be learning new skills.

2 Label these items with the words in **bold** from the text in **1**.

1 _____

It was agreed that Jonas will
- look at ways of cutting spending
- talk to the bank about a loan
- aim to balance the books in 6 months.

2 _____

Sunhills community project

Completed: wiring and plumbing
Ongoing: plastering and tiling
Still to do: decorating and
            furnishing

3 _____

June

5 June: complete decorating
6 June: safety checks
10 June: official opening

4 _____

Venue:	€2,000
Catering:	€4,000
Transport:	€350
Total:	**€6,350**

5 _____

- Accomplished in bookkeeping.
- Knows how to operate a variety of computer software.
- Speaks English and Spanish.

6 _____

7 _____

8 _____

3 06▷ Samira is telling someone about the volunteer project that she is working on. Listen to these extracts from the conversation and answer questions 1–2.

1 Which items in **2** does she talk about?
2 What does she say about each one?

4 06▷ Listen again and complete the phrases that Samira uses in column A. Then work with a partner. Take turns to cover column A while your partner tests you using the definitions in column B.

> *Example:* **A** *How can you say 'finish on time'?*
> **B** *'Meet the deadline'?*
> **A** *Yes.*

A		B
1 _____ the deadline	=	finish on time
2 fall _____ schedule	=	make slow progress
3 catch _____	=	get back to the original schedule
4 be back _____ track	=	work to the predicted schedule
5 finish _____ schedule	=	finish before the planned date
6 _____ resources	=	make use of people, money, time
7 stay _____ budget	=	spend the right amount of money
8 _____ tasks	=	give people different responsibilities
9 get _____ a task	=	do a job
10 _____ updates	=	receive reports on progress

5 Work in small groups. A colleague has been asked to take over running a project for someone who is off sick. He / she has never managed a project alone. He / she has asked you for advice about how to manage the project and the project team. Discuss what advice you will give him / her. Then tell the class.

> *Example:* *He / she needs a realistic schedule to meet the deadline.*

>> For more exercises, go to **Practice file 2** on page 104.

ⓘ >> Interactive Workbook >> Glossary

Tip | *in time* and *on time*

In time means having enough time to be able to do something.
> *If we leave now, we'll be there **in time** for the meeting.*

On time means at the correct time.
> *I have to be at work at 9 a.m. and I always arrive **on time**. I'm never late, but I don't like to be early either.*

Meetings | Updating and delegating tasks

TO DO:

Call Samira Khan (community centre)

Check re:

– deadline – can they meet it?

– decorating?

– lighting?

– carpets?

– action?

1 07▷ Jamie Ortega oversees several volunteer projects in the Chicago area. He is calling Samira Khan to ask about the progress of the community centre project she is **working on**. Listen to their conversation and makes notes on Jamie's notepad.

2 07▷ **Listen again and complete these phrases.**

1 How _____ over there?

2 Well, so far _____.

3 Everything's _____.

4 So what's _____ the decorating?

5 We're _____ the ceiling …

6 And where _____ the lighting?

7 We've _____ …

8 So, _____, the painting's nearly done, …

9 So it's all going according _____.

3 Put the phrases from **2** into these categories.

a Asking for an update: _____

b Giving an update: _____

c Summarizing: _____

4 Work with a partner. Look at this schedule for an office move. Ask and answer questions about the project using phrases from **2**.

> *Example:* ***A*** *What's happening with the headed stationery?*
> ***B*** *We've ordered it.*

Office move progress update 11/05

Task	Deadline	Date finished
Order headed stationery	10/05	09/05
Order new furniture	10/05	10/05
Send new address cards to clients	11/05	To do
Issue staff with new badges	11/05	10/05
Pack up paperwork	15/05	ongoing

5 08▷ **Listen to this meeting between Samira, Jamie, and team members, Josie and Bruno. Who agrees to**

1 meet the carpet suppliers? _____

2 buy the paint? _____

3 paint the ceiling? _____

Tip | Dates

Dates are written differently in the US and the UK. In British English the day comes before the month. In American English the month comes before the day.

the tenth of May = *10/05* (British English); *05/10* (American English)

6 08▷ Listen again. Mark 1–10: *A* (allocating a task), *O* (offering / agreeing to do a task), *D* (declining to do a task), or *S* (summarizing).

1 We need somebody to be here then to open up. _____

2 Can you do it? _____

3 Leave it with me. _____

4 I can go there this afternoon if you want. _____

5 Why don't I go there now? _____

6 I'd prefer not to if that's OK. _____

7 I'll come with you, then. _____

8 You can carry on with the rest of this paint. _____

9 I'm sorry, I have an appointment. _____

10 So, you two are going to get the paint … _____

>> For more exercises, go to **Practice file 2** on page 104.

7 Work with a partner. Some students are visiting your company and you need to: book a room for the talk (task 1), get name badges (task 2), organize refreshments (task 3). Have a conversation using this flow chart.

| **A** Ask B to do task 1. |
| **B** Agree, and ask A to do task 2. |
| **A** Decline and give a reason. |
| **B** Offer to do task 2. |
| **A** Offer to do task 3. |
| **B** Recap. |

8 Work with a partner. Two project update meetings took place yesterday. Student A, turn to File 03 on page 136. Student B, use the information below.

Student B: You went to the Project 2 meeting. Your partner went to the Project 1 meeting. Your partner will call you. Tell him / her about Project 2, then find out what is happening with Project 1. These are the things you need to know.

Project 1 – organizing a training day for staff
- Venue for training session?
- Hotel for trainers?
- Lunch?
- Information pack for trainees?
- Other?

Project 2 – raising money for a local children's charity
- Posters and leaflets – printing now
- 10 km sponsored run – need to contact council about using municipal ground
- Charity sale – all staff have received a memo
- Need someone to organize collection boxes

ⓘ >> Interactive Workbook >> **Email**

Practically speaking | How to start and end phone calls

1 Complete phrases a–f below. Which ones can you use to

1 start a call? _____   2 end a call? _____

a I'm returning your _____.   c _____'s (name) here.   e What can I _____ for you?

b Thanks _____ your help.   d _____ for calling.   f I'm _____ about / for / to …

2 Work with a partner. Have three phone calls using phrases from **1**.
- You want to know the time of a meeting tomorrow.
- You want an expenses authorization form.
- You are calling someone back with information about your holiday dates.

Key expressions

Asking for an update
How are things going?
What's happening with …?
Where are we with …?

Giving an update
So far so good.
Everything's on track.
We're (+ -ing) …
We've finished / completed …, etc.

Allocating a task
Can you …?
You can …
I / We need somebody / you to …

Offering to do something
Why don't I …?
I'll …
I can … if you want.
Leave it with me.

Declining to do something
I'm sorry, I can't.
I'm afraid I'm busy.
I'd prefer not to (if that's OK).

Summarizing
So, to recap …
X is / am / are going to …
It's all going according to plan.

ⓘ >> Interactive Workbook
>> **Phrasebank**

Language at work | Present simple and continuous

1 Look at the verbs in **bold** in these two sentences. Which tenses are used and why?
  1 I'm **calling** for an update.
  2 I **get** updates from people every two days.

2 Read these two questions. Are they talking about now or in general? Why do they use different tenses?
  1 What's happening with the decorating?
  2 What else do we need to do at the moment?

3 Complete these rules with *simple* or *continuous*.
  1 Use the present _____ to talk about general facts or regular actions.
  2 Use the present _____ to talk about a current action or temporary project.
  3 Some verbs are not used in the present _____ when they are talking about states, not actions. For example: *understand, like, know, believe, mean, need.*

4 Choose the correct answer from the words in *italics*.
  1 What *is he doing / does he do* in my office?
  2 He *fixes / is fixing* your computer.
  3 He *is knowing / knows* what is wrong with it now.
  4 He *repairs / is repairing* computers every day – that's his job.

  ≫ For more information and exercises, go to **Practice file 2** on page 105.

5 Work with a partner. Ask and answer questions using these prompts.
  1 what / you / work on / this week?
  2 you / like / travelling?
  3 how often / you / work late?
  4 you / have / any problems at work / at the moment?
  5 who / you / talk to / right now?
  6 how many people / be / in your English class today?
  7 what / you / think / at the moment?
  8 you / understand / the word 'deadline'?

6 Write notes on the notepad below about some current events or activities in your life.
  1 Give a mini presentation to the class using your notes.
  2 Listen to other members of the class and prepare two questions on their presentations.

Training or education:

Planning a holiday:

My work:

My free time:

Ways of practising my English:

Other:

ⓘ ≫ Interactive Workbook ≫ **Exercises and Tests**

Planning a launch party

Background

The sustainable dance club

Enviu is an international organization which helps young people develop profitable business ideas that have a positive effect on the environment and the local community.

Enviu is working in partnership with the architectural firm Döll on an exciting new project – a sustainable dance club in the city of Rotterdam.

The club will have a low impact on the environment, recycle energy, and raise awareness among young people of social and environmental issues.

Enviu and Döll are cooperating with the Technical University of Delft and the Development Board of Rotterdam. Around 80 volunteers, mostly students and young professionals, are working on the project. They're helping to construct and equip the club ready for the launch party in a few weeks' time.

The Expert View

The project planning process should ensure that the work (scope) can be done within the deadlines (time) and budget (cost), and to the right specification (quality). These four elements (variables) are inter-related, and together make up the project baseline. If one of them changes – for example a reduction in time or budget, or an increase in scope – then the others need to be adjusted to keep the baseline business benefit. A good project manager is able to judge what the trade-off is if one of the variables changes. This requires clear thinking during planning, and careful tracking during the execution of the project.

Chris van der Hoven, Lecturer in Innovation
Cranfield School of Management

Discussion

1 In what ways are nightclubs environmentally unfriendly?

2 How could you make one more environmentally friendly?

3 09 ▷ Listen to one of the volunteers talking about the project. Compare what she says with your answers to 1 and 2 above.

Task

1 You are part of the project team planning to open a sustainable club in your city or town. The project is nearly complete and you are now planning the launch party which will take place in one month. Read about the key tasks that need to be done in this table.

The venue	The launch party	Publicity
Finalize installation of electrical equipment	Confirm all DJs and special events	Print leaflets and posters
Finish the decoration	Confirm orders with food and drink suppliers	Start distributing leaflets and posters, send out invitations
Equip the relaxation zone	Receive delivery from food and drink suppliers	Update the website
Install kitchens and toilets	Hire and train staff	Organize a radio advertisement

2 The project team has divided into groups, A, B, and C. Each group has different responsibilities. Read the information for your group. Group A, turn to File 04 on page 136. Group B, turn to File 11 on page 138. Group C, turn to File 20 on page 140.

3 When you have read your information, hold a meeting to discuss the key tasks. Make sure you know at the end of the meeting exactly what needs to be done, who will do it, and when.

- Update the other members of the project team.
- Make a note of the tasks that are complete and of all the tasks that still have to be done.
- Discuss as a team how you will proceed.
- Allocate tasks and create a schedule for completing them.

Case study

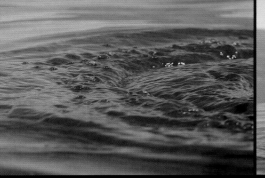

3 | Leisure time

Starting point

1 What is 'work-life balance'?

2 Why should employers care about work-life balance?

3 Is there a 'long-hours' working culture in your country?

Working with words | Work-life balance

1 Read this article and answer questions 1–3.
1 Do you work similar hours to Todd Einck in his old job or his new job?
2 What does Todd tell his employees? Do you think he is right?
3 Could you do the same at your workplace? Why / Why not?

No more late nights

After working fifteen-hour days for most of his career, Todd Einck, 42, left his sales job and started JLT Mobile Computers. He wanted to create an organization where he could control his schedule and have time for his wife and young children. Nowadays, Todd leaves work by 5.10 p.m. almost every evening and he tells his fifteen employees to do the same. Working at the weekend or taking assignments home is also not allowed.

2 This is a quiz about your work-life balance.
1 Complete the quiz. Then add up your scores and turn to File 02 on page 135.
2 Do you agree with your results?

Find out your work-life balance

Write *2* if the statement is true for you, *1* if it's mostly true and *0* if it's not true.

1 I have plenty of time for outside interests and hobbies. ☐

2 I occasionally do overtime if it is paid. ☐

3 I work flexitime or am able to organize my work and home life around each other. ☐

4 I leave my 'to do' list on my desk and rarely work from home. ☐

5 I regularly relax by doing exercise or socializing with friends. ☐

6 I regularly play sports in order to make useful work contacts. ☐

7 I take all my paid leave every year and go on holiday. ☐

3 **10▷** Work with a partner. Listen to this conversation between two colleagues, Nina and Florin. Student A, listen to Nina. Which parts of the quiz can you answer for her? Student B, listen to Florin. Which parts of the quiz can you answer for him? Now compare Nina and Florin's work-life balance. Who do you think has a better work-life balance?

4 Match these verbs from the quiz in **2** and audio **10▷** to the words in 1–4.

take   make   do   work

1 _____ exercise / work / overtime
2 _____ me somewhere / some holiday / paid leave / time off
3 _____ late / from home / flexitime
4 _____ time / useful contacts / progress

5 Work with a partner. Talk about the following using words from **4**.
- a typical week (***Example:*** *I regularly work from home* …)
- this week or last week (***Example:*** *I made a lot of progress last week* …)
- your holidays this year (***Example:*** *I'd like to take three weeks* …)
- the company policy on overtime (***Example:*** *We do three hours extra* …)

6 Work with a partner. Use adjectives from the list to describe the activities in the pictures.

exciting   boring   relaxing   exhilarating   tiring
interesting   frightening   enjoyable   hard work

7 Work with a partner. Take turns to describe what you do outside work and why.
Example: *I cook a lot because it's relaxing and interesting to create new dishes.*

8 **11▷** A lot of adjectives in **6** can have an *-ing* ending or an *-ed* ending. Listen again. Which ending do you hear? Which form of the adjective describes how a person feels?
1 I got home at about midnight. I'm really *tired / tiring*.
2 I'm taking the kids camping tomorrow. They're so *excited / exciting*.
3 I made dinner and watched a *bored / boring* documentary about plants.

▶▶ For more exercises, go to **Practice file 3** on page 106.

9 Work with a partner. Say what you are
- interested in
- tired of
- excited about
- bored with
- exhilarated by
- frightened of.

10 What's your ideal balance of work and leisure time? Think about the following. Then work with a partner. Take turns to describe the current situation in each area, how you might like to change things, and how this would make you feel.
- hours worked in the week
- hours in the office
- type of job
- activities outside work
- number of weeks' holiday per year
- types of holiday

ⓘ ▶▶ Interactive Workbook ▶▶ **Glossary**

Unit 3 | Leisure time

Tip | *really* and *so*

Use *really* or *so* to add emphasis.
 I'm **really** excited.
 I'm **so** tired.
 I **really** like cycling.
 It's **so** exhilarating.
Note that when you use *really* with the negative form you can say either of the following
 1 I **really don't** like cycling.
 2 I **don't really** like cycling.
The position of *really* in 1 adds greater emphasis. The speaker in 1 dislikes cycling more than the speaker in 2.

Exchanging information | Talking about leisure | Exchanging contact details

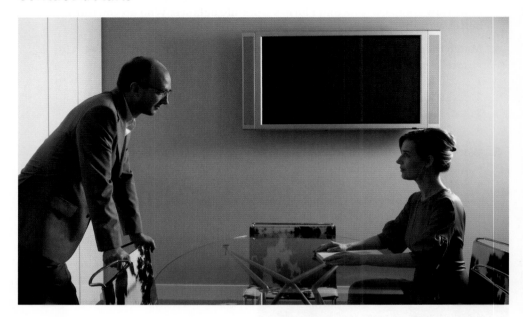

1 12▷ Mirella Lyrio from Brazil is on a three-month work placement at a Swedish company. It is the end of her first week and she meets her line manager, Leif Gunnarsson. Listen and complete her notes.

> Department in week 1: _____
>
> Department in week 2: _____
>
> Travel to: _____
>
> Weekend plans: _____
>
> Need to buy: _____

2 12▷ Listen again and complete these questions. Can you remember Mirella's answers to Leif's questions? Listen again and check if necessary.
1 _____ working in (HR)?
2 _____ your first time in (Europe)?
3 _____ things do you like doing?
4 _____ the accommodation?
5 _____ the family?

3 Work with a partner. You are both working abroad on a six-month work placement / contract. Decide what country and department you are in. Then take turns to ask and answer the questions in **2**. Change the information in brackets.

4 12▷ Match the phrases from the list to the words in *italics* in 1–4. Then listen again and check your answers.

isn't keen on   isn't crazy about   's interested in   's fond of

1 She *wants to know more about* Human Resources. _____
2 He *really likes and cares about* Brazil. _____
3 She *is not enthusiastic or excited about* shopping. _____
4 She *doesn't really like* museums. _____

Tip | *like* + *-ing* or the infinitive
You can use the infinitive or the *-ing* form after the verb *like*. In British English *like* + *-ing* is normally used to talk about enjoyment and leisure activities. *Like* + the infinitive is used for choices and habits. In American English, *like* + the infinitive is normally used for both.
*Do you **like reading** novels?* / *I **like to relax** at the weekend.* (British English)
*Do you **like to read** novels?* (American English)

5 Work with a partner. Talk about things you like or dislike and about your interests using this table.

Example: I'm really interested in marketing.

I'm (not)	(really)	interested in fond of keen on crazy about	area of work, e.g. computers. city / country, e.g. Paris. subject, e.g. mathematics. activity, e.g. cooking. sport, e.g. golf. friends.

6 13▷ Listen to the rest of Mirella's conversation with Leif and complete her notes. How does Mirella check her spelling?

Extension no.: _____

_____ for an outside line.

Company no.: _____

Email: _____

7 Write down two telephone numbers and two email addresses.
1 Tell your partner your email addresses and telephone numbers.
2 Listen to your partner's email addresses and telephone numbers and write them down.
3 Check you both got them right.

>> For more exercises, go to **Practice file 3** on page 106.

8 Work with a partner. Read the information for Student A and Student B below and plan what questions you might ask or what you might say about the following.
- accommodation
- work responsibilities
- free time and interests

Student A: You are on a placement at a new company. It is the end of your first week.

Student B: Your partner is on a placement at your company. Check that he / she is happy with everything.

Have the conversation and exchange contact details for the weekend.

ⓘ >> Interactive Workbook >> Email

Practically speaking | How to end a conversation

1 Which of these expressions signal the end of a conversation?
1 Anyway, I'd better get on.
2 I need to go now, I'm afraid.
3 I'll get back to him in a minute.
4 I should get back to work.

2 14▷ Listen to the ends of three conversations and check your answers in 1.

3 14▷ Listen again. How do the people respond to the phrases you chose in 1?

4 Work in small groups. Have conversations on the following subjects. End the conversations politely before starting the next one with a different person.
- what you did yesterday evening
- a problem you're having at work
- a phone call to check on the time of a meeting

Key expressions

Talking about leisure and interests
Do you like playing tennis / to relax in the evening?
Is this your office / favourite restaurant?
What sort of music do you like / things do you like doing?
How is your hotel / often do you play?
How do you find our country / your job?

Talking about likes and dislikes
I like / really like / love (+ -ing / to … / noun)
I don't like / hate (+ -ing / to … / noun)
I enjoy / don't enjoy (+ -ing)…
I'm (not) interested in / keen on / fond of / crazy about (+ -ing / noun)

Saying telephone numbers
00 = double zero / zero zero / double oh (British English)
Say telephone numbers in groups of three or four: 096 … 745 … 6745

Saying email addresses
/ (forward) slash
. dot
_ underscore
– dash
@ at
lower case / UPPER CASE

Checking spelling
S for sugar
E for egg
P for Paris, etc.

ⓘ >> Interactive Workbook
>> Phrasebank

Language at work | Past simple and present perfect

1 Work with a partner. Think of questions for these answers. Compare your ideas with the rest of the class.

Good, thanks.

Yes, I did. It was fascinating.

Yes, a couple of times.

No, I haven't.

2 15▷ It is Monday morning. Mirella Lyrio is waiting for her manager, Leif, outside his office. Listen for the answers in **1**. What were the questions?

3 15▷ Listen again. Decide if these sentences are true (*T*) or false (*F*). How do you know which sentences are false? Discuss your ideas with a partner.
1 Mirella waited for Leif and then left. ____
2 She went to the museum on Saturday. ____
3 Leif went there a couple of times on Saturday. ____
4 Miriam has never met Mirella. ____
5 Miriam has organized a desk for Mirella and it's ready for her to use. ____
6 We don't know when Leif played tennis. ____
7 Before the weekend, we don't know when Leif last played tennis. ____

4 Match sentences a–d below to meanings 1–4.
1 Talking about a finished action that took place at a specified time: ____
2 Asking about an action / event – the speaker doesn't say / know / ask when it took place: ____
3 Talking about a very recent action / event: ____
4 Asking about an action / event – the speaker asks / knows when the event took place: ____

a I**'ve** just **organized** a desk for you to work from.
b **Did** you **go** to the museum on Saturday?
c Leif **played** tennis at the weekend.
d **Have** you **met** Mirella?

5 Complete these sentences with *since* or *for*.
1 I haven't played tennis _____ ages. = _____ + a period (days, months, years)
2 I haven't seen you _____ January. = _____ + a specific time (day, date, year)

6 Work with a partner. Choose the correct answer from the words in *italics*.
1 I *booked / have booked* the hotel yesterday.
2 *Have you ever been / Did you ever go* to India?
3 I live in London now, but I *have lived / lived* in Paris from 2000 to 2002.
4 I *haven't seen / didn't see* him recently.
5 Last year I *have changed / changed* jobs.
6 *Did you go / have you been* to the meeting last week?
7 He has worked here *since / for* eight years.
8 She has been the CEO *since / for* December 2005.

>> For more information and exercises, go to **Practice file 3** on page 107.

7 Work with a partner. Ask and answer questions about the following. Start the questions with the word in *italics*.
- your present job / company (*How long have …?*)
- date you joined (*When did you …?*)
- previous job (*What was …?*)
- education (*Where did you …?*)
- travel (*Have you ever been …?*)
- people (*Have you met …?*)
- other subjects (*I still haven't asked you about …*)

Tip | Conversations

The present perfect is often used to start conversations. Speakers often use the past simple to continue the conversation and ask for / give more details.

A *Have* you *been* to Brazil?
B *Yes I have.*
A *When* *did* you *go*?
B *I went two years ago.*

ⓘ >> Interactive Workbook >> **Exercises and Tests**

Corridor conversations

Work in small groups. Each player places a counter on 'Start'. Take turns to roll a dice and move to another square.

Green squares – ask all the players a question using the phrase.
Blue squares – move to the nearest square another player is on and speak to that player.
Pink squares – a player talks to one other player.
Purple squares – follow the instructions.
The player who lands on 'End' first is the winner.

Start	Move to another player's square. Ask him / her about last night.	*Have you met …?*	**End**
Do you like …?	Move to another player's square. Say hello and ask a question.	Ask another player what he / she thinks of Mexican food.	Check the spelling of another player's name.
You make a useful contact. Have another go.	Move to another player's square. Ask him / her a question about his / her leisure time.	Where did you go when you last went abroad? Move to join a player who has also been there.	Work some unpaid overtime. Miss TWO goes.
Check another player's telephone number.	Take a day off. Miss a go.	*(…) did you …?*	Ask another player what he / she thinks of football.
How do you find …?	*What sort of …?*	Check another player's email address.	Move to another player's square. Talk to him / her about last weekend then end the conversation politely.

Activity

23

4 | Services & systems

Learning objectives in this unit
- Talking about services and systems
- Explaining how something works
- Introducing information
- Making comparisons

Case study
- Improving systems

Starting point

1 **What services do you use regularly?**

2 **What do you like about them?**

3 **What makes services good or bad?**

Working with words | Service

1 **Read these website reviews.**

1 Which of the extracts is about a website for
- Lloyds TSB (a bank)?
- The Guardian (a newspaper)?
- Expedia.com (an online travel agency)?

2 Would you be interested in these services? Why / why not?

a Instead of continuously visiting websites to see if there are new articles and updates, you can have them delivered directly to you. Its user-friendly service gives you access to all the most up-to-date and accurate news and information on the web.

b This service is free and gives you immediate access to your accounts when it's convenient for you. The system also protects your personal financial information and ensures that you stay secure.

c This system is really time-saving and efficient, because consumers can combine multiple flights, hotel bookings, car rentals, and local activities all from just one website. Users can customize their bookings to fit their needs and there are many discounts and special prices, so it's really cost-effective.

2 **16 ▷ Listen to three speakers. Which website in 1 would they be interested in?**

3 <u>Underline</u> the adjectives in the reviews in **1** that would attract the three speakers.

4 Work with a partner. Which of the adjectives you underlined in the texts in **1** might describe these services? Do you use services like these?

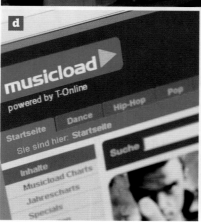

5 17 ▷ Listen to four people talking about a service from **4**.
1 Which service is each person talking about?
2 How does the service make their life easier or what does it allow them to do?

6 Work with a partner. Make sentences using the words in this table.
   Example: *Search engines allow people to find relevant websites.*

Search engines	help	me	infinitive
Telecommunication companies	allow	you	(with *to* …)
	make it easier for	organizations	
Financial advisers		companies	
Call centres		people	
Consultants	let	the world	verb (without *to* …)
Legal services			

▶▶ For more exercises, go to **Practice file 4** on page 108.

7 Make a list of the type of services your company offers or services you often use. They might be financial, travel, legal, or medical. Tell your partner about the benefits of these services.
   Example: *My financial adviser helps me to plan my future.*
   Booking tickets online is really efficient and more cost-effective than using a travel agent.

ⓘ ▶▶ Interactive Workbook ▶▶ Glossary

Tip | *let*
The verb *let* is followed by a noun and then a verb without *to*.
Don't say:
~~Online banking lets me to manage my account from home.~~
Do say:
*Online banking **lets me manage** my account from home.*

Presenting | Explaining how something works | Comparing new with old

1 Why do companies need databases? What sort of information do they keep? Do you use a database? If you do, is the system easy to use?

2 18▷ A hotel chain has a new customer database for all its hotels. It is being presented to the hotel manager and her staff for the first time. Listen and answer questions 1–5.

  1 What was one of the disadvantages with the old database?
  2 When can they use the new database?
  3 How is it similar to the old database?
  4 What is new about it?
  5 What does the hotel manager suggest is a problem with the new system?

3 18▷ Match 1–8 below to a–h to make pairs of phrases. Then listen again and check your answers.

  1 The good news is …, _____
  2 It might seem a bit difficult to use at first …, _____
  3 It looks very similar to …, _____
  4 As soon as you …, _____
  5 In other words, as well as (-ing) …, _____
  6 The more …, _____
  7 On the one hand …, _____
  8 One downside is …, _____

  a but what's different is …
  b it also …
  c but the bad news is …
  d but on the other hand …
  e but in fact it's very simple.
  f the (better) …
  g but on the plus side …
  h it starts to …

4 Put the phrases in 3 into these categories.
  a Comparing and contrasting: _____
  b Describing what something does or how it works: _____

▶▶ For more exercises, go to **Practice file 4** on page 108.

5 Work with a partner. Imagine your company has some new software for storing customer information. Make sentences using some of the phrases from **3** and these prompts.

Example: *The good news is we have new software, but the bad news is we need six months' training.*

1 new software + need six months' training
2 press this button + look for the customer's name
3 the old system + the quantity of information it can store
4 storing basic information + finds more information
5 information you get + easier it is to target customers
6 the system is more complicated + it is faster

6 Work with a partner. Compare the functionality of the objects, systems, or services in 1–3. Make a list of the benefits and drawbacks of each of the more recent objects / systems.

Example: *Compared to CD players, MP3 players store more songs, are smaller, and more expensive.*

1 CD players   MP3 players
2 filing cabinets   folder storage systems on PCs
3 going into a bank   using an online bank

7 Now work with a different partner. Take turns to talk about the functionality of 1–3.

Example: *On the one hand, the MP3 player is expensive, but on the other hand, it can store thousands of songs.*

8 Think of something that has recently changed at work. Tell your partner about the benefits and drawbacks of the change. It might be a change to

- working hours / breaks
- how supplies are ordered
- measuring customer satisfaction.

ⓘ ≫ Interactive Workbook ≫ **Email**

Practically speaking | How to introduce information

1 19 ▷ **Listen to 1–5. Notice the stressed words in bold and the pauses (/) after the introductory phrases.**

1 As you **know**, / we have a new customer database.
2 So the **purpose** of today / is for you to start to become familiar with it.
3 As I **say**, / the good news is …
4 **Now**, / up on the screen you can see …
5 In **other** words, / as well as giving the customer more of what they want …

2 Match the sentences in **1** to functions a–e.

a Repeating something you have already said: ____
b Explaining a feature in a different way: ____
c Giving information that is already common knowledge: ____
d Explaining what is going to happen: ____
e Introducing a new item: ____

3 Give a one-minute presentation to your partner about how an object in your classroom or office works. For example, the CD player or the answering machine. Try to use all five of the introductory phrases from **1** in your presentation.

Key expressions

Explaining how something works
Let me explain how it works.
One / the main thing to note is …
What happens is …
Basically, …
It's a bit like …
You can see what happens when you …
As soon as you …, it starts to …

Explaining additional features and benefits
One other useful feature is that …
As well as (+ noun / -ing) …, it also …
The more …, the better (the) …

Asking questions about functionality
Will it let me … (+ verb)?
Will it allow me … (+ infinitive)?
How does it know what to do?
What happens when …?

Comparing
On the one hand …, but on the other hand …
The good news is …, but the bad news is …
Whereas before …, we now …
It looks very similar to …, but what's different is …
It might seem …, but in fact it's …
One downside is …, but on the plus side …
One benefit is that …, though a drawback might be …

ⓘ ≫ Interactive Workbook ≫ **Phrasebank**

Language at work | Comparative forms

1 A hotel manager has received these comments from staff on using the new customer database. Complete their comments with the correct form of the adjectives in brackets.

1 ❛It takes a little _____ (long) to learn how to use it.❜

2 ❛When customers call, it's slightly _____ (easy) to find their information.❜

3 ❛It's definitely not as _____ (slow) as the old system was.❜

4 ❛Even the customers seem to be noticing the differences. They are far _____ (positive).❜

5 ❛In general, I think it's a great deal _____ (good).❜

2 Read the comments in **1** again. For each comment, decide if the improvement of the new database is big or small or if there is no improvement.

3 Correct the mistakes in this dialogue about a new office.
1 **A** This office is more noisier than the last one.
2 **B** Yeah, but at least it's not as darker as the old one.
3 **A** That's true. I just wish it was biger.
4 **B** It's much convenienter for teamwork though.
5 **A** Yes, but it's much more worse for concentration.
6 **B** I think it's as good than the last office, but in different ways.
7 **A** Well, you've always been more tolerant that me.

4 Decide if these intensifiers indicate a big (*B*) or small (*S*) difference.

slightly ____   a great deal ____   nearly as … as ____   not anything like as … as ____
a little ____   significantly ____   far more ____   much less ____   marginally ____
not nearly … as ____   a lot ____

▶▶ For more information and exercises, go to **Practice file 4** on page 109.

5 Work with a partner. Your local supermarket has changed its layout and updated its website. Take turns to ask and answer questions from this customer feedback form using the adjectives in brackets. Circle *0*, *1*, *2*, or *3* to show your partner's opinion.

> *Example:* **A** *What do you think of the choice of goods?*
> **B** *The choice is slightly **wider** than before.* (Student A circles ② on the form.)

Feedback form

Level of improvement (0 = got worse, 1 = none, 2 = some, 3 = big):

What do you think of the choice of goods? (wide)	0	1	2	3
How easy is it to find items? (easy)	0	1	2	3
What do you think of the wait at the checkout? (long / short)	0	1	2	3
What do you think of the café and children's area? (good / bad)	0	1	2	3
What do you think of the website? (user-friendly)	0	1	2	3

6 Work with a partner. Compare your present job with your last job. Choose your own adjectives or use some from the list to talk about the areas below.

friendly   long   stressful   challenging   helpful   modern
convenient   fast   comfortable   difficult   interesting

- your colleagues
- your office / work place
- your responsibilities
- your working hours
- your journey to work

ⓘ ▶▶ Interactive Workbook ▶▶ **Exercises and Tests**

Improving systems

Background

Travelling responsibly at Nike HQ

When Nike World Headquarters relocated to a suburb outside Portland, Oregon in the USA, the management decided to save money by building fewer car parking spaces at the new site. At this time, 98% of Nike's employees drove alone to work, and there were too many cars for the number of parking spaces.

Management soon realized they needed to encourage fewer people to drive to work alone. They started an incentive-based programme – employees who shared car journeys, cycled to work or used public transport received money towards their travel costs, or vouchers that they could spend in the cafeterias at work and at Nike stores. It was a popular programme, but it was expensive and difficult to monitor. They then introduced a new system called TRAC – Travelling Responsibly? Accept the Challenge. TRAC gave employees information about public transport, cycling routes, and car-sharing and offered monthly prizes to employees. The company also started to pay 72% of the cost of bus and rail passes.

The percentage of employees driving alone to work is now 78%. However, the company would like to reduce this figure still further.

Discussion

1 **What are the advantages of not driving to work for**
   1 the employees?   2 the company?   3 the local community?

2 **What could the company do to reduce the number of employees driving alone to work even further?**

3 **What alternative means of transport would you consider using to get to work? Give your reasons.**

Task

1 **Work with a partner. You both work for a large manufacturing company. The commuting situation at your company needs to improve. Read this information.**
   - Your company employs 30% more people than it did two years ago. As a result there are too few parking spaces and it is unable to get more space for employees' cars.
   - Traffic in the area is getting worse and employees travelling by car are often stuck in traffic jams and arrive at work late, feeling very stressed.

2 **Hold a meeting with your partner. Take turns to report some recent relevant data. Make notes as you listen. Student A, turn to File 05 on page 136. Student B, turn to File 12 on page 138.**

3 **Make a list of ways to improve the situation. Will you need to change the system of parking? Can you change the working hours? Perhaps you can encourage alternative means of transport for employees.**

4 **Present your ideas to the class. Explain how the new system will work and explain its benefits compared to the current situation. Your audience may want to ask you questions about how it will work.**

The Expert View

Why change?
If staff are dissatisfied (D) with the current situation, and if there's a vision (V) for improvement and a clear process (P), then the cost of not changing (C) is more than the cost of changing (DxVxP>C). Change is resisted if dissatisfaction, vision and / or process don't exist.

What 'change process'?
Try a typical four-stage process: 1 awareness of the need for change, 2 interest in the process, 3 willingness to try the changes, 4 acceptance. Different stages need different tactics, but the 'platinum rule' is – do for other people what they would do for themselves!

Cora Lynn Heimer-Rathbone, Programme Director, Centre for Customized Executive Development
Cranfield School of Management

Case study

5 | Customers

Learning objectives in this unit

- Talking about customer service
- Getting information
- Making and changing arrangements
- Starting a conversation on the phone
- Using the present simple and continuous to talk about the future
- Managing customer feedback

Case study

- Managing customer feedback

Starting point

1 Who does your company sell products or provide services to?

2 Which departments and employees in your company need your services or products to do their job?

3 Your answers to **1** are your *external customers*. Your answers to **2** are your *internal customers*. Compare your answers to **1** and **2** with a partner's answers.

Working with words | Customer service

1 Read this information. What does Technogym do? Who are its customers?

Technogym

Nerio Alessandri built his first fitness machine in his garage in 1983 and founded Technogym. The company is now a market leader in fitness and biomedical rehabilitation equipment. Its products have been chosen by over 30,000 fitness centres and 20,000 private homes worldwide. It was the official supplier at the Sydney 2000 and Athens 2004 Olympics and Paralympics, and at the Turin 2006 Winter Olympics.

2 Complete these sections of a website homepage with words from the list.

requirements   care   satisfaction   services   expectations

We're here to help
Whatever you require, our call centres are open to assist you with all issues concerning our products and ¹_____.

The design team
Our in-house design team assesses the proposed area of development to give the best layout of equipment. It then monitors every stage of the installation for complete ²_____.

After-sales
The After-Sales Service extranet site provides online ³_____ and support 24/7.

Technical support
Our technical support team ensures that the equipment is always in perfect working order and matches your ⁴_____.

Tailor-made courses
We tailor our courses to meet the specific ⁵_____ of our clients, with in-house training courses.

3 Which sections of the website in **2** should these customers click on?

1 " I want to download a copy of the instructions for your treadmill. "

2 " We're interested in having a small gym for employees in our office building but I don't think there's space for it. "

3 " Would it be possible to get some more information about your products? "

4 " I'd like all of my staff to understand how the machines work. "

5 " I can't seem to change the speed of the treadmill. "

4 Complete this table with words from **1** and **2**.

	Noun	Verb	Adjective
1	_____	serve	–
2	_____	satisfy	satisfied
3	_____	supply	supplied
4	_____	care	caring
5	_____	expect	expected
6	_____	require	required
7	_____	produce	–

5 Complete this text with the correct form of words from the table in **4**.

Customers always ¹ _____ a company to ² _____ them with top-quality goods and ³ _____ . They are ⁴ _____ if their ⁵ _____ are met. If their ⁶ _____ are not met, however, it is the role of the customer ⁷ _____ department to try to sort out any problems. If the customer receives efficient and helpful ⁸ _____ and feels that the company really ⁹ _____ about them, this will result in a happy customer who is more likely to buy the company's ¹⁰ _____ and services again.

6 Complete these questions with the correct form of words from the website sections in **2** to match the words in brackets.

1 What kind of customers do you _assist_ ? (help) What do they usually _____ ? (need)
2 How do you _____ their needs? (evaluate)
3 Is there a department at your company which continually _____ customer service? (checks)
4 What do you think is one way to _____ customer satisfaction? (guarantee)
5 Are you able to _____ 24-hour-a-day support to your customers? (give)
6 Is it important to be able to _____ your products or services? (adapt)

» For more exercises, go to **Practice file 5** on page 110.

7 Work with a partner. Ask and answer the questions in **6** using the words you found in the website sections in **2**.

8 Think of a service you know well. It could be your own company's product or service, or one you have recently bought or used. Present this product or service to the class, as if you are trying to promote it to them. Explain what makes it so good.

ⓘ » Interactive Workbook » Glossary

Tip | *customer, client, and consumer*
A *customer* is someone who buys a standard product or service.
A *client* is someone who buys an individually designed product or service, for example, financial advice.
Consumer is a general term to talk about any person who buys things, not a specific product or service.

31

Exchanging information | Getting information | Making and changing arrangements

1 20▷ Listen to this phone call between Elena Schenker, the facilities manager of a hotel chain, and Sergio Lanese, a Technogym representative. Complete Sergio's notes. What information does he ask for?

2 20▷ Listen again and complete these phrases for getting information.
1 I'd like to _____ your services ...
2 Can you _____ a little more?
3 We're _____ updating ...
4 Is that something you _____?
5 Would it be _____ someone to ...?

3 Work with a partner. Student A, you are a hotel facilities manager. Turn to File 06 on page 136. Student B, you are a sales representative for Technogym. Answer your partner's phone call and ask for the same information as in the notes in **1**. Then change roles. Student B, turn to File 14 on page 138. Student A, use the notes in **1**.

4 21▷ Listen to the end of Sergio and Elena's phone conversation and answer questions 1–3.
1 What do they arrange?
2 What is planned for the 30th?
3 What is planned for the 1st?

5 21▷ Listen again and complete these sentences.
1 Can we _____ a meeting then?
2 _____ about Tuesday the 31st?
3 I _____ the Wednesday.
4 The 1st of February? Yes, that _____ me.

6 Work with a partner. Take turns to answer the phone and make arrangements for the situations below. Use this flow chart and your own diaries if you want.

A Answer the phone.

B Suggest an arrangement.

A Agree and suggest two possible dates / times.

B State your preferred date / time.

A Agree and say goodbye.

- meeting to plan new website
- celebrating your birthday
- playing golf or tennis
- visiting your new company headquarters
- an anniversary dinner

Notepad:

2.15 p.m.

1 _____ ?
A chain of 4- and 5-star hotels in Switzerland.

2 _____ ?
Ten years old.

3 _____ ?
Eleven in total.

4 _____ ?
Not known.

Tip | make

Make has many uses. Here it means *to attend.*
   *I can't **make** the meeting. = I can't attend the meeting.*

7 22▷ **Sergio calls Elena again. Listen and answer questions 1–4.**

1 What is the main reason for his call?
2 What else do they talk about?
3 What can't Sergio make?
4 What do Sergio and Elena move back?

≫ For more exercises, go to **Practice file 5** on page 110.

8 **Read this sentence and then change the diary page below.**

❝ Fabio can't make the 27th, so we'll bring the meeting forward a day and move the tour back a day. ❞

9 **Repeat your calls in 6 but now you can't make the appointments. Change the arrangements to a new time. Use this flow chart and your own diaries if you want.**

A Answer the phone.

B Give your reason for calling. Apologize and explain. Suggest alternative dates / times.

A State your preferred date / time.

B Agree and say goodbye.

ⓘ ≫ Interactive Workbook ≫ **Email**

Practically speaking | Starting a conversation on the phone

1 23▷ **The first time we speak to someone on the phone we are usually quite formal. After that the calls may be more conversational. Match phrases 1–5 to responses a–e. Then listen to five conversations and check your answers.**

1 Sorry for calling so late. _____
2 How are things? _____
3 Is this a busy time for you? _____
4 What's the weather like? _____
5 Hello, Anna. This is James. _____

a No, I'm not too busy at the moment.
b It's really beautiful and clear.
c Everything's going fine, thanks.
d Hello. How are you?
e Don't worry – I don't usually finish before 7.00.

2 **Work with a partner. Start a phone call. Use phrases from 1 or your own conversational openers.**

Key expressions

Stating interest
I'd like to find out about …
We're interested in …

Asking for information
Can you tell me a little more …?
Is that something you deal with?
Would it be possible for …?

Suggesting arrangements
Can we fix / arrange a date for the meeting?
What / How about the 30th of January?

Stating a preference
I'd prefer the Tuesday.
Tuesday would be better.
The 31st is good for me
Thursday suits me.

Changing arrangements
Sorry, I can't make the Thursday.
I'm afraid I can't come on / make Thursday.
Can we move it back to Friday?
Can we bring it forward to Wednesday?
The afternoon is free / convenient.

ⓘ ≫ Interactive Workbook ≫ **Phrasebank**

Language at work | Present simple and continuous for future use

1 24▷ **Listen to these sentences. Choose the correct answer from the verbs in *italics*.**
1 We *come* / *'re coming* to Switzerland next month.
2 Customers often *comment* / *are commenting* on this.
3 I *call* / *'m calling* for some information.
4 My trip *begins* / *is beginning* on the 30th of January.

2 **Which sentences in 1 are about the future?**

3 **Which of the sentences you selected in 2 describes**
a an arrangement? ____   b a schedule / timetable? ____

4 **Complete these sentences with *simple* or *continuous*.**
1 Use the present _____ to talk about an arrangement for the future.
2 Use the present _____ to talk about a scheduled or timetabled event in the future.

>> For more information and exercises, go to **Practice file 5** on page 111.

5 **Complete this email with the present simple or present continuous form of the verbs in brackets.**

> Dear Elena
>
> I ¹_____ (write) to confirm that we ²_____ (meet) on Thursday at 2.00 p.m. My train ³_____ (arrive) at 12.30, so there shouldn't be any problems. One of our technicians ⁴_____ (come) with me. He's called Mario.
>
> We look forward to seeing you.
>
> Sergio

6 **Work with a partner. Look at the diary and make sentences in the present simple or present continuous using prompts 1–9.**

Example: *I'm going to a conference next week.*
                 *The conference **starts** on Tuesday.*

1 go / conference	4 conference / start	7 first session / start
2 have / team meeting	5 fly / Paris	8 flight / leave
3 have / lunch	6 speak / at conference	9 presentation / start

May

	a.m.	p.m.
6 Monday	10.00 Team meeting	
7 Tuesday	9.30 First session	—— CONFERENCE ——
8 Wednesday		—— CONFERENCE —— 14.00 My presentation
9 Thursday		—— CONFERENCE —— 12.30 Lunch with Sally and Remi
10 Friday	To Paris.	14.20 Flight from LHR.

Tip | Action and state verbs

Remember that some verbs (state verbs) are not used in the present continuous when they are talking about states, not actions. For example: *understand, like, know, believe, mean, need.*

ⓘ >> Interactive Workbook >> **Exercises and Tests**

Managing customer feedback

Background

Limewood Spa is an exclusive country house hotel and spa. It has a very good reputation, but recently it has received negative customer feedback on several websites.

Limewood Spa

Set in its own country garden, Limewood Spa believes in combining state-of-the-art facilities with natural therapies. Limewood Spa is unique in being able to offer long, quiet walks in its fifty-acre forest followed by vigorous exercise in the fitness centre. We assess your fitness on your first morning and tailor your programme. Our five-star restaurant is run by chefs specializing in healthy cooking.

Customer feedback

'This hotel is set in a most beautiful location. The problem was the restaurant. The service was poor and the food itself was expensive and not very good. When we mentioned this to the manager, she said that we were the only people complaining so things couldn't be that bad!'

'The room was very nice, and the setting is wonderful. It's a shame the staff aren't more helpful.'

'The hotel was very clean and you could see that the rooms had been refurbished recently. The health spa in the basement was of a really high standard. The main problem was that the staff didn't seem interested, and only really attended to our needs when we asked them.'

'We arrived in the restaurant at 9.34 (to be exact), only to be told that the kitchen closed at 9.30 and we were too late for dinner!'

Discussion

1 Based on the information in their brochure, what would you expect as a customer at Limewood Spa? Do you think they are living up to their good reputation? Why / why not?

2 Is it important to act on customer feedback? How much do customers' comments affect business?

3 How should Limewood Spa respond to the negative customer feedback?

Task

1 Limewood Spa needs to do something about the bad feedback it has received from some customers. The hotel manager has decided to contact a firm of business consultants for advice. Work with a partner. Student A, turn to File 07 on page 137. Student B, turn to File 13 on page 138. Read the information and follow the instructions.

2 You are now at the arranged meeting. Brainstorm some ideas for how the hotel can offer better customer service and guarantee customer satisfaction. Discuss your ideas and what you are going to do.

3 Present your ideas to the rest of the class.

The Expert View

In any business, it is a mistake to invest in facilities for customers without training staff in customer care. Success means building good relationships with customers, and good service means loyal customers. Poor customer service and poor maintenance of customer relations can mean long-term damage to an organization's reputation and, eventually, loss of profitability. Solutions include better staff training and rewards for good customer care, a commitment to maintaining good customer relations, and an effective system for responding to complaints and feedback.

Lynette Ryals, Professor of Strategic Sales and Account Management

Cranfield School of Management

Unit 5 | Customers

Case study

6 | Guests & visitors

Starting point

1 How often do you have business guests or visitors?

2 Why do they come to see you?

3 How do you entertain them (if at all)?

4 How often do you travel for work?

5 What do you think of the hospitality you receive when you travel for work?

6 How much free time do you have for sightseeing or enjoying yourself?

7 Do you prefer being the visitor or the host? Why?

Working with words | Business travel

1 Read this information from a recent survey of business travellers and answer questions 1–2.

1 Are most business travellers positive or negative about business travel?

2 How close are the views of the travellers in the survey to your own views?

Travelling for business – love it or hate it?

Most business travellers (87%) believe that technology such as email and 'virtual' meetings cannot replace face-to-face contact.

Over three-quarters of business travellers enjoy travelling for business (78%). Of these, 66% like the variety, 62% appreciate the opportunity to see the world, and 51% enjoy experiencing a new culture. But only 8% say it makes them feel important.

Of those who don't enjoy travelling for business – 58% find it tiring and stressful, 55% say it affects their personal life, 46% don't like being away from home, and 32% just find it boring. Almost a third of business travellers (30%) have experienced a cancellation, a missed flight, or a delay.

2 25, 26▷ Seville is an important destination for business travellers. It hosts many conferences and exhibitions. The local chamber of commerce is doing a survey at the airport to find out why business travellers come to Seville. Listen to two interviews and complete this table.

	Traveller 1	Traveller 2
Reason for visit		
Where they are staying		
Plans (professional / personal)		

3 25▷ **Listen again. Match the words from the list to definitions 1–10.**

conference   entertainment   exhibition   excursion   venue
facilities   hospitality   nightlife   sightseeing   speciality

1 visiting interesting buildings and places as a tourist: _____
2 a large meeting where people with the same work or interests come together: _____
3 the place where a conference or a big event is held: _____
4 space, equipment, and services provided (e.g. by a hotel): _____
5 friendly and welcoming behaviour to guests: _____
6 a type of food or product that a restaurant or place is famous for: _____
7 things to do in the evening (e.g. bars, restaurants, etc.): _____
8 somewhere you go to see different products or works of art: _____
9 a short, organized trip made for interest or pleasure: _____
10 activities which people do for fun and relaxation: _____

4 **Work with a partner. Cover up your answers in 3 and take turns to test each other with the definitions.**

5 26▷ **Listen again. Match a word from A to a word or phrase from B to make a new phrase. Then match each new phrase to pictures a–h.**

A	B
freshen	out
pick	around
look	(someone) off
check	up
meet	(someone) up
show	in
drop	up with
eat	(someone) around

➤➤ For more exercises, go to **Practice file 6** on page 112.

6 **Work with a partner. Two visitors are coming to speak at a conference in your nearest city. You have to look after both of them. Use the information below to create a plan for their visit. Decide what will happen (and when) from the time you pick them up from the airport. Use words and phrases from 3 and 5.**

	Visitor A	Visitor B
Arrival	Friday 16.30	Friday 10.30
Time of presentation	Saturday 9.30–11.00	Saturday 11.30–13.00
Departure	Saturday 16.30	Saturday 15.00
Preferences / requests	• wants to see conference venue and facilities on Friday • wants an early night on Friday • likes traditional food • wants to see the city	• needs one hour on Saturday to prepare / set up presentation • likes lively evening entertainment • wants to see the city • wants to go shopping

Tip | *travel, trip,* and *journey*

Travel is mainly used as a verb.
 *I like to **travel** by train.*
There are some exceptions:
business travel, travel arrangements, and *travel agents.*
Don't say:
 ~~Did you have a good travel?~~
Do say:
 *Did you have a good **journey** / **trip** / **flight**?*
Journey is the period spent travelling to your destination.
Trip is a short visit with a specific purpose (e.g. *a business trip*).

Socializing | Welcoming visitors

1 When someone comes to visit your place of work, what do you show them? Are there any areas which are 'off-limits' (private or secret)?

2 27▷ Jacinta Ross works for HYB Electronics. She meets Marvin Bernstein at reception. He is visiting the company for the day. Listen to their conversation and complete the agenda for Marvin's visit.

Agenda for Marvin Bernstein's visit to HYB Electronics
Monday 2 October

Morning:
Lunchtime:
Afternoon:

3 27▷ Listen again and complete these phrases that Jacinta uses.

1 _____ our new facility.
2 It's nice to _____ in person.
3 So, how was _____?
4 And did you have _____ finding us?
5 Here, _____ your coat.
6 Can I _____ a coffee?
7 OK. Come this way and I'll _____ today's programme.
8 So, first of all, I _____ join a tour of the facility this morning.
9 Then, _____ at lunchtime.
10 He's introducing the tour this morning, but _____ to meet up with him over lunch.
11 You'll need this ID card to get around the site. _____ you keep it on you at all times.
12 Yes, _____ that. I'll clear it with Facilities.

4 Work with a partner. Match these responses to phrases 1–8 in **3**.

a Likewise. ____
b Thank you. ____
c OK. ____
d That sounds interesting. ____
e Yes, please. Black, no sugar. ____
f I'll hang onto it, thanks. ____
g Not really, it was easy. ____
h It was fine, thanks. ____

5 Work with a partner. Have a conversation with a visitor to your place of work using this flow chart. Student A is the visitor and Student B is the host. When you have finished, change roles.

A Introduce yourself to B.	
	B Identify yourself and welcome A.
A Respond.	
	B Ask about A's journey.
A Respond.	
	B Offer tea, coffee, etc.
A Respond.	
	B Talk about schedule.
A Respond and ask to meet another colleague.	
	B Respond.

6 Work with a partner. Imagine you are welcoming a new person to the class today. Have a short conversation about their journey to the office / classroom and go through the schedule for the lesson.

7 28▷ It is the start of the tour. Listen to this welcome speech and answer questions 1–3.
   1 Who is Dilip Patel?
   2 How is the day organized?
   3 What piece of advice does Dilip give the visitors?

8 28▷ Dilip's speech is more formal than Jacinta's conversation with Marvin. Listen again and find formal equivalents to these phrases.
   1 Welcome to …: _____
   2 You'll get a chance to …: _____
   3 Remember …: _____
   4 Make sure you …: _____

>> For more exercises, go to **Practice file 6** on page 112.

9 Work in small groups. Prepare and give a short welcome speech to a group of first-time visitors to your place of work or study.

ⓘ >> Interactive Workbook >> **Email**

Key expressions

Welcoming
Welcome to …
It's nice to meet you in person.
Likewise.
Good morning. / Good afternoon.
On behalf of …
It gives me great pleasure to welcome you to …

Asking about a journey
How was your journey?
Did you have any trouble finding us?

Being hospitable
Can I get you a coffee?
Let me take your coat.
Have a seat.

Explaining the programme
Let me run through / go over today's programme.
First of all, I thought you could …
We'll catch up again later / at …
You will have the opportunity to …
You'll get a chance to …
We're going to begin with …

Giving extra information
Make sure you …
Please be sure to …
Don't worry about (+ noun / -ing) …
Can I remind you that …
For your own safety, …

Ending
Before I hand over to …
May I wish you all an enjoyable visit.

ⓘ >> Interactive Workbook
   >> Phrasebank

Practically speaking | How to make and respond to offers

1 Which of these offers are more / less formal?
   1 Would you like a drink?   3 Do you fancy a drink?
   2 Do you want a drink?   4 Can I get you a drink?

2 29▷ Complete these responses to the offers in **1** with words from the list. Then listen to six conversations and check your answers.

   would   sounds   fine   time   love   please

   1 No thanks, I'm _____.   4 A drink _____ good.
   2 That _____ be great, thanks.   5 I'd _____ one.
   3 Yes, _____. A coffee would be nice. 6 I'm afraid I don't have _____.

3 One of you is the host and the other is the guest. Decide if the guest is: your boss, a colleague, a visitor you haven't met before, or a regular visitor to your company. Offer your guest these things then change roles.
   • dinner this evening   • a quick tour of the plant   • lunch in the canteen

Tip | *catch up*

Catch up has several meanings.
Used with *with*, *catch up* means *see someone again*.
   We'll **catch up** (**with** each other) later.
Used with *on*, *catch up* means *to get back on schedule with work*.
   I'm working late this evening as I have a lot of work **to catch up on**.

Language at work | Obligation, necessity, and prohibition

1 30▷ **Aruna Singh is showing visitors around her company. Listen and answer questions 1–3.**

1 What happens in the clean room?
2 What is the biggest enemy?
3 What are the rules about
   a clothing?
   b jewellery?

2 30▷ **Listen again and complete this table.**

necessary	not necessary	against the rules
room is dust-free		

3 **Put sentences and questions a–h below into categories 1–6.**

1 Talking about a prohibition: _____
2 Talking about necessities / obligations: _____
3 Talking about an absence of obligation or necessity: _____
4 Asking if there is a prohibition: _____
5 Asking if something is necessary: _____
6 Talking about a rule that is not very strict: _____

a Everyone **has to** wear a special overall.
b **Do** we **have to** get undressed?
c No, you **don't need to** worry.
d You **don't have to** undress.
e You **mustn't** wear any natural fibres.
f You're **not supposed to** wear jewellery.
g We **need to** follow a very strict procedure.
h **Are** we **allowed to** go inside?

>> For more information and exercises, go to **Practice file 6** on page 113.

4 **Work with a partner. Finish these sentences so that they are true for you.**
- In my organization we have to …
- Luckily, we don't have to …
- At work we're not supposed to …
- Where I work no one is allowed to …
- If you work here, you mustn't …

5 **Work with a partner. One of you is welcoming a new colleague to your place of work. Tell him / her about the rules you have to follow. The other should ask questions about the rules. Talk about**
- taking breaks
- phone and Internet for private use
- identification and security
- health and safety
- what to do about receiving guests on site
- car parking
- leaving PCs on overnight
- any other rules you can think of.

ⓘ >> Interactive Workbook >> Exercises and Tests

Tip | Softening rules and regulations
Use *supposed to* to talk about a rule which is often broken, or to make the rule you give sound 'softer'.
*We're not **supposed to** eat or drink in the computer room, but often we're so busy that we have a sandwich while we're working.*

Solving an intercultural problem

Background

AKA telecommunications in India

AKA is a Swedish software technology and design company. They create products and services for the computer and telecommunications industries. Six months ago they started work on a major project with an Indian software developer based in Bangalore. A number of project managers from Sweden, some of them women, relocated to India to manage the different parts of the project. They are working with local managers, and software designers and engineers.

Since the Swedish managers arrived, things have not gone as well as AKA hoped. The standard of work is very high, but the project is behind schedule, and several important delivery dates have been missed. Also, the relationship between the Swedish managers and their Indian teams is getting worse. Meetings to review progress and make decisions are often very long, and the outcome is not always clear. There have also been some communication problems, even though everyone speaks 'good' English.

The Swedes now see their Indian colleagues as disorganized, inefficient and unwilling to take responsibility. The Indians think the Swedes are too informal and relaxed at work, don't say what they want, and are unable to make decisions.

Discussion

1 Make a list of the main problems. What are possible reasons for these problems?

2 How could management improve the situation?

3 If you were relocated to a different country to work on a joint venture, how would you prepare yourself?

4 Imagine someone from a different cultural background comes to work for your company for a year. How would you explain your work culture? Think about: dress code, hierarchy and status, attitudes towards time and deadlines, the working day, attitudes towards meetings and communications at work, etiquette / politeness (e.g. using first or last names).

Task

You and your partner work for two companies involved in a joint venture in the same situation as AKA and their Indian partner. Student A, you are the Human Resources Director of the Swedish company and Student B, you are the Human Resources Director of the Indian company. Try to find out the reasons for the problems with the joint project and work together to make some recommendations as to how the situation could be improved.

1 You have each received a number of complaints from your own employees about the current situation. Have a meeting to find out why things are going wrong. Student A, turn to File 10 on page 137. Student B, turn to File 17 on page 139. Make a list of the issues to resolve.

2 Work with your partner and discuss how to deal with each issue in 1.
   Example: We could ask the Swedish managers to send a memo out saying they would appreciate punctuality at meetings. / We could advise Swedish managers to get someone to call them once everyone has gathered for a meeting.

3 Work together. Look at the suggestions in File 15 on page 138. Discuss the pros and cons of each suggestion then choose one to recommend to the management of the joint venture (Swedish and Indian). Present your choice, giving reasons, to another group.

The Expert View

National culture is patterns of behaviour and attitudes that are learned and shared among a group. Problems between people from different cultures can occur because of their different responses to particular situations. For example, some cultures value personal relationships more than the rule of the law; others believe regulations must be obeyed, independent of friends or family. To deal with intercultural problems you need to understand your own culture, be sensitive to other people's behaviour and attitudes, and be interested in other people's viewpoints.

Dr Michael Dickmann, Senior Lecturer, Director MSc International HRM

Cranfield School of Management

Unit 6 | Guests & visitors

Case study

7 | Security

Starting point

1 **What security measures can / do you use to protect your home and possessions?**

2 **Which of these security measures do you use at work?**

3 **Why is security an important issue for companies?**

Working with words | Security at work

1 **Read these articles and answer questions 1–3.**
   1 In each article, what was the security breach?
   2 What was stolen in each case?
   3 Who were the victims of each theft?

Credit agency reports security breach

More than 1,400 Canadians have been notified of a major security breach at Equifax Canada Inc., a national consumer-credit reporting agency. According to reports, unauthorized access was gained to the personal, detailed credit files which contained social insurance numbers, bank account numbers, home addresses, and job descriptions. With identity theft in Canada rising in one year from 8,100 to 13,000 reported cases, the industry is once again asking how to safeguard databases against identity theft, and deter people from entering the system without passwords.

Burglar doing 'overtime'

Police arrested a man last week for stealing from his company's warehouse. Over a period of three months, the employee used his own security pass to open up the warehouse in the middle of the night and load a van in full view of security cameras. The boxes contained DVDs and CDs. When police questioned security staff who were paid to monitor for such activity, they said, 'We thought he was just doing overtime.' A member of staff finally reported the man when he saw him selling DVDs in a street market on a Saturday afternoon. The company has decided to review its security procedures.

2 Find words in the articles in **1** to put into these categories.

Security measures	Security breaches
password	

3 Work with a partner. Discuss questions 1–3.

1 Has there ever been a security breach at work? If so, what happened?
2 What do you need authorized access for at work?
3 Which members of staff are responsible for security? What do they monitor?

4 Find verbs in the articles in **1** to complete these verb + preposition phrases.

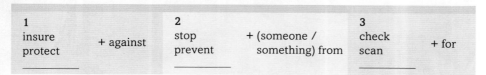

1 insure protect + against	**2** stop prevent + (someone / something) from	**3** check scan + for
_____	_____	_____

>> For more exercises, go to **Practice file 7** on page 114.

5 Look at these extracts from a credit card company information leaflet. Use a verb + preposition phrase from **4**. Then work with a partner and compare your answers.

1 You can _____ your card _____ loss for as little as €1 per month.

2 To _____ anyone else _____ getting your card by mistake, all cards are sent recorded delivery.

3 _____ the envelope _____ any signs that it might have been opened before you accept the delivery.

4 To _____ anyone else _____ using your card, make sure you sign it immediately.

5 To _____ _____ fraud, never write your PIN (Personal Identification Number) down – keep it in your head.

6 Make sure you _____ your monthly bank statement _____ any unauthorized use of your card.

6 Work with a partner. Take turns to choose one of the security measures below and describe what it's for, using a verb + preposition phrase from **4**. Your partner must guess what you are talking about.

- PIN number
- password
- burglar alarm
- X-ray machine
- security pass
- CCTV
- lock and key
- antivirus software

Example: **A** *We use it to safeguard against other people taking our money.*
B *Is it a PIN number?*
A *Yes.*

7 Work with a partner. Think about your answers in the Starting point. Tell your partner why those security measures are in place.

ⓘ >> Interactive Workbook >> Glossary

Tip | *safety* and *security*

Safety and *security* have different meanings. *Safety* is when someone / something is not in danger or at risk.

I am concerned about the ***safety*** *of the lifts in this building.*

Security means the activities involved in protecting a person / country / building, etc.

We need to introduce new ***security*** *measures to prevent thefts.*

Presenting | Explaining and asking about changes

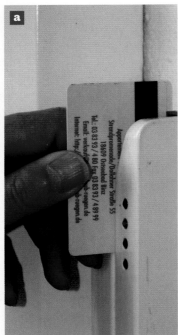
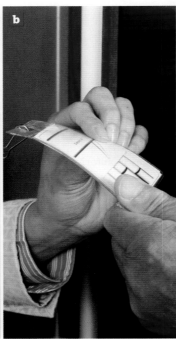

1 The pictures show some security measures for entering a building. What are the advantages and disadvantages of each?

2 31▷ Listen to two extracts from a meeting and answer questions 1–2.
1 What is the current security system? What is the new system?
2 What are the advantage and the disadvantage of the new system?

3 31▷ Match 1–12 to a–l. Then listen again and check your answers.
1 What I want to do today, … ____
2 I'll talk about … ____
3 As you know, we've recently … ____
4 Up to now, … ____
5 Because of this … ____
6 So, first, I'd like to update you … ____
7 As a result, … ____
8 What's the reason for … ____
9 It's because security … ____
10 Can you tell us … ____
11 Do you mean that … ____
12 The current situation, as it stands, … ____

a more about them?
b we've decided to upgrade the system.
c changing the current system?
d no one has stolen anything …
e been having a few problems …
f is to explain …
g on the plans for changes to …
h the background to the situation …
i we have to swipe every time …?
j can't always check …
k simply doesn't prevent …
l we've been installing …

4 Put the phrases in **3** into these categories.

a Introduce a talk: _____1_____

b Give background information: _____

c Ask for information / clarification / an explanation: _____

d Give an explanation / reason: _____

» For more exercises, go to **Practice file 7** on page 114.

5 Work with a partner. Student A, turn to File 08 on page 137. Student B, turn to File 18 on page 139. Make notes on the information in your email. Then take turns to give an update using this flow chart.

A Give background information and describe changes to the security system.

B Ask for an explanation.

A Give an explanation.

B Ask for further clarification / information about how the new system will work.

A Give more details about the new system.

6 Work with a partner or in small groups. Think of a situation at work that changed, either recently or in the past. Explain the original circumstances, what the change was, and the reasons for it. Be prepared to answer any questions or requests for further explanation. It might be

• a new security system
• a reorganization of your working space
• a reorganization of your team structure
• a new pricing system
• a new delivery system
• a change in your way of travelling to work.

ⓘ **»** Interactive Workbook **»** Email

Unit 7 | Security

Key expressions

Introducing a talk
What I want to do today is …
I'll talk about …
I'll run through …

Giving background information
As you know, we've recently …
As you are aware …
Up to now …
I'd like to update you on …
The situation / problem now is that …
We expect the situation to …
The situation, as it stands …

Asking for an explanation
What's the reason for …?
I don't quite understand how it works.
Can you tell us (more) about …?
What do you mean by …?

Giving an explanation
It's because of the fact that …
As a result, …
Because of this …
By (+ -ing) …, we can / hope to …

Checking information
So, if I understand you correctly …
Do you mean that …?
I'm not sure I follow you.

ⓘ **»** Interactive Workbook
» Phrasebank

Practically speaking | How to introduce and respond to news

1 Which of these phrases help to create interest (C)? Which phrases show interest in what the other person is saying (S)?

1 You're kidding! ___

2 How long have you known about that? ___

3 Have you heard the news? ___

4 Guess what I've just seen? ___

5 I've just heard something really interesting! ___

6 I've never heard that before! ___

7 What's happened? ___

8 Really? ___

2 32▷ Listen to four conversations and check your answers in **1**.

3 Think of two pieces of recent news, one true and the other false. Work with a partner. Take turns to tell your news and guess which piece of news is false.

Language at work | Present perfect simple and continuous | Connectors

1 Which of the sentences a–b below is about

  1 an unfinished action continuing up to now? _____

  2 a completed action / completed actions in an unfinished time period? _____

  a We've recently **been having** a few problems.

  b We've **had** three incidents reported since the beginning of the month.

2 Which sentence in **1** uses the present perfect simple and which uses the present perfect continuous?

>> For more information and exercises, go to **Practice file 7** on page 115.

3 Choose the correct answer from the verb forms in *italics*.

  1 We've *worked / 've been working* on this current project for five months now.

  2 They*'ve completed / 've been completing* the proposal and here it is.

  3 How many times have you *been meeting / met* the CEO?

  4 Sorry, but I don't think I*'ve understood / 've been understanding*.

4 Work with a partner. Take turns to ask and answer questions using the prompts below, starting with *Have you …?* or *How long …?* In some cases it may be possible to use either the simple or continuous form.

    Example: *How long* **have you been studying** *English?*

            Have *you ever* **studied** *English before?*

  1 study / English

  2 live / in your current home

  3 be / current position

  4 work / current project

  5 have / problems at work

  6 have / your car

  7 use / new mobile phone

  8 know / your English teacher

5 Read sentences 1–4. Does the word / phrase in **bold** in each sentence show the reason for an action or the result of an action? Write *reason* or *result*.

  1 An employee has had her bag stolen from her office desk. **Consequently**, we've decided to install a new PIN number system of security. _____

  2 **In order that** visitors can be allowed into the building, you have to inform security the day before. _____

  3 We have to change the current system **because of** the fact that security can't always check everyone's badge. _____

  4 We need to give everyone a password **in order to** prevent unauthorized access.

    _____

6 Match these words to the words in *bold* in **5**.

    so   due to   therefore   so that   to   as a result

>> For more information and exercises, go to **Practice file 7** on page 115.

7 Work with a partner. Take turns to make sentences or questions about things that have happened or have been happening at work. Use one of the words from the list and a connector from **5** or **6** in each of your sentences. Answer your partner's questions.

    recently   still   ever   never   for   yet   since

    Example: *I've* **recently** *been taking very short lunch breaks because of the fact that I have such a heavy workload.*

ⓘ >> Interactive Workbook >> **Exercises and Tests**

Improving data security

Background

Company faces high costs because of security breach

CastCard Corp. (CCC) processes data for a number of major credit card companies in the United States. The company, based in Arizona, recently announced that information on more than 40 million credit cards may have been stolen.

The security breach happened when an unauthorized person from outside the company was able to enter the CCC network and access cardholder data. It was discovered during a routine check for credit card fraud. Although the person was able to get information on customers' credit card numbers, the cards themselves do not hold personal information like social security numbers or dates of birth. The information could be used for credit card fraud, but not to steal customers' identities.

CCC is working with the police to investigate the security breach. All the credit card companies have said that CCC will be responsible for any illegal transactions and customers will not lose any money. Security procedures at the company are now being changed.

Discussion

1 What could happen to CastCard Corp. as a result of this security breach? Why?

2 What can the company do to make its customers feel better about the situation?

3 How could CCC change its security measures to stop this happening again?

Task

You work for a financial company. Many of your competitors have experienced security breaches. These have cost them a lot of money and have created bad publicity. Your company wants to safeguard against these problems and is considering some changes to its security measures.

1 Read these possible options. Think about the advantages and disadvantages of each option.

Memo | Company security policy

1 Check the background of all potential employees before recruiting them.

2 Restrict the number of employees who are allowed to take laptops home.

3 Restrict the number of employees who have access to confidential information.

4 Do not allow employees to use personal USB devices at work.

5 Run training programmes for employees to inform and update them about good security procedures. Also, explain what will happen if they break the rules.

6 Reward loyalty so that fewer people leave the company, taking information with them. For example, paying people bonuses related to how long they have worked for the company.

7 Don't keep any confidential data stored on laptops. Keep all the data at the office and use remote access to view the data when working on laptops outside the office.

8 Use an encryption system (coding system with password access) for data on laptops.

2 Work in small groups. Discuss all the options. Decide which are the three most important options for the company.

3 Present your ideas to another group. Be prepared to answer questions about your decisions. Can both groups agree on three options for a company action plan?

The Expert View

To protect their reputations, companies don't commonly publicize the fact that 80% of all fraud is internal. In an attempt to reduce security breaches in today's increasingly regulated and complex global recruitment market, most employers carry out pre-employment screening in the following three areas: CV verification – checking an applicant's experience and qualifications; background screening – checking an applicant is who they say they are, and that they don't have a criminal record; medical checks – ensuring that the applicant is fit and able to do the job.

Eyal Ben Cohen, Managing Director, Verifile Limited, MBA graduate
Cranfield School of Management

Case study

8 | Working together

Learning objectives in this unit
- Talking about working in teams
- Presenting and discussing plans
- Encouraging people
- Using *will*, *going to*, and modal verbs to talk about your goals

Case study
- Creating a plan for effective teamwork

Starting point

1 Match these eight names to make four partnerships.
John Lennon, Domenico Dolce, Douwe Egberts, Crédit Lyonnais, Philips, Paul McCartney, Tour de France, Stefano Gabbana

2 Which sectors do / did the companies / people work in?

3 What is / was the nature of their partnership?

4 What do you think are possible benefits of teams and partnerships?

Working with words | Teamwork and partnerships

1 What skills and abilities do the people in these pictures need?

2 How important are teamwork and regular meetings where you work?

3 Some companies use psychological tests to check if someone will be a good team player. Do this questionnaire and compare your results with a partner.

	Agree	Disagree
1 Life is easier when someone else tells you what to do.	☐	☐
2 I would rather work on my own than with other people.	☐	☐
3 I prefer to work with people who are different from me.	☐	☐
4 Winning is more important than getting on with other people.	☐	☐
5 I usually welcome suggestions from other people.	☐	☐
6 Colleagues are often more dangerous than business rivals.	☐	☐

4 33 ▷ Harriet and Conrad work in the project management section of a large finance group. They are looking for someone to join their team. They are discussing a candidate's responses to the questionnaire in **3**. Listen to their conversation. Which choices did the candidate make?

5 33 ▷ Match the words in **A** to the words in **B** to make phrases. Then listen again and check your answers.

A	B
take	skills
team	forces
work	responsibility
join	benefit
complementary	alliances
common	closely
form	venture
joint	goals
mutual	player
shared	ground

6 Work with a partner. Match the phrases you made in **5** to definitions 1–10.
1 when two people have different abilities that work well together: _____
2 come together to form a team: _____
3 put yourself in a position to be blamed if something goes wrong: _____
4 advantageous to both sides: _____
5 make partnerships: _____
6 have a strong working relationship with: _____
7 project that is being worked on by two or more parties: _____
8 similar objectives: _____
9 someone who works well in a team: _____
10 similar ideas or experience in something: _____

» For more exercises, go to **Practice file 8** on page 116.

7 Work with a partner. Think of a current or future project one of you is working on. This could be at work or at home. You have to form a team of four, including you and your partner, and two people from the list below, to complete this project.
1 Decide which two people would be best in your team. Think about the skills you and they can offer.
2 Tell the class why you have chosen these two people.

> Greta: Quiet and hard-working. Very methodical. Good at statistical analysis. Good at detail. Quite shy.
>
> Carlos: Friendly. Good team player and very easy to talk to. No special skills, but quite good at everything. Has a lot of experience of dealing with clients.
>
> Billy: Very good communication and presentation skills. Can get angry and aggressive. Has a lot of friends and colleagues in the business. Likes to lead and be dominant.
>
> Penny: Clever with words. Quite creative and artistic. Sometimes lazy, needs others to keep her on track.
>
> Stevie: IT specialist with good financial skills. Not very good with people. Can be difficult.
>
> Tessa: Experienced office manager. Good at logistics and systems. Gets on well with most people. Cool and organized. Not very imaginative or creative.

ⓘ » Interactive Workbook » **Glossary**

Tip | *rather*

Use *would rather* to state a preference between two things.
  A Do you want to eat in the canteen or go out?
  B I'd rather go out.
Use *rather than* to express a better option.
  We should keep to the original teams rather than change them.

Meetings | Presenting and discussing plans

1 Merging companies or departments can be difficult. Work in small groups and talk about the problems that might happen in the following areas.
  1 personal relationships and teamwork
  2 working space
  3 old and new hierarchies
  4 ways of doing things

2 34▷ Quoteus Insurance is merging with Buckler Insurance Services. Quoteus managers, Carmen and Nikos, are meeting with Erica and Dieter, their counterparts from Buckler. They are discussing how to overcome feelings of suspicion between staff. Listen and make notes on Erica's notepad.

> Nikos's plan:
>
> How it will work:
>
> Timescale of the plan:
>
> What he needs before he can launch it:

3 What other way of breaking down barriers do they discuss?

4 34▷ Listen again and complete these phrases.
  1 We _____ to be ready on schedule.
  2 Where does this _____ us?
  3 _____ the next few weeks …
  4 … I _____ to hold a series of small meetings.
  5 How long will it _____ to involve all the staff?
  6 I _____ to have seven or eight sessions.
  7 What's the _____ on this?
  8 _____ the end of next month.
  9 What's the next _____?
  10 It is _____ that …
  11 … there'll be a few problems in the short _____
  12 But the _____ are …
  13 … there won't be too many personality clashes in the _____ run.

Tip | *likely* and *pretty*

These adjectives can mean something different from what you might immediately think. *Likely* can mean *probable*.
  *Share prices are **likely** to go down after this disaster.*
Pretty can mean *reasonably*.
  *I'm **pretty** sure that won't happen.*

5 Put the phrases from **4** into these categories.

a Talking about a future hope, a plan, or expectations: _____

b Asking and talking about time needed: _____

c Asking and talking about an action needed: _____

⟫ For more exercises, go to **Practice file 8** on page 116.

6 Work with a partner. Continue the meeting from **2**. There are two other important topics on the agenda – organization of office space and creation of the new departmental organigram. Student A, turn to File 19 on page 139. Student B, use the information below. Read your information before you start.

Student B

You are creating the new departmental organigram (diagram which shows the hierarchy of the department).

This is a very sensitive subject because of the status of different job titles in different companies.

Your plans are to
- conduct individual interviews with key staff
- prepare a draft document for discussion.

By the end of the month: have small working parties
In six weeks' time: have proposal for both Quoteus and Buckler
In two months' time: make decision and inform staff

1 Your partner will describe his / her plans for the project he / she is working on.
2 Tell your partner what you are working on, how you expect it to go, and describe your plans.

---

7 Think about the next twelve months at work. Look in your diaries if you want. Make short notes about your immediate plans and your long-term plans. Tell the class.

ⓘ ⟫ Interactive Workbook ⟫ **Email**

Practically speaking | How to encourage people

1 35▷ Listen to five extracts from conversations. Which of the phrases a–e below show the speaker is

1 very happy about something? _____

2 not very sure about something? _____

a Well done!

b It's a start.

c Great work, everyone.

d That's an excellent idea.

e That has potential.

2 Work in small groups. You have two minutes to do one of the following.
- Come up with an idea to improve something in your workplace.
- Write a new slogan for your company.
- Design a visual diagram of your company's activities and partners.

3 Look at everyone else's creations or listen to their ideas. Take turns to comment on them.

Key expressions

Describing plans and intentions
We're also going to …
X is going to …

Expressing future hopes and expectations
We expect to …
We hope to …
I plan to …
I intend to …
The chances are …
It is likely to / that …

Asking how much time is needed
How long will it take to …?
What's the timescale on this?

Asking about immediate action
Where does this leave us?
What's the next step?

Time expressions
Over the next few weeks …
By the end of the / next month …
By Tuesday …
In the short / medium / long term …
In the long run …

ⓘ ⟫ Interactive Workbook
⟫ **Phrasebank**

Language at work | Talking about the future – *going to, will,* and modal verbs

1 Carmen works for Quoteus Insurance. She has written to her colleague, Kirsten, with an update on how plans are going for a merger between their company and another insurance company. Read her email and answer questions 1–2.

  1 How optimistic is Carmen about the schedule?

  2 What predictions does she make?

Dear Kirsten,

I just wanted to let you know that Erica is **going to** prepare a list of key people to consult on the new hierarchy and departmental structure. Based on feedback I've received from staff meetings, I can see that this is **going to** be a sensitive issue for some people, but the steps we are taking **should** reduce problems. There **could** be trouble, and I expect that a few people **will** leave.

Anyway, the basic message is that everything is on schedule, so we **should** be in the new premises by the end of June. By the way, it **might** be useful for you to come to the next meeting. We're going to discuss the allocation of work space. There **could** be some issues which affect you directly. I'**ll** keep you posted on any developments in the meantime.

All the best,

Carmen

---

2 Complete sentences 1–6 with the words in **bold** from the email in **1**.

  1 Use _____ to make a confident prediction.

  2 Use _____ and _____ when we are less confident but think something is possible.

  3 Use _____ for predictions which are based on evidence we can see in front of us.

  4 Use _____ to make a prediction based on what is usual or expected.

  5 Use _____ for an intention to do something.

  6 Use _____ for a spontaneous offer, promise, or decision.

3 Complete sentences 1–6 with words from **2**.

  a There _____ be a train in two minutes; there is usually one at that time.

  b The price of commodities _____ definitely continue to rise.

  c I think I'_____ come in on Saturday – there's just so much to do.

  d This decision _____ cause problems if we don't handle it carefully.

  e What terrible sales figures! We are _____ go bankrupt if things don't improve.

  f He's _____ apply for the manager's job.

  ⟫ For more information and exercises, go to **Practice file 8** on page 117.

4 Work with a partner. Read situations 1–5 and decide what you would say.

  1 Your boss is worried about you missing a deadline. Reassure him / her.

  2 Your colleague usually arrives at work at 9.30. It's 9.15. Somebody asks you where she is.

  3 With a quarter of the year left, you've only reached half of your sales target.

  4 Your head of department has just been promoted. Someone asks you if you want to apply for his / her job. You are not sure.

  5 You sent a document by post to a client. They need it in two days. You are fairly confident that this is OK. They want to know where it is.

5 Make notes about your short- and long-term goals in your job and at home. Work with a partner or in small groups. Tell each other what your goals are.

ⓘ ⟫ Interactive Workbook ⟫ **Exercises and Tests**

Tip | Adding extra information and changing topic

Use *by the way* and *incidentally* to add extra information or thoughts.

By the way, *you should try to come to the next meeting.*

Incidentally, *Erica is bilingual.*

Creating a plan for effective teamwork

Background

Virtual teamwork at Nortel

Nortel creates Internet technologies, and has 80,000 employees located in 150 countries. It conducts business 24 hours a day, seven days a week with people on different continents and in different time zones.

The HR Director works at the head office in Ontario, Canada, but as a member of a virtual team, she has colleagues as far away as Europe and China. She trained her virtual team of 60 finance and legal employees on deal-making skills. Since they were located throughout the world, she used a group meeting technology tool called Meeting Manager. Virtual participants were on individual PCs and also on a teleconference line.

The meeting took place in real time from team members' desktops. Charts from the presenters were uploaded onto Meeting Manager, which allowed for group viewing. The chair was able to control the order of the meeting and the viewing of the charts. Participants posted questions on an electronic white board, which could be answered online or by phone.

The Expert View

Early in a project it's important to create a positive working environment where team members can learn to trust and support each other. Social interaction and understanding of cultural differences are essential to obtaining commitment from all members. It's also important to identify individual strengths and role preferences. The team needs to appoint a leader to provide a framework for working towards defined outcomes or collective goals. As the project becomes more task focused, the team dynamic may shift from performing as a group to becoming a collection of individuals.

Raj Mulvadi, Manish Singh, Simone Taylor, David York, Full-time MBA graduates
Cranfield School of Management

Discussion

1 What is a 'virtual team'? How does the team meet?

2 What are the advantages and disadvantages of virtual teamwork?

3 Why might an international company decide against virtual teamwork?

Task

1 You work for a global company. It has five key regions: North America; Latin America; Europe; the Middle East and North Africa; and Asia. The head office is in the Netherlands. You need to set up new working practices to allow for better and more effective teamwork across the different regions. Read this information about the international meetings, training sessions, and conferences that take place throughout the year.

Event	When / where	Who travels	Details
Sales conferences	One per year in June / July	All sales managers from all regions	Attend three-day conference in one of the regions.
Product training sessions	Four per year in varying regions	Product manager and several product developers from head office	Run two-day sessions for local sales reps covering several new products.
Marketing meetings	Several times per year in each of the regions	Marketing and R&D personnel from head office	Visit regional sales teams to discuss sales and marketing strategy.
Finance meetings	Several times a year in different regions	Finance controllers from head office	Visit finance teams in all the regions for a one-day meeting to look at the books and discuss future strategy.
General conferences	One every two years in the Netherlands	Managers and senior workers from all regions	To analyse results, share ideas and develop strategy. Includes social events.

2 Work in small groups, divided into two parts – A and B. Group A turn to File 21 on page 140. Group B, turn to File 28 on page 142. Read the information and make notes.

3 Share the information from your files and discuss what to do about all the international meetings, etc. in 1. Decide what changes you will make and when.

4 Present your plans to the rest of the class.

Case study

9 | Logistics

Starting point

1 What does the term 'logistics' mean?

2 Have you ever experienced problems with delivery of goods at home or at work? What happened?

Working with words | Logistics and supply chains

1 How long would you expect to wait for a new computer after ordering it?

2 Read this article and answer questions 1–2.
   1 How does Dell do business differently from other companies?
   2 How does this affect its suppliers?

Dell does it differently

Conventional **manufacturers** have to keep supplies of **raw materials** in order to produce their goods. Ordinary **retailers** too, have to keep the appropriate stock levels to satisfy their **clients'** needs. Enormous sums of money are tied up in this **inventory**. By contrast, Dell only builds once it has received an order and delivery takes on average seven to ten working days from the date the order is placed. By dealing directly with consumers through mailshots, advertisements, and the Internet, it bypasses distributors and shopkeepers. And Dell's performance is truly breathtaking: its factories construct 80,000 machines per day and it can operate without **warehouses**. When an order is placed, the firm orders **components** from their **suppliers**. In addition, suppliers are expected to give credit even though Dell is paid in advance. This means that Dell has already been paid by its customers before it has to pay its own bills. Everything is so **streamlined** that it demands expert logistics and management of the **supply chain**.

3 Match the words in **bold** from the text in **2** to definitions 1–11.
   1 people who sell products to the public: _____
   2 stock: _____
   3 the place where goods are stored: _____
   4 parts you need to construct something: _____
   5 designed for optimal efficiency: _____
   6 the series of processes and companies involved in making and selling a product: _____
   7 customers: _____
   8 the 'middleman' between the manufacturer and retailer: _____
   9 providers of goods: _____
   10 producers: _____
   11 the basic substances used to make something: _____

4 Work with a partner. Talk about the differences between Dell and a traditional supply chain. Use words from the list to complete the two flow charts.

distributor   retailer   manufacturer (x2)   *customer* (x2)   ~~*supplier*~~ (x2)

1 Traditional supply chain

supplier _____ _____ _____ _____

2 Dell supply chain

supplier _____ _____

5 36▷ **Steve Zackon also works in the computer business. Listen to this interview and answer questions 1–3.**
1 What are the main differences between his business and Dell?
2 How does he keep control of his stock?
3 How does Steve follow the progress of his orders?

6 36▷ **Listen again. Complete the phrases in *italics*.**
1 We have to keep a lot of components _____ *stock*.
2 How do you make sure that you don't *run* _____?
3 It tells us what we have left, if it's _____ *order* …
4 You never want to *run* _____ *of* basic items.
5 It's really not good to be _____ *of stock*.
6 It just warns us we're *low* _____ stock.
7 You don't want to *stock* _____ *on* components …
8 If there's an essential package, I _____ *track of* it very closely.

7 Match five of the phrases in *italics* from **6** to pictures a–e.

>> For more exercises, go to **Practice file 9** on page 118.

8 Work with a partner. Ask and answer questions 1–6. Talk about work and / or home.
1 Have you got anything on order at the moment?
2 What important supplies are you running low on?
3 How often do you run out of something essential?
4 When was the last time something you wanted to buy was out of stock?
5 What do you like to stock up on?
6 How do you keep track of your spending?

9 Work with a partner and take turns to
• say what you can do to make sure you don't run out of essential supplies at work
• describe what you know about your company's supply chain.

ⓘ » Interactive Workbook » **Glossary**

Exchanging information | Placing and handling orders

1 Gisele Kern works for a computer assembler in Hamburg. Read her email to Composource, a Singapore-based supplier, and answer questions 1–4.

1 What does she want to order?
2 Is she a regular customer?
3 When does she want delivery?
4 How will she pay?

From: giselekern@abracomp.com
Subject: Order – motherboards

Dear Sir / Madam

I would like to place an order for 2,000 motherboards. This is a repeat order. We need these urgently so please send them asap. Please charge it to our account as usual.

Kind regards,
Gisele Kern
Abracomp

---

2 Underline the useful phrases for placing an order in the email in **1**.

3 37▷ Two weeks later, Gisele is still waiting for the components. She calls her supplier, Composource, to find out what is happening. Listen and complete the supplier's information.

Account: *Abracomp*   Quantity: *2,000*

Account reference: Dispatched: Yes / No

Date of order: Date and time dispatched:

Product description:

---

4 37▷ Listen again and complete these phrases.

1 I'm _____ an order I placed two weeks ago.
2 I'd like to _____ what has happened to it.
3 I see. Can I take your _____?
4 When did you _____ the order?
5 We put it _____ to our warehouse.
6 _____ my information, it was dispatched that afternoon.
7 Something _____ gone wrong.
8 I'm not _____ this at all.
9 Could you _____ for me?
10 Certainly, _____ immediately.
11 This is a _____ problem for me.
12 I'll be _____ I can.
13 I really want to know what's _____ to it.

» For more exercises, go to **Practice file 9** on page 118.

Tip | Clarifying

Remember that to clarify spelling, we can use common words (names, cities, countries) to illustrate a letter.

That's P for Peter, A for Australia. For easily confused numbers (18 and 80, etc.), say each individual digit after the number.

The number is eighteen – one, eight.

5 Work with a partner. Take turns to role-play two situations using this flow chart. In one situation you will be a customer, and in the second situation a call handler. In each situation you will have two conversations. Student A, turn to File 22 on page 140. Student B, turn to File 30 on page 142.

Conversation 1

Call handler Answer the phone.

Customer Identify yourself and say you want to place an order.

Call handler Ask for the account number and details of the order.

Customer Give your details.

Call handler Give the order reference and say goodbye.

Conversation 2

Call handler Answer the phone.

Customer Say you are checking on / unhappy with an order.

Call handler Ask for the account details and the order reference.

Customer Give your details.

Call handler Explain the problem.

Customer Ask for a solution / new delivery time.

Call handler Propose a solution.

Customer Agree and say goodbye.

ⓘ **»** Interactive Workbook **»** Email

Practically speaking | How to leave a voicemail message

1 38▷ Listen to three recorded messages. What are the instructions?

2 Put phrases a–h below into categories 1–4.

1 Leaving a contact number: _____
2 Giving the time of your call: _____
3 Identifying yourself: _____
4 Giving a reason for the call: _____

a Hi / Hello, this is …
b Call me back on …
c This is a message for …
d I was just wondering if …
e It's 6.30 p.m.
f You can reach me on …
g I'm calling at …
h I was just calling about / to …

3 39▷ In what order would you do 1–4 in 2? Listen to a message and compare it with your answer.

4 Work with a partner. Take turns leaving these messages.

1 You are arriving at the airport at 3.30 p.m. Your flight number is HG781. You hope someone can meet you. Your mobile number is 0773 654989.
2 You want to know when you car will be ready. Leave a message at the garage. Give your contact details.

Key expressions

Placing an order
I'd like to place an order.
This is a repeat order.
Please send them asap.
Please charge it to my account.

Asking for details
Do you have an account with us?
Can / could I take / have your account details, please?
When did you place the order?
Can I ask when you placed the order?

Checking on an order
I'd like to find out about an order.
I'm chasing / following up an order.
Could you check it out for me?
I really want to know what's happened to it.

Explaining what happened
We put it (straight) through to …
According to my information, …
It was dispatched on …

Complaining
I'm not happy about this.
This is a real problem for me.
This is unacceptable.

Promising action
I'll look into it immediately.
I'll check it out straight away.
I'll find out.
I'll get back to you (within the hour).
I'll be as quick as I can.

ⓘ **»** Interactive Workbook **»** Phrasebank

Language at work | Reported speech

1 40▷ **Linda works for Composource. She is checking on an order for their customer, Gisele Kern. Listen to their conversation.**

1 What is the problem with the order?

2 What solution does Gisele ask for?

2 Read sentences 1–4 and write what was actually said.

1 I asked the warehouse to check what had happened to it.
  'Can you _____?'

2 They told me it had gone two weeks ago.
  'It _____.'

3 They said they'd sent it by sea.
  'We _____.'

4 I asked if they knew where it was.
  'Do _____?'

3 Put sentences a–e below into categories 1–4.

1 Reporting statements: _____

2 Reporting questions: _____

3 Reporting requests: _____

4 Reporting orders: _____

a I **asked the warehouse to** check what had happened to it.

b They **told me** it had gone two weeks ago.

c They **said** they sent it by sea.

d I **asked if** they knew where it was.

e I'm sure I **told them to** send it by courier when I placed the order.

4 Complete these rules with *say* or *tell*.

1 We _____ something.

2 We _____ someone something.

3 We _____ something to someone.

>> For more information and exercises, go to **Practice file 9** on page 119.

5 41▷ **Gisele is listening to a voicemail message from Linda. Listen and complete her notes.**

Message from: _____

Time: _____

Message: Have sent _____ by _____

Linda told carrier this was _____

Arriving in _____

Reference / tracking number: _____

6 Gisele's boss, Peter, is very unhappy about the mix-up. Work with a partner and role-play a conversation between Gisele and Peter. Gisele – report back on Linda's message. Peter – ask questions and make comments.

7 Work in small groups. Think of a time when you had a disagreement or a problem with a colleague, a client, or a supplier. Tell your group what happened and what was said.

ⓘ >> Interactive Workbook >> **Exercises and Tests**

Solving a logistics problem

Background

DIY retailer calls in logistics experts

Castorama Polska belongs to the Kingfisher group of companies. Kingfisher is the third-largest home improvement retailer worldwide and has over 680 stores in eleven countries.

Castorama is the market leader in Poland with more than 30 stores and over 6,000 employees. Its products are sourced from around 700 suppliers in Asia, Europe, and Poland. Castorama's first store opened in Warsaw in 1997. In the following years the business in Poland grew rapidly, but so did their operational and economic challenges. As the number of stores grew, and demand for their products increased, it became more and more difficult to distribute stock to all their customers on time.

Each Castorama store operated as a 'logistically independent' unit – they each had different stock requirements and different ordering systems. Because there was no overall strategy, it was difficult to coordinate supply and demand. As a result, stock was often delayed or even lost, and orders quickly became outdated. The company's logistics costs went up, delays in orders increased, and customer satisfaction started to go down, ultimately leading to lost sales.

The company needed help to solve this problem. They called in the logistics consultants, Maersk Logistics, to help improve their supply chain, reduce costs, and increase customer satisfaction.

The Expert View

Logistics is the process of creating a framework for the flow of resources within a business. Supply chain management is the management of relationships with suppliers, distributors and customers – its aim is to coordinate the different processes within the business, and between customers and suppliers.
For effective supply chain management, both individuals and organizations need to learn how to build relationships and work together. To solve logistics and supply chain problems we need Technical Intelligence (IQ) as well as Emotional Intelligence (EQ) – our ability to build relationships.

Richard Wilding, Professor of Supply Chain Risk Management

Cranfield School of Management

Unit 9 | Logistics

Discussion

1 What kind of products do Castorama sell?

2 What went wrong? Why did these things happen?

3 What are the benefits of a well-designed logistics system?

4 What changes would you advise Castorama to make?

5 Turn to File 24 on page 141 to find out how Maersk helped Castorama to make changes. Did you have the same ideas?

Task

You and your partner work for a logistics consultancy like Maersk Logistics. You have been called in by Toyztime, a large, growing chain of toy stores based in England. Toyztime is losing sales because of logistics problems. Like Castorama Polska, each of the 150 Toyztime stores operates as a 'logistically independent' unit.

You and your partner have collected information from people who were once regular customers and from employees at Toyztime. You will discuss and analyse this information and then make recommendations to the company directors.

1 Student A, turn to File 32 on page 143. You have collected information from Toyztime customers. Student B, turn to File 42 on page 145. You have collected information from employees. Take turns to report your findings to your partner.

2 Work with your partner. Make a list of the six logistics problems that need to be solved and discuss what can be done. Use your own ideas and ideas from Maersk Logistics' solution for Castorama (see File 24 on page 141).

3 Present your solution to another group.

Case study

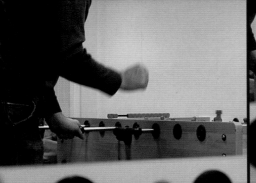

10 | Facilities

Learning objectives in this unit
- Describing your place of work
- Making suggestions and recommendations
- Linking ideas
- Using nouns and quantifiers to talk about facilities

Case study
- Organizing a cause marketing event

Starting point

1 Name as many places of work as you can. Which ones would you most like to work in and which would you least like to work in? Why?

2 Look at the picture of the building in the text on this page. What sort of place do you think it is? Would you like to visit it? Why / why not?

Working with words | Describing a place of work

1 **Read this article and answer questions 1–3.**
1 What makes this place of work really different?
2 What facilities does it offer visitors?
3 How many different words for buildings can you find?

Dream factory

Does this complex look like an opera house? Actually, it has hosted Dresden Opera's highly successful production of *Carmen*, but ordinarily, it is tourists and customers who are welcomed to this state-of-the-art car plant. For a start, the Volkswagen 'Glass Factory' houses an interactive experience for learning about VW. A well-equipped and spacious customer centre invites buyers to choose the most up-to-date model, with specific colours and interiors. The ground floor houses a fine restaurant, but the amazing thing is that it stands in a city-centre park next to Dresden's beautifully-maintained baroque museums and churches.

---

2 **Find words in the text in 1 that mean the opposite of these negative adjectives.**

1 badly-equipped: _____
2 old-fashioned: _____
3 cramped: _____
4 run-down: _____

3 42▷ **Listen to people visiting three different workplaces. Which adjectives from 2 can be used to describe each workplace they talk about?**

4 The speakers in **3** use adverbs like *very* to intensify the adjectives. Complete this scale with other adverbs from the list.

pretty   fairly   quite   not exactly   extremely   really

weak intensifier ●————————————————————● strong intensifier

1 _____ 2 _____ 3 _____ 4 _____
                              _____
                              _____

» For more exercises, go to **Practice file 10** on page 120.

5 Work with a partner. Add a suitable adverb from **4** to sentences 1–7 and take turns saying them.

1 Your new offices are amazing.
2 It's all well designed.
3 All the machines are old.
4 Everyone is motivated.
5 It's state-of-the-art.
6 The offices are not modern.
7 This is a successful company.

6 42▷ Listen again and compare your sentences in **5**.

7 Work with a partner. Look at this website with a range of offices for rent. Take turns to choose a property and describe it to your partner. Use adjectives from the list and adverbs from **4**. Your partner must guess which property it is.

well maintained   wide   spacious   well equipped   well located   secure

Example: A *These offices are fairly well located. The meeting room is not exactly spacious but there's a pretty wide range of telecom services.*
B *Is it property 1?*

Top Office Rentals
Our rating: 5 = Excellent, 1 = Poor

Property 1: **Fallows Court Offices**

5 individual offices on 3rd floor of four-storey building
Location: 3 (mainline station 1 km)
Maintenance / presentation: 2
Range of telecom services: 4
Conferencing facilities (1 meeting room): space = 2; equipment = 5
Security: 4

Property 2: **High Towers**

1 open-plan office (10 people) + 3 individual offices located on ground floor
Location: 5 (mainline station 500 m)
Maintenance / presentation: 4
Range of telecom services: 3
Conferencing facilities (3 meeting rooms): space = 4; equipment = 3
Security: 5

Property 3: **Watson's Wharf**

Up to 30 individual offices + 2 open-plan offices (up to 20 people in each)
Location: 2 (mainline station 3 km)
Maintenance / presentation: 4
Range of telecom services: 5
Conferencing facilities (6 meeting rooms): space = 5; equipment = 4
Security: 4

8 Work with a partner. Take turns to describe the following. Use as many adverb + adjective combinations as you can.

- your place of work
- your favourite building in the world
- your company headquarters
- a place where you relax

ⓘ » Interactive Workbook » **Glossary**

Tip | Asking for descriptions

When asking for a description of a person, place, film, job, etc. say:
*What is / are … **like**?*
Don't say:
~~*How is … **like**?*~~
Do say:
*What are your new offices **like**?*
*What is the CEO **like**?*

Meetings | Making suggestions and recommendations

1 How do you make suggestions in your company? By email? Comment forms? Do you use a suggestion box?

2 Complete the comments below from a suggestion box using phrases from the list.

why don't   have you thought about   we could always   couldn't we do

Comment form

Because so many women work here now, ¹_____ we have a crèche for young children? Then parents wouldn't have so many problems with childcare. And ² _____ see our children at lunchtimes, which would also be good for motivation.

Comment form

I don't want to complain about the new relaxation room – it's extremely comfortable and spacious. But ³_____ having some entertainment in there? I read about employees at Microsoft where they have a special room called an Anarchy Zone. They can play computer games, table football, or watch MTV. ⁴_____ something like that?

3 43▷ An architect is making initial recommendations to a facilities manager for a new office layout. They have looked at employee suggestions and started to draw up plans for it. They are discussing ideas for a crèche and a relaxation area. Listen and answer questions 1–2.
1 Why can they only choose one of the ideas?
2 Which one do they choose and why?

4 Choose the correct answer from the words in *italics*.
1 Well, it might prove *difficult / difficulties* to have both.
2 I think we should consider *have / having* …
3 Besides, I have a few *reserves / reservations* about …
4 You might be *better / the best* off without it …
5 I'd rather not *have / having* it.
6 I'd recommend *to put / putting* it here.

5 43▷ Listen again and tick (✓) the responses you hear in the meeting.
1 I really like it. ____
2 Good idea. ____
3 Sorry, but I don't think that would work. ____
4 I'm not sure. ____
5 Great! ____
6 Exactly. ____

>> For more exercises, go to **Practice file 10** on page 120.

6 Work with a partner. An architect is redesigning your office space. Look at these two styles of office and read about some advantages and disadvantages for each in the table below. Can you add any more?

	Style A	Style B
Advantages	friendly, easy to communicate	good for concentration, private
Disadvantages	noisy, harder for private conversation	not as social, old-fashioned

7 Now prepare and give your recommendations for one of the office styles in **6** using phrases from **4**. Student A, promote style A. Student B, promote style B. Respond to the recommendations you hear. Try to come to an agreement with your partner.

> *Example:* **A** *I'd recommend having an open-plan office because …*
> **B** *I think we should consider building closed offices because …*

8 Work in small groups. Imagine your company lets you have an Anarchy Zone – an area to relax and forget about work for a few minutes – with four items in it.

1 Make suggestions for what you would put in your Anarchy Zone. For example, a TV, computer games, books, etc. Give reasons for these suggestions. Respond to others' ideas. Decide on four items you will have in the zone.

2 Present your final recommendations to the rest of the class.

3 Comment on the other groups' recommendations.

ⓘ **≫** Interactive Workbook **≫ Email**

Practically speaking | How to link ideas

1 Read sentences 1–5. <u>Underline</u> the two reasons given in each sentence. What word or phrase links the reasons?

1 I can't apply for the job because it's in Madrid. Besides, I don't have the right experience.

2 We chose this design because it's very modern and on top of that, it's cheaper.

3 Starting work at 8.00 a.m. means I avoid rush hour and also have longer evenings.

4 I like it here – my new colleagues are very helpful, as well as being friendly.

5 The company offers flexitime, which creates a better working atmosphere, and in addition to that, we have increased productivity.

2 Work with a partner. Talk about the topics below. Join the two reasons using the linkers from **1** above.

> *Example:* *I want a new job because I dislike my current boss and also, the pay is very low.*

1 New job: dislike my current boss + pay is very low

2 Buy new car: current car is ten years old + it often breaks down

3 Take a holiday: very tired + no days off work for a year

4 Study English: important for work + useful for holidays abroad

Key expressions

Suggesting
What / How about (+ -*ing*)?
Why don't we (+ verb)?
Maybe we should (+ verb) …
Maybe / Perhaps we could (+ verb) …
Couldn't we (+ verb) …
Have you thought about (+ -*ing*) …
We could always (+ verb) …

Recommending
I think we should consider (+noun / -*ing*) …
We might be better off (+ -*ing*) …
It's probably worth (+ -*ing*) …
It might prove (+ adjective) …
I have a few reservations about (+ noun / -*ing*) …
I'd rather not (+ verb) …
I'd recommend (+ *that* / -*ing*) …
It would be better (+ infinitive) …

Responding
I really like it.
It's / That's a good idea.
Sorry, but I don't think that would work.
I'm not sure.
Great.
Exactly.

ⓘ **≫** Interactive Workbook **≫ Phrasebank**

Language at work | Nouns and quantifiers

1 Work with a partner. Make a list of all the facilities that a workplace can have. Compare your lists with another pair.

2 44▷ Listen to three employees commenting on their facilities at work. Which of the facilities in pictures a–c does each employee comment on?

1 _____ 2 _____ 3 _____

3 44▷ Listen again and complete sentences 1–7.

1 There isn't _____ *space* in them to put personal belongings.
2 And when I get changed, they don't hold _____ *clothes.*
3 Perhaps if we had _____ *shelves,* it might help.
4 It would be a great idea to have _____ *running machines* …
5 _____ *employees* only have _____ *time* after work …
6 There aren't _____ *places* in the factory to relax.
7 There are _____ *chairs* in that room …

4 Put the nouns in *italics* from **3** into these categories.

1 Countable nouns: _____
2 Uncountable nouns: _____

5 Complete this table with the quantifiers you wrote in **3**. Some words can go in both columns.

quantifiers for uncountable nouns, e.g. *time*	quantifiers for countable nouns, e.g. *chairs*	
some	*some*	

6 Which of the quantifiers from **5** can you use to

1 talk about small quantities / amounts? _____
2 talk about large quantities / amounts? _____
3 ask questions about quantities / amounts? _____
4 make negative statements about quantities / amounts? _____

7 Complete sentences 1–5 with words from **6**.

1 There is _____ extra space in my office – most of my cupboards are empty.
2 Have you got _____ spare time?
3 There's only _____ coffee left.
4 _____ people use our fitness room – but most people don't have _____ time.
5 We don't have _____ space, I'm afraid.

>> For more information and exercises, go to **Practice file 10** on page 121.

8 Work with a partner. Changes have been made to the workplace facilities in pictures a–c in **2**. Turn to File 29 on page 142 and talk about the changes.
Example: There's **a lot of space** in the lockers now.

9 Work with a partner. Make a list of the facilities you have or would like to have at work. Tell your partner why and how they are used, and what you think of them.
Example: We have a canteen because there **aren't many** restaurants nearby.
There **aren't any** showers because there **isn't enough** space.

ⓘ >> Interactive Workbook >> **Exercises and Tests**

Organizing a cause marketing event

Background

All for a good cause

Cause marketing is a type of marketing where a typical, 'for profit' business and a non-profit organization (for example, a charity like Unicef or Médecins Sans Frontières) work together. This cooperation has benefits for both partners. In the United States, companies spend more than a billion dollars per year on cause marketing and this amount is increasing.

Example 1

The French-owned company, Yoplait®, specializes in yogurt and desserts, and offers some 2,500 products in approximately 50 countries worldwide. In the United States, Yoplait® is working with the Susan G. Komen Breast Cancer Foundation to help raise awareness and money for research into breast cancer through its Save Lids to Save Lives® programme. This asks customers to send the company their pink Yoplait® yogurt lids. For every lid received, the company gives a sum of money to the Foundation.

Example 2

The UK-based mobile-phone company, Vodafone, is well known as a sponsor of the European football UEFA Champions League. Vodafone is also working with the National Autistic Society (NAS) to provide help for people with autism and their families. The company's role includes:

- setting up a database of services for people with autism which can be accessed online or by mobile phone
- paying for advertising and marketing campaigns to publicize the work of NAS and to raise awareness about autism
- recycling old mobile phones and giving the profits to NAS.

The Expert View

Marketing a corporate brand today means developing sustainable business practices, and being more socially responsible. Major supermarkets like Tesco and Wal-Mart have started to improve all aspects of their businesses, from energy use and transportation to store merchandizing. This also involves the cooperation of their suppliers, from the big multinationals like Unilever and Frito-Lay, to smaller local suppliers. International banks, such as HSBC, are committing billions of dollars to promote research into climate change and to support the development of sustainable products and services. Businesses need to decide how they can reduce their effect on the environment, and what advantage their brand image will gain as a result.

Simon Knox, Professor of Brand Marketing
Cranfield School of Management

Unit 10 | Facilities

Discussion

1 What are the advantages of cause marketing for both partners?

2 Why do you think these companies chose to work with these charities?

3 What possible disadvantages are there in this kind of arrangement?

Task

Your company produces bicycles. For the last two years the company has worked with a children's charity to promote health and fitness among young people. Last year, you held an open day at the factory for local people. The aim was to raise the company's profile in the community, and to create interest and raise money for the charity. You are on the committee to plan and organize another similar event this year.

1 Work in groups of three. Student A, turn to File 23 on page 140. Student B, turn to File 31 on page 142. Student C, turn to File 35 on page 144. Read the information in your files.

2 Take turns to make recommendations for this year's event. Respond to each others' recommendations and make further suggestions.

3 Decide on your final recommendations and present these to the class.

Case study

11 | Decisions

Learning objectives in this unit
- Talking about decision-making
- Participating in a discussion
- Being persuasive
- Using the first and second conditionals to talk about future possibilities

Activity
- The decision game

Starting point

1 Read how four people make decisions. Who are you most like?

'I trust my instinct. If I think too much about something, I often get it wrong.'

'Sometimes I rush into decisions too quickly and I often regret what I have done.'

'I make a list of the advantages and disadvantages of each option before I decide.'

'I ask people I trust what they think before I make up my mind. I find it hard to make decisions on my own.'

2 Is there a difference between the way you make decisions at work and at home?

Working with words | Decision-making

1 Read these texts and look at the diagrams of three decision-making processes. How are they different?

Suma is a large healthfood wholesaler. The company is a cooperative and practises a democratic decision-making process. All employees can take part in the decision-making.

Mitsubishi Motor Sales of America is changing the way it does business. 'We now have a completely collaborative process using a consensus decision-making model,' says Pierre Gagnon, Executive Vice President. This means that ideas are put forward by management, and are passed to other company employees to get their opinions.

At the Ford Motor Company, senior management members of the Strategy and Business Governance group decide on the direction of the company and make the necessary decisions.

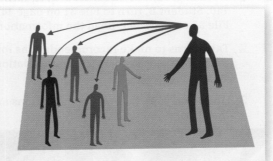

2 45, 46, 47▷ Franz, Stella, and Aidan are talking about how decisions are made where they work. Listen and match them to the companies in 1.

66

3 Which decision-making process in **1** is closest to that in your place of work?

4 45▷ **Listen to Franz again. Complete these words.**

1 a discussion where different expert opinions are heard before a decision is made: *con_____*

2 an argument or open conflict: *con_____*

3 something you agree to accept or do in order to reach an agreement or end an argument: *con_____*

4 an agreement where you get part of what you want: *com_____*

5 general agreement between a group of people: *con_____*

5 46▷ **Listen to Stella again. Match words from the list to definitions 1–9.**

*go for   brainstorm   options   in favour of   majority
hierarchy   backing   put forward   carry out*

1 the power and decision-making structure of an organization: _____

2 generate ideas imaginatively and energetically: _____

3 present / propose: _____

4 choices / alternatives: _____

5 support / approval: _____

6 most of the people: _____

7 for, not against: _____

8 choose: _____

9 perform / execute: _____

6 47▷ **Match the verbs in A to the nouns in B to make phrases. There is sometimes more than one combination. Then listen again and compare your answers.**

A	B
put forward	your mind
have	major decisions
express	a consensus
make	an idea
reach	confrontation
evaluate	a suggestion
carry out	a say
avoid	ideas
make up	an opinion

>> For more exercises, go to **Practice file 11** on page 122.

7 Work with a partner. Ask and answer questions using the phrases you made in **6**.

    Example: **A** *When did you last put forward an idea that was accepted?*
              B *I last put forward an idea that was accepted about a month ago.*

8 Work in small groups. Have a discussion on these two topics.
- You have to decide on a dress code (what to wear at work) for all members of staff.
- Someone has suggested that everybody should have the same salary, whatever their position in the company or their responsibilities.

9 Tell the rest of the class how your discussion went.

1 What different stages did you follow?

2 How much confrontation, consensus, compromise, and consultation were involved?

3 Who put forward some good ideas and who expressed opinions?

ⓘ >> Interactive Workbook >> **Glossary**

Tip | How to introduce a question

To signal that you are going to ask a question, you can begin with *so, now,* or *and*.

    So what happens if the workforce doesn't agree?
    And does this lead to strikes?
    Now how do you agree on something like that?

Meetings | Participating in a discussion

1 **48▷** In 2002, Stefan, Ilse, and Patrick founded an independent computer games shop in the backstreets of a large historic town. It is popular with students and young people who live in the area. A new shopping centre is opening outside town and they are discussing whether they should move their business there. Listen to three extracts from their discussion. Who

1 thinks they should start to think about growing? ____
2 mentions how easy it will be to park at the shopping centre? ____
3 reminds everyone about who their customers are? ____
4 suggests keeping the shop in town as well as going to the shopping centre? ____
5 is worried that there won't be any well-located shops left in the shopping centre? ____
6 would like to wait and see what big retailers plan to do? ____
7 suggests asking for independent advice? ____

2 **48▷** Listen again. Put phrases a–l below into categories 1–6.
1 Giving an opinion: _____
2 Agreeing: _____
3 Asking if there is a general agreement: _____
4 Acknowledging what someone else says: _____
5 Summarizing what someone has said: _____
6 Asking for suggestions for future action: _____

a Personally, I think we should …
b I agree with you, …
c I hear what you're saying, (but) …
d That's a nice idea, (but) …
e As far as I'm concerned, it's …
f I take your point, (but) …
g According to …,
h So if I've understood you correctly, …
i So, where do we go from here?
j So are we all agreed, then?
k Yes, that's fine with me.
l Me too.

⟫ For more exercises, go to **Practice file 11** on page 122.

3 Work with a partner. Take turns to choose a statement about using email from the list of pros and cons and exchange opinions. Use expressions from **2**. You can add your own ideas if you want.

> *Example:* **A** *As far as I'm concerned, email is the best form of communication in business because it's so fast and inexpensive.*
>
> **B** *I hear what you're saying but you don't always get an answer straight away.*
>
> **A** *Yes, good point.*

Pros: Email is the best form of communication in business because
- it's so fast and inexpensive
- you can send documents as attachments – no need to wait for the post
- you can pick up messages wherever you are in the world
- it gives you more time to think than a phone call does
- it means you have an accurate record of communications with a customer.

Cons: Email is not that great because
- you don't always get an answer straight away
- it's not as private as a letter
- you don't always have access to a computer
- it's not as personal as a handwritten letter
- it's easy to delete messages by mistake and therefore lose important information.

---

4 Work in small groups. A number of people where you work want your organization to become more ethical and democratic. Have a discussion on these proposals and decide whether to accept them or not.

---

1 All decisions will be made democratically using a 'works parliament'. Each member of staff will have one vote for every year they have worked at the firm (with a maximum of five votes).

2 For the health of employees, from now on the staff restaurant will only serve sugar-free soft drinks, decaffeinated coffee, and vegetarian meals.

3 As parking at the company is limited, only cars which carry at least two employees will be permitted to park.

4 At the moment, the highest paid worker earns ten times more than the lowest paid. This will be reduced to a four-to-one ratio.

ⓘ ›› Interactive Workbook ›› **Email**

Practically speaking | How to be persuasive

1 49▷ Listen to these extracts and note down the four phrases the speakers use to sound more persuasive.

1 _____   3 _____

2 _____   4 _____

2 Match the phrases in **1** to meanings a–d.

a I am about to mention something important we shouldn't forget. ____
b Be reasonable. ____
c I am going to tell the truth as I see it. ____
d We need to be realistic. ____

3 Work with a partner or in small groups. Discuss the following statements. Give yourself a point for each time you use one of the phrases from **1**.
- First impressions are nearly always the most reliable.
- Private health insurance creates inequality among people who are ill.
- All workers should receive a share of the company's profits.
- Two heads are always better than one.

Key expressions

Giving your opinion
Personally, I think / feel …
I think we should …
In my opinion, …
From my point of view, …
As I see it, …
As far as I'm concerned, …

Giving someone else's opinion
X says that we should …
According to X …
X maintains that …

Agreeing / disagreeing
I agree.
Exactly.
Absolutely.
I couldn't agree more.
I don't agree.
Yes, but …
I'm not (quite) sure about that …
That's fine with me.

Acknowledging what someone else says
Yes, good point.
I take your point.
I hear what you're saying, …
I can understand what you're saying.
Yes, fair enough.

Checking understanding
So what you're saying is …
So if I've followed what you've said, …
So if I understand you correctly, …

Reaching a decision
Does everyone agree?
Are we all agreed?
Is everyone happy with that?

ⓘ ›› Interactive Workbook
›› **Phrasebank**

Language at work | First and second conditionals

1 Read this email. What advice do you think Jeff will give?

> Dear Jeff
>
> I am writing to you to ask for your expert advice. We've got the opportunity to relocate our computer games shop to a new out-of-town shopping centre. If we ¹*had / have* more money, we would keep the shop in town and open up at the shopping centre too. However, that's not an option for us. If we ²*don't keep / won't keep* this shop, we'll lose most of our current customers who are local students without cars. However, if we move, we ³*would / will* have a larger base of potential (and wealthy) customers.
> We'd greatly appreciate it if you could advise us on this matter. Please could you let us know if you are able to do so asap.
>
> Many thanks and best wishes
>
> Ilse

2 Choose the correct answer from the words in *italics* in the email in **1**.

3 Match sentences a–c below to meanings 1–3.
1 Something that might or might not happen and the result: ____
2 Something that is impossible or very unlikely to happen: ____
3 Something that is likely to happen: ____
a If we **had** more money, we **would keep** the shop.
b If we **don't keep** this shop, we**'ll lose** most of our current customers.
c If we **move**, we **will have** a larger base of potential customers.

4 Which word / phrase in *italics* in 1–2 means 'just imagine'? Which means 'if not'?
1 They won't be able to get to the shopping centre *unless* they have a car.
2 *What if* we kept the shop here and opened up in the shopping centre?

>> For more information and exercises, go to **Practice file 11** on page 123.

5 Work with a partner. Complete 1–7 using the meter on the left which tells you how likely the event is (*I* = impossible / unlikely, *C* = certain / likely).

1 If I _____ (win) salesperson of the month competition, I _____ (go) to Prague to celebrate.

2 If our bosses _____ (listen to) us more it _____ (avoid) so much confrontation.

3 We _____ (understand) her arguments better if she _____ (explain) herself more clearly.

4 If people _____ (cooperate) more willingly, we _____ (make) faster progress.

5 What _____ (you / do) when you _____ (retire)?

6 What _____ (you / do) if they _____ (offer) you the job in New York?

7 How _____ (you / react) if your company _____ (relocate) to the other side of the country?

6 Work with a partner. Discuss what you will / would do if your
- company is / was relocated to another part of the country or abroad?
- firm is / was taken over by its main competitor?
- partner gets / got a new job a long way from home / abroad?
- boss's job becomes / became vacant?

ⓘ >> Interactive Workbook >> **Exercises and Tests**

The decision game

Work in small groups. You work at the Central Bank, a British bank with branches in most towns and cities. All of your call centres are based in the UK, in areas of high unemployment. You must make a series of decisions which will affect the future of these call centres. Work together and make your first decision by choosing option **a** or **b**. Start at **1**. Follow the instructions.

1
Senior management want you to cut costs and improve profitability. In India, call centre workers are paid five times less than in the UK. You decide to
a keep the call centres in the UK and accept higher costs. **Go to 6**.
b investigate more fully the cost and benefits of moving the call centres. **Go to 2**.

6
Shareholders complain that you are less profitable than rival banks. They are still putting pressure on you to cut costs. You decide to
a please shareholders by closing some less profitable branches. **Go to 9**.
b organize a newspaper campaign explaining to the public why you want to keep the call centre jobs in the UK. **Go to 4**.

11
Your negotiations with the union have reached a crossroads. The union wants to reduce UK job losses to a minimum. You decide to
a keep just 150 UK call centre jobs and risk a strike. **Go to 14**.
b keep 400 UK jobs which will satisfy the union. **Go to 5**.

2
If you close the UK call centres, 1,000 jobs will be lost. You do not want to cause unnecessary panic because you are still at the investigation stage. You decide to
a be open about your plans. **Go to 8**.
b keep your plans confidential for the moment. **Go to 15**.

7
Customers are even angrier when they receive your letter. They don't care what your motives are. You decide to
a ignore the complaints. **Go to 13**.
b invest more money in staff training. **Go to 3**.

12
Union negotiations have been successful. Both sides have compromised. You have agreed to keep 250 UK jobs. The bank offers you a tough new mission which involves closing other unprofitable branches. You decide to
a accept their tough new mission. **Go to 10**.
b stay where you are, happy that you have survived a difficult moment. **Return to 1 or end here**.

3
The India call centre is now a success and complaints have dropped. However, an Indian worker now costs a third as much as a UK worker and soon will cost half as much. You will now have to look for a cheaper alternative or think of other places where costs might be cheaper. **Return to 1 or end here**.

8
UK call centre employees have heard about your possible plans to go to India. They want full consultation with the union. You decide to
a involve the union and discuss the plans with them. **Go to 11**.
b ignore the union and go ahead with your plans. **Go to 14**.

13
Angry customers contact Head Office and name you as personally responsible for the problems. Senior managers are happy to use you as a scapegoat. You are moved to manage a small branch in the countryside. It is the end of your ambitions. **Return to 1 or end here**.

4
A newspaper has run a campaign praising you as the patriotic bank. This is good for your image, but means that your hands could be tied in the future. **Return to 1 or end here**.

9
Your plan to close smaller branches will cost 500 jobs. This causes protest from the union and from customers who live near the small branches. You decide to
a carry on with the closures. **Go to 10**.
b reconsider other ways of cutting costs, including the call centre option. **Go to 2**.

14
There have been three one-day strikes in selected branches. You decide to
a face up to the union and refuse to change your position. **Go to 13**.
b re-open negotiations with the union. **Go to 12**.

5
Now you have solved the union problems, the call centre is going ahead. However, UK customers say there are often communication problems with the Indian-based call handlers. You decide to
a ask senior management to invest more money in staff training. **Go to 3**.
b send a letter to customers explaining the need to set up in India. **Go to 7**.

10
Going ahead with the branch closures loses the bank several thousand customers and gets a lot of negative publicity. You lose your job! **Return to 1 or end here**.

15
Someone has leaked the story about the India plans to the union. You are attacked in the press as an exporter of British jobs. You decide to
a deny everything and go ahead with the plans in secret. **Go to 14**.
b open up negotiations with the union. **Go to 11**.

Activity

12 | Innovation

Learning objectives in this unit

- Talking about innovation and new ideas
- Giving a formal presentation
- Responding to difficult questions and comments
- Using superlative forms to talk about extremes

Case study
- Presenting innovative products

Starting point

1 Work with a partner. Put these twentieth-century innovations and inventions in order from the earliest (*1*) to the most recent (*6*).

_____ photocopier

_____ Velcro

_____ handheld calculator

_____ vacuum cleaner

_____ instant coffee

_____ parking meter

Check your answers in File 09 on page 137.

2 Which inventions and innovations of the twentieth century do you think were the most
- important?
- useful?

Working with words | Innovation and new ideas

1 When and where do you get your best ideas? At work? After lunch? In the middle of the night? When you're exercising? In the car?

2 Read this article and answer questions 1–2.
1 Why did Mitchell Ditkoff and John Havens invent The Breakthrough Café?
2 Would you like to go there?

Food for thought

The Breakthrough Café is the **brainchild** of Mitchell Ditkoff and John Havens. The aim is that customers will have at least one **'a-ha' moment** during an evening that is a combination of 'party, restaurant, and brainstorming session'.

Over a three-course meal, customers begin by meeting each other and reading their name badges. The name badge also contains the words 'How can I ...?' Each customer completes this with a question about an idea or **obstacle** in their life. For example, 'How can I start my own catering business?', 'How can I find someone to invest in my **prototype**?', 'How can I get a new job?' As well as discussing and giving advice to each other, there are 'Innowaiters' who serve food and drink, but also act as **facilitators** to encourage **innovative** ideas.

Ditkoff explains how he first **came up with** the **concept**. 'I've asked thousands of people: "Where do you get your best ideas? What is the **catalyst**?" Less than one per cent of people say they get their ideas at work. They get their ideas when they are happy, away from the office, late at night, and in the company of friends.'

3 Match the words in **bold** from the text in **2** to definitions 1–9.
1 an idea for something new: _____
2 an idea or invention of one person or group of people: _____
3 new and original: _____
4 when you suddenly realize or understand something: _____
5 people who help you: _____
6 something to cause change: _____
7 think of a new idea or plan: _____
8 something stopping you: _____
9 the first form of something new: _____

4 50▷ The article in **2** gives three examples of questions people might ask at the café. Listen to three conversations at the Breakthrough Café. Which question from the article does each person have on his / her badge?

1 _____ 2 _____ 3 _____

5 50▷ Listen again. Tick (✓) adjectives each speaker uses to describe the three categories in the table.

	Job / Company	Technology	Idea
dynamic	✓		
original			
reliable			
revolutionary			
simple			
sophisticated			
traditional			

>> For more exercises, go to **Practice file 12** on page 124.

6 Work with a partner. Dicuss these questions and give reasons for your answers.
1 Which of the adjectives in **5** describe your company or job?
2 How would you describe the technology you use?

7 Read these quotes from people talking about ideas and obstacles in their lives. Work in small groups. Think of different ways to help these three people. Then tell the class.

1 ❝ I have this really simple idea for setting up a cleaning company where we clean local companies and people's houses. The only problem is I have two small children who aren't at school yet. How can I do both? ❞

2 ❝ My brainchild is a motorbike that runs on hydrogen, not petrol. I've already built a prototype, but how can I get the money to manufacture and market it? ❞

3 ❝ I've retired with a pension but I'm bored. I have some money, but I don't know what to do with it. I don't want to work too hard. What could I do? ❞

8 Think back to all the ideas and discussions in **7** and answer questions 1–4.
1 During the group discussion, did you hear any ideas which were
   • innovative? • original?
   • simple? • other?
   • revolutionary?
2 Which was the best 'brainchild' you heard?
3 Who was the most useful facilitator or catalyst in your group?
4 What obstacles did you encounter?

9 Work with a partner and compare your answers to **8**.

10 Write your own *How can I …?* question.
1 Tell the class your question and ask each person to give you an idea / solution.
2 Choose your favourite idea and explain why you like it.
   Example: I like the idea that Antje came up with because it's simple but also very innovative and original.

ⓘ >> Interactive Workbook >> **Glossary**

Tip | *invention* and *innovation*

An *invention* is a design of something new. An *innovation* is an idea or way of doing something that is completely different from anything that has gone before.

Presenting | Giving a formal presentation

1 Read this company mission statement. Do you have something similar for your company?

> Bertran RL aims to create innovative and state-of-the-art conferencing technology products of the highest value, with the greatest reliability and simplicity we can offer. We achieve this with employees who deserve the very best in professional support and development.

Agenda

1 How we want to be seen

2 Current company situation

3 Finding a mission statement

2 51▷ The PR Manager of Bertran RL is giving a presentation about rewriting their mission statement. Listen to her introduction. Correct the agenda.

3 51▷ Put these phrases from the PR manager's introduction in the right order 1–7. Then listen again and check your answers.
_____ **a** First, I'm going to talk …
_____ **b** Feel free to ask questions …
_____ **c** We have a lot to do, so let's start.
_____ **d** Good morning, everyone, and thanks for coming.
_____ **e** I'd like to begin by explaining …
_____ **f** And finally, after coffee, we'll try to …
_____ **g** Then, we'll try to …

sophisticated
simple
traditional
innovative
up-to-date
reliable

4 52▷ Listen to the next part of the presentation. What do the coloured words on the slide represent?

5 52▷ Listen again and complete phrases 1–3 for referring to visuals.
1 First of all, _____ slide.
2 _____ it has a number of words that describe our company.
3 _____ some words are in blue and some are in red.

6 53▷ Listen to the final part of the presentation. Why does Rudi criticize mission statements? Do you agree with him?

7 53▷ Correct the mistakes in 1–5. Then listen again and check your answers.
1 That's everything I want to tell for the moment.
2 Thank you all for listen.
3 The best reason for this meeting is to …
4 Are there any answers?
5 We think it a good idea because …

>> For more exercises, go to **Practice file 12** on page 124.

8 Prepare and give a short presentation using as many of the phrases in **3**, **5**, and **7** as possible. Talk about one of the objects below. You have one minute to convince your partner why this object is the best or most useful in the world. Follow the four stages in the flow chart.

- pen
- MP3 player
- mobile phone
- paper
- laptop
- cash card

1 Introduce your object
I'm going to tell you about …

2 Show your object
As you can see …

3 Explain why
The best thing about it is …

4 End the presentation
Thanks for listening …

9 Prepare and give a longer presentation to your partner or the rest of class about how your customers view your company, service, or product. Design a slide with adjectives you think your customers would use. Organize the presentation like this.

- Introduce the aim and structure of the presentation.
- Present the slide and explain the main reasons for each adjective.
- Close the talk and answer any questions.

ⓘ **»** Interactive Workbook **»** **Email**

Practically speaking | How to respond to difficult questions and comments

1 54▷ Listen to the final part of a presentation. Tick (✓) the methods of responding to questions the presenter uses.

1 Ask for the question again. ____
2 Compliment the question. ____
3 Explain that you will answer the person later. ____
4 Understand their opinion, but disagree. ____
5 Say you don't understand the question. ____
6 Understand their opinion. ____

2 Match 1–6 in **1** to a–f.

a Sorry, I couldn't hear you. ____
b Yes, I know what you mean, but … ____
c Good question. ____
d Sorry, I don't think I follow you. ____
e I totally agree with you. ____
f Can I get back to you on that one? ____

3 Work with a partner. Here are some difficult questions and comments from a presentation. Take turns to ask / say them, and answer using some of the techniques above.

❝ Why did the company have its lowest profits ever this year? ❞

❝ Why are sales of our latest product so low? ❞

❝ What's the current sales situation in Brazil? ❞

❝ How do you propose to satisfy increasing customer demand? ❞

❝ I think we are risking losing our profit margin. ❞

Key expressions

Starting
Good morning and thanks for coming.
I'm here today to …
Let's start.
My name's … and I'm going to tell you / talk about …
I'd like to begin by (+ -ing) …

Previewing
First, I'll / I'm going to …
Then, we'll …
And finally …
Feel free to ask questions.
I'll take questions at the end.

Referring to visuals
Let's look at this …
As you can see, …
You'll notice that …

Explaining reasons / benefits
The main reason for this meeting is …
The best thing about this is …
We think it's a good idea because …

Closing
That's everything I want to say.
That brings me to the end of my presentation.
Thanks for listening.
Are there any (more) questions?

ⓘ **»** Interactive Workbook
» **Phrasebank**

Language at work | Superlative forms

1 Read this extract from a sales brochure for a Bertran RL conference-call system and correct the mistake in each line.

> **CallTerminal VVX 1000**
> Your conference room phone is one of your most valuablest assets. Multicell's
> CallTerminal VVX 1000 delivers best sound quality and picks up speech
> from six metres away – that's a furthest of any on the market.
> Conference-call participants are happyest with Multicell!

2 Read this article and answer questions 1–2.
1   What is DreamWorks famous for?
2   What is its new innovation?

> For most people, DreamWorks Animation (DWA) is probably best known for
> producing films like *Toy Story* and, recently, *Shrek 2*, which was the third highest-
> grossing film of all time. However, the company's latest release isn't a film, but what
> may be the most sophisticated videoconferencing system the world has ever seen.

3 <u>Underline</u> the superlative forms in the article in **2**.

4 Match extracts a–c to rules 1–3 about using the superlative.
1   To describe the maximum or minimum: _____
2   To place something in a position after first place: _____
3   With the present perfect to describe our experience of something: _____

a   … **the most sophisticated** videoconferencing system the world has ever seen.
b   … the company's **latest** release …
c   … the **third highest-grossing** film of all time.

>> For more information and exercises, go to **Practice file 12** on page 125.

5 Work with a partner. Using the words in the table below, take turns to ask and answer questions. You will need to use the superlative form of the adjectives.

> *Example:* A   *What's **the worst** decision you've ever made?*
> B   *Leaving my first company.*
> A   *So what's **the second worst** decision you've ever made?*
> B   *Joining this one!*

What's / Who's the (second / third)	bad good big nice beautiful friendly exciting	country / place film decision person hotel idea experience	you've ever	met? made? had? seen? stayed at? visited? heard?

6 Work with a partner. Make a list of ways to communicate with colleagues and clients.
1   Which do you like best and why?
2   Which do you like least and why?
> *Example: I like email **the best** because it's **the quickest** and **easiest** way to contact someone.*

ⓘ >> Interactive Workbook >> **Exercises and Tests**

Presenting innovative products

Background

Clever products

A clever car

The Kenguru is a car with a difference, designed specifically for wheelchair users. Built in Hungary, it is small, stylish and easy to park and gives users greater freedom and independence.

The Kenguru holds one passenger in a wheelchair. It doesn't have doors or seats like a normal car. To get in, the driver opens the extra large back door and rolls inside without leaving the wheelchair. The chair automatically locks into place inside the car. The controls are simpler than a normal car too – a joystick instead of a steering wheel means that drivers with limited arm mobility can easily control the vehicle.

The Kenguru is electrically powered. It has a range of up to 60 km and a top speed of 35–40 km/h, and costs about the same as a small family car.

An intelligent water pump

Tom Smith, a science graduate from Cambridge in the UK, has developed a new kind of pump which is powered by the sun's heat. This means it can be used in places that do not have electricity.

Tom is working on two possible uses for the pump. One use is to help supply water to farmers in parts of the developing world. The other, more commercial use is to create a more energy-efficient way of circulating hot water in central-heating systems.

The pump can raise water from several metres under the ground, so it is very useful for farmers in the developing world.

The pump has no moving parts and it can be produced very cheaply.

The Expert View

How can organizations become more innovative? Many senior managers want their companies to develop products and services that create new market opportunities. However, this is challenging because there are many elements to managing innovation. Companies need, for example, to develop better ways of discovering customer needs and to create the right 'culture of innovation'. These are issues that top managers need to devote sufficient time to. Don't neglect innovation – if you do, your organization will never reach its true potential.

Keith Goffin, Professor of Innovation and New Product Development

Cranfield School of Management

Unit 12 | Innovation

Discussion

1 What are the particular selling points of these two products?

2 Who are the customers for these products?

3 How can these products be marketed effectively?

Task

1 **Work with a partner or in small groups.**

   1 Brainstorm things that you would like to improve in your everyday life – for example, at home, in your workplace, in your local community.

   2 Choose one of these problems and brainstorm ways to improve or solve it. It could be a new product, invention, or idea for a new way of doing things or for adapting an existing product.

2 **Prepare and give a presentation of your new brainchild to the class. You will need to**

- open the presentation
- show a simple design of the new item / idea
- explain why it is the best idea
- describe your target market and explain how you would promote your product
- close the presentation and answer any questions.

Case study

77

13 | Breakdown

Learning objectives in this unit
- Talking about breakdowns and faults
- Discussing problems and offering advice
- Checking someone understands
- Using the language of advice and recommendation to offer help

Case study
- Managing a breakdown in service

Starting point

1 What kinds of breakdown can you think of?

2 Is it acceptable to produce goods and provide services that are not 100% perfect?

3 Which of these products would you be prepared to buy at a discounted price if they had a defect? Why / why not?
- furniture
- jewellery
- food products
- clothing
- toys
- electronic equipment
- books
- cars

Working with words | Breakdowns and faults

1 Read these extracts 1–3 from defect policy statements and match them to the products in pictures a–c.

1
In the case of product **failure**, please contact the number below to obtain a returns code. Please return the **defective** unit to us in its original packaging together with a description of the fault and a note of the returns code.

2
If you are not completely satisfied with the quality of our products or if the packaging is **damaged**, please retain the product and the packaging and return to the address above within 48 hours of receipt. Please include a note about the nature of the problem and state whether you would prefer a refund or replacement.

3
Products may be returned for product dissatisfaction, size changes and manufacturer **defect**. If a product is damaged we will pay for shipping.

2 Match the words in **bold** from the texts in 1 to definitions 1–4.
1 with a mistake or fault in it: _____
2 harmed or spoiled: _____
3 a mistake or fault: _____
4 case of something not working / functioning as expected: _____

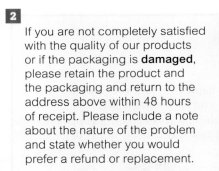
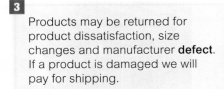

3 Match 1–8 to a–h.

1 The campaign has **gone wrong** … ____
2 We can't do any work on our computers at the moment … ____
3 We didn't get the products in time for Christmas … ____
4 It has definitely **broken down** … ____
5 I need to exchange my new keyboard … ____
6 I can't open this file … ____
7 There must have been a **misunderstanding** … ____
8 We'll have to use the stairs … ____

a because it's **faulty** – the space bar doesn't work.
b because the lift is **out of order**.
c because the product has a major **flaw** and it won't be ready in time for the launch.
d because I asked for 40 but I got 14!
e because our supplier **let** us **down**. They are very **unreliable**.
f because the format of it is **incompatible** with the software I use.
g because the server is **down**. There must be a **bug** that needs to be fixed.
h because it won't do anything and this red light is on.

4 Which words in **bold** from the texts in **1** and from **3** would you normally use to talk about these things? Some words may go in more than one category.

1 people   2 objects   3 companies

» For more exercises, go to **Practice file 13** on page 126.

5 Work with a partner. Describe and analyse the possible problems in these pictures. Use as many words from **2** and **3** as possible.

6 Work in small groups. Discuss the problems you might have with the following.
- two teams from different countries working together
- a very old office building
- a traditional office hierarchy
- buying electrical or electronic products abroad
- buying a second-hand computer
- buying things online

    Example: *If you buy a product abroad and it is faulty, it is very difficult to get it fixed or replaced.*

ⓘ **»** Interactive Workbook **»** Glossary

Exchanging information | Discussing problems

1 What kind of problems do you have with office equipment or computers? How good are you at fixing them yourself?

2 55▷ Listen to two conversations and complete this table.

	Problem	Diagnosis	Solution / cure
1			
2			

3 55▷ Listen again and complete the phrases in *italics*.
1 Hi, Magda. *What's the _____?*
2 My boss _____ *on* giving me extra work.
3 *What do you _____ by* 'extra work'?
4 Well, *it looks _____* you have a communication problem to me.
5 *Have you _____* talking to her?
6 Well, I'd ask to speak to her *if I _____ you.*
7 *I _____ you should* ask for an extension on the deadline.
8 *That should _____ it out* temporarily.
9 Good afternoon. _____ *can I help?*
10 OK. *What's wrong with it _____?*
11 Well, *it's _____* crashing.
12 *When you _____* 'it's always crashing', *do you _____ ...?*
13 Well, *it _____ as though* it could be a battery problem.
14 *The _____ thing would be* to buy a new battery.
15 *That _____ fix it.*

4 Which phrases in *italics* in 3 express the following ideas?
a Do you have a problem? _____
b He / She / It ... all the time. _____
c Give me more details. _____
d I think the problem is ... _____
e My advice is ... _____
f That should solve the problem. _____

5 Put this conversation in the right order 1–10. Then work with a partner. Read the conversation.
___ **a B** Someone in your accounts department.
___ **b A** It sounds like a problem with our telephone system. Who were you trying to speak to?
___ **c A** The best thing would be for me to give Accounts your details and get them to call you. That should sort it out.
___ **d A** Have you tried dialing their direct line?
___ **e B** Yes and it's always when I've just managed to get through to the right person.
___ **f A** When you say 'cut off', do you mean that the line just goes dead?
_1_ **g A** Good afternoon. How can I help?
___ **h B** I'm trying to speak to someone at your company but I keep getting cut off.
___ **i B** OK. Thanks. My number is 01654 543321.
___ **j B** Yes, I have. But the same thing always happens.

>> For more exercises, go to **Practice file 13** on page 126.

Tip | *always*

We use *always* + present simple to talk about a habit or regular activity.
*She **always takes** the bus to work.*
We use *always* + present continuous to talk about an annoying habit.
*She**'s always taking** my stapler.*

6 Work with a partner. Have conversations about the two problems below using this flow chart.

A Ask about the problem.	
	B Explain the problem.
A Ask for more details.	
	B Respond.
A Make a diagnosis.	
	B Respond.
A Suggest action.	
	B Respond and thank A.

1 Your team members often have meetings without you, so you don't know what is happening with the project.

2 You have received fifteen complaints in the last week about one of your products not working. It is a piece of software that doesn't work on some systems.

7 Work in groups and try to speak for at least a minute on these subjects. Then listen to the others in your group. When they have finished, ask for more details and offer a solution.
- a problem with a piece of office equipment
- a communication breakdown at work
- an unreliable or untrustworthy colleague

ⓘ **»** Interactive Workbook **»** Email

Practically speaking | How to check someone understands

1 56▷ Listen to four conversations. Match 1–4 to a–d.
1 Do you know … ____
2 Does that … ____
3 Is that … ____
4 Do you … ____

a make sense?
b clear?
c see?
d what I mean?

2 56▷ Listen again. Does the listener understand what the first person is saying?

3 Which of these responses show the person understands? Which ones show they don't understand?
1 Absolutely.
2 Kind of, but …
3 I don't get …
4 I see what you mean …

4 Work with a partner. Take turns to explain the following to your partner and check that he / she understands
- why it is important to get on with your colleagues
- what you want to change about your working conditions and why
- how to make a domestic appliance work
- how to book time off from work

Key expressions

Asking what the problem is
What's the matter?
How can I help?
So what appears to be the problem?

Explaining the problem
It keeps on (+ -ing).
It's always (+ -ing).
It won't (+ verb).
It means that …

Asking for details
What's wrong with it exactly?
What do you mean by …?
What sort of noise / smell is it?
When you say …, do you mean …?

Diagnosing the problem
It looks / sounds like …
It looks / sounds as though …
It could be …
It might be …

Advising
The best thing would be to …
I'd advise you to …
If I were you, I'd …
Have you tried (+ noun / -ing)?
I think you should …

Confirming a solution
That should fix it.
That should sort it out.
That should solve the problem.

ⓘ **»** Interactive Workbook
» Phrasebank

Language at work | Advice and recommendation | *too* and *enough*

1 **Put a–g below into categories 1–4.**

   1 Asking for advice: _____

   2 Giving advice: _____

   3 Introducing an option: _____

   4 Giving an instruction: _____

   a I think you **should** ask for an extension.

   b You **have to** get it approved by management.

   c **I'd** ask to speak to her if I were you.

   d Well, you **could** just use the electrical lead.

   e What **should** I do?

   f What **would** you do in this situation?

   g I **would** buy a new battery.

2 **Read 1–3. <u>Underline</u> the adjectives and circle the nouns.**

   1 Is the job too difficult?

   2 I don't have enough time.

   3 It's easy enough to do.

3 **Do we use *enough* with nouns or with adjectives?**

4 **When do we use *too*?**

5 **Choose the correct answer from the words in *bold italics*.**

   1 We use *too* before ***nouns / adjectives*** to emphasize them.

   2 We use *enough **before / after*** nouns and ***before / after*** adjectives.

>> For more information and exercises, go to **Practice file 13** on page 127.

6 **Work with a partner. Take turns to give and receive advice and instructions. Student A, turn to File 33 on page 143. Student B, turn to File 37 on page 144.**

7 **Work with a partner. Look at these pictures and identify the problems. Take turns to be the people in one of the pictures. Ask you partner for advice. Have conversations using phrases for advice and recommendation and *too* and *enough*.**

---

i >> Interactive Workbook >> **Exercises and Tests**

Managing a breakdown in service

Background

A community-minded company

One World Bazaar sells handmade products from developing countries in Africa, Asia and Latin America, with an emphasis on quality and good design. It sells the products online via their website and also supplies over 300 independent shops in Europe.

What makes One World Bazaar different from most companies is that it was set up to benefit the producers of the products it sells, rather than the customers. The producers are craftmakers in some of the poorest parts of the world and their work helps to build up communities, relieve poverty and improve social and environmental conditions.

All the products come from cooperatives set up by the producers in their local communities. The producers are paid a realistic amount of money for the job, which takes account of the local cost of living and the amount of skill involved. One World Bazaar always pays them on time and adds an extra payment, called a 'community surcharge', to prices when market conditions allow. The cooperatives use the extra money to benefit the whole community. The company also provides working capital to producers who need money for materials or equipment, and any remaining profits from sales are also reinvested in projects to benefit the local community.

Discussion

1 **Who benefits from the way a company like One World Bazaar operates? Do you think this is good? Why / why not?**

2 **Think about the way One World Bazaar sells their products and who they supply them to. What problems might a company like this have as a result of the way it operates?**

The Expert View

Producers do not maintain relationships with customers only for the customers' benefit. However, a close working relationship between producers and customers has many benefits for both parties. The value of such a working relationship can be considered as a trade-off between these benefits, and the sacrifices that both parties expect to make. For a good long-term relationship to develop, the benefits need to be greater than the sacrifices. The mutual benefit and value of the relationship may be put in danger if either party fails to fulfil the requirements of the other – for example, by failing to provide the expected level of service support.

Dr Bob Lillis, Lecturer in Service Operations Management

Cranfield School of Management

Task

The company is currently experiencing some problems. Hits to the website are up by 30% but the number of orders is down by 20%. The company profits have fallen by 10%. There is an increasing number of complaints which fall into these three categories

- problems using the website for online ordering
- poor quality / condition of goods received
- problems with supply and delivery times.

1 **Work in groups of three. You are holding a meeting to discuss the problems at One World Bazaar. Read some of the customer complaints about**
   - online ordering – Student A, turn to File 34 on page 143
   - products – Student B, turn to File 38 on page 144
   - supply and delivery – Student C, turn to File 26 on page 141.

2 **Summarize the complaints for your colleagues.**

3 **Listen to your colleagues' summaries and ask for more details if necessary.**

4 **Discuss the complaints and suggest possible solutions.**

5 **Decide what the company needs to do in order to improve its service to its customers.**

Case study

14 | Processes

Learning objectives in this unit
- Talking about processes
- Making and changing future plans
- Getting someone's attention
- Using the passive to talk about processes

Case study
- Introducing new processes

Starting point

1 **Work with a partner. Brainstorm the stages for any of the following processes.**
   - applying for a job
   - moving your office
   - buying a house

2 **Compare your stages with another pair. Who has the most stages? Are they all necessary?**

Working with words | Processes

1 **Read this company information and answer questions 1–2.**
   1 What kind of fuel do you use in your car? How is biodiesel different?
   2 Is the oil from the jatropha plant a recent discovery?

D1 Oils Building its biodiesel business

D1 Oils is a UK-based global producer of biodiesel. We design, build, own, operate, and market biodiesel refineries. Our vision is to be the world's leading biodiesel business.

Our refinery can produce 8,000 tonnes of biodiesel per year from vegetable oils, including jatropha.

The jatropha plant originated in South America, where its leaves and seeds were used as medicines. It has also been used for centuries to make oil lamps.

2 57▷ **A biofuels company wants to open a new refinery. The CEO, Dr Karl Kirstler, is explaining the process to potential investors. Listen and answer questions 1–3.**
   1 Is the basic procedure complex or simple?
   2 What are the main stages of the process?
   3 What is the end product?

3 57▷ **Listen again and complete sentences 1–6.**

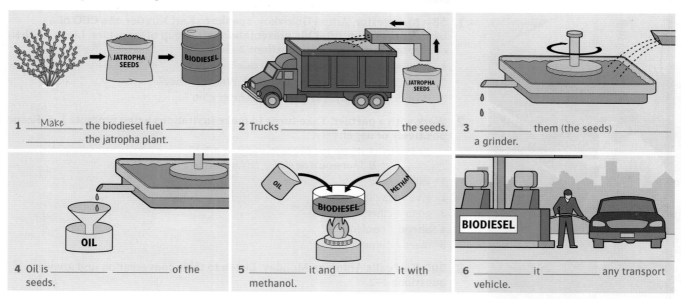

1 ___Make___ the biodiesel fuel _____ _____ the jatropha plant.

2 Trucks _____ the seeds.

3 _____ them (the seeds) _____ a grinder.

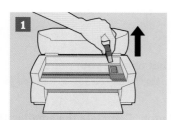

4 Oil is _____ _____ of the seeds.

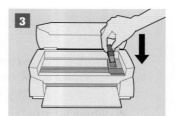

5 _____ it and _____ it with methanol.

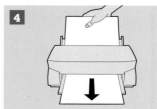

6 _____ it _____ any transport vehicle.

4 Work with a partner. Look at this process of recycling printer ink cartridges. Which verb phrases in **3** can you use to describe the actions in stages 1–4?

> *Example:* *Take the cartridge out of the printer.*

5 These phrases are from audio 57▷. Put them in the order (1–6) you would use them in to describe the process in **4**.

____ **a** Once …, you're ready to …
____ **b** The basic procedure is …
____ **c** Essentially, there are … main stages.
____ **d** First of all, …
____ **e** Having done / finished / brought, etc. …, you …
____ **f** Finally, …

>> For more exercises, go to **Practice file 14** on page 128.

6 Choose one of these processes and list the main stages using the phrases from **5**.
- loading new software on to a computer
- interviewing people for a job
- preparing for a business trip
- going through an airport – from arriving at the entrance to getting on the plane

7 Work with a partner. Take turns to describe your processes from **6**. Does your partner think you included every stage?

8 Work with a partner. Prepare a visual aid to show the stages of a process you are very familiar with. Then present the process to the rest of the class.

ⓘ >> Interactive Workbook >> Glossary

Tip | pick up

The meaning of *pick up* is different here from the one you learnt in Unit 6. Here it literally means *to take hold of something and lift it up.*

Socializing | Planning future contact

1 58▷ An investor, Anton Golovkov, speaks to Karl Kirstler, the CEO of a biofuels company, after his presentation to a group of investors. Listen to their conversation and answer questions 1–3.

  1 Why is Anton interested in Karl's talk?

  2 Anton makes two invitations to Karl. What are they?

  3 How does Karl say 'yes'? How does he say 'no'?

2 Work with a partner. Take turns to make invitations using prompts 1–5. Respond positively or negatively.

  Example: *A Would you like to join us for a drink?*

               B That would be nice. / I'd love to, but I …

  1 join / drink

  2 give / training session

  3 go to / cinema

  4 attend / conference

  5 meet / dinner

3 59▷ Karl calls Anton on Monday. Listen to their conversation and answer questions 1–2.

  1 What is the change of plan?

  2 What is the main reason for the change?

4 59▷ Listen again and complete these sentences.

  1 There's been a slight _____.

  2 _____, we won't be able to give you a date at this stage.

  3 I _____. These things happen.

  4 It's _____ that we can't meet soon.

5 Work with a partner. Use the situations in **2** again but change your plans.

  Example: *I'm sorry, but there's been a slight change of plan. I won't be able to join you for a drink because …*

6 Three months later, Karl receives an email from Anton. Complete the email with the more formal phrase, **a** or **b**, from 1–6 below.

Dear Dr Kirstler

You may remember that about three months ago we met at your investors' presentation in Tallinn. At the time ¹___ which, as a result, meant we weren't able to proceed with your proposal.

²___ for ³___. However, since then the position is clearer and ⁴___ Moscow to present your investment proposal to a group of investors. We ⁵___ meet you. Please find full details of the group in the attached document. ⁶___ too short notice for you to join us in Moscow?

I look forward to hearing from you.

Sincerely
Anton Golovkov

---

  1 **a** there was a slight change of plan / **b** something came up

  2 **a** I would like to apologize / **b** Sorry

  3 **a** messing you around / **b** any inconvenience caused

  4 **a** I would now like to invite you to / **b** how about joining us in

  5 **a** 'd love to / **b** would all appreciate the opportunity to

  6 **a** I was wondering if next week would be / **b** Would next week be

7 Karl has to change his plans. Read his email to a close colleague. Complete it with five of the less formal phrases in **6**. You may need to change the form of the verb.

Hi Robert

I ¹_____ meet you here next week, but ²_____.
Do you remember Anton Golovkov from the Tallinn seminar. Well, he's finally invited me to Moscow. ³_____ for ⁴_____ but you know how important this is. ⁵_____ Stockholm the week after?
Best wishes
Karl

>> For more exercises, go to **Practice File 14** on page 128.

8 Work with a partner. Have two phone calls. Use phrases from **6**.

	Student A	Student B
Call 1	You invited B to speak to a group of your colleagues on 13 May. However, you need to change this to 20 May. Call B.	You were invited to speak at a company on 13 May. The organizer, A, calls you.
Call 2	You have a meeting on 16 June with your close colleague, B. He / she calls you about it.	Call your close colleague, A, to change your meeting on 16 June because you are giving a talk that day.

9 Work with a partner. Using your own diaries, make a series of phone calls. Take turns to invite each other to an event from your schedule. Accept or decline the invitations according to your availability. If you accept, make another call to change the arrangement and explain why.

ⓘ » Interactive Workbook » **Email**

Practically speaking | How to get someone's attention

1 Which response a–g below can you *not* use to respond to phrases 1–6?

1 Have you got a minute? ____
2 Are you busy? ____
3 Is this a good time? ____
4 Sorry to bother you … ____
5 Can I interrupt you for a second? ____
6 Can I talk to you for a moment? ____

a Yes, what can I do for you?
b Well, actually it's not a good time.
c Yes, sure.
d No, not at all.
e Well, I am rather busy at the moment.
f I am a bit busy, sorry.
g That's OK.

2 Work in two groups, Group 1 and Group 2.
1 Group 1, begin chatting with a partner or in small groups.
2 Group 2, after a few moments, try to politely get the attention of one of the people in Group 1, then continue a conversation with them.
3 Those in Group 1 with no partner must now try to get the attention of someone else. Continue until you have used as many of the expressions in **1** as possible.

Key expressions

Inviting
I'd like to invite you to …
I was wondering if you would like to …
I'd be delighted if you would …
Would you like to join me …?
How about joining …?

Accepting
That would be great / nice.
I'd be delighted to.
OK. I'll …

Declining
I'd love to, but I'm afraid I …
Sorry, but I can't …
Thanks, but …
Sorry, but I'm a bit tied up …

Changing plans and giving reasons
There's been a slight change of plan … which means / because …
As a result, we won't be able to …
I would like to apologize for any inconvenience.
Something's come up.
Sorry to mess / for messing you around, but …?

Responding to a change of plan
That's a pity.
I understand.
I'm sorry to hear that.
Maybe next time.
It can't be helped.
It's a shame that …
Not to worry.
These things happen / take time.

ⓘ » Interactive Workbook
>> **Phrasebank**

Language at work | Passive forms

1 In your country, is most business done in the office or at social events, such as parties and business lunches? How important is meeting people socially or 'networking' for you?

2 60▷ Listen to someone speaking at a training event on effective networking. Tick (✓) the points the speaker mentions.

> **Effective networking: How business is really done**
>
> – Do your research before the event.
> – Make sure you meet new people.
> – Start conversations by mentioning someone you both know.
> – Pay attention to the speaker.
> – Introduce other people to each other.
> – Find someone to introduce you to the person you want to meet.
> – Learn people's names and don't forget them.
> – Don't leave without the numbers of important contacts.

3 61▷ Complete these sentences with the correct form of the verbs in brackets. Then listen and check your answers.

1 Business is _____ (do) through networking and meeting people.
2 A contract, or a job, can be _____ (win) or _____ (lose) on first impressions.
3 If you've been _____ (invite) out to a business dinner, …
4 Hello, I was _____ (give) your name by a colleague.
5 Try to be _____ (introduce) by someone else.

4 Match the sentences in 3 to verb forms a–e.

a infinitive form: ____   c past simple: ____   e present simple: ____
b present perfect: ____   d modal: ____

5 Match sentences a–d below to uses of the passive 1–3. More than one answer is sometimes possible.

1 To emphasize the result, rather than the person or cause: _____
2 When the person who does the action is unknown, unimportant, or too obvious to mention: _____
3 To talk about a process or how something is done: _____

a I **was given** your name by a colleague.
b Jatropha plants **are grown** in hot climates.
c Fiat cars **are produced** in Turin.
d A mistake **has been made**.

>> For more information and exercises, go to **Practice file 14** on page 129.

6 Read these statements. Are they true or false for you? Make the false statements true for you and tell a partner.

❛My company was founded over twenty years ago.❜

❛Most of my work is done on the phone and by email.❜

❛Employees can be sacked for being late where I work.❜

❛It's always important to be liked by the boss.❜

❛Most of my colleagues have been employed by other companies at some stage.❜

7 Work with a partner or in small groups. Prepare a short presentation for the rest of the class on one of the following processes.

• Disciplinary procedures at work   • How to get promoted quickly
• How my company was founded

Introducing new processes

Background

Airline needs to check on its check-in system

Air27 is a low-cost airline operating on routes throughout Europe. The company is very successful. It carries over 30 million passengers a year and has a total revenue of over two billion euros.

But Air27 is facing problems. It has kept fares low by using traditional check-in desks and not investing in alternative technology like some of its competitors. This means that the average passenger check-in time is more than two hours. At busy times, the company does not always have enough staff to check in everyone on time. This leads to long queues, unhappy passengers, more stress for check-in staff, and flights being delayed or taking off without passengers.

Passenger feedback suggests some people may not want to fly with Air27 again – they like the low fares but not the check-in experience. The situation is not helped by recent increased security measures. These slow down passengers' progress through the airport even more.

However, passenger numbers are increasing. The UK Department for Transport forecasts the number of air passengers will increase from 228 million in 2006 to 465 million by 2030. The current growth in UK passengers is 6.4% a year. Air27 knows it needs to invest in different methods of checking in passengers if it is to remain competitive.

Discussion

1 Would you choose to fly with Air27? Why / why not?

2 What other methods of checking in could Air27 consider?

3 What are the advantages and disadvantages of automatic check-in systems for passengers? And for airlines?

Task

Work in groups of three. You need to find a solution to Air27's problem. You will need to keep the current check-in system, but also decide which automatic systems the company should choose. The money for investment in two additional systems is available.

1 Read about alternative automatic check-in systems. Student A, turn to File 27 on page 141. Student B, turn to File 36 on page 144. Student C turn to File 43 on page 146.

2 Explain how your system works to the other members of the group.

3 Discuss the different check-in systems and decide which two are the best combination to solve Air27's problems.

The Expert View

Introducing a new process often meets with resistance from employees. Frequently, the organization is trying to improve efficiency by developing or streamlining its activities. In this case, it helps to involve the people who will be affected by the new process – they can help identify ways to improve efficiency. If reducing costs also means reducing staff numbers, employees will want to know how the changes will affect them. If new processes are the result of opportunities created by new technology, it's important to involve employees and customers in pilot schemes. Organizations should be prepared to listen to feedback and review their approach if necessary.

Graham Clark, Senior Lecturer in Operations Management

Cranfield School of Management

Case study

15 | Performance

Starting point

1 How do you assess your performance at work? What about activities outside of work, such as sports, parenting, friendships, education, language classes?

2 How do you define success? Which things on this list are important? What else would you add?
- money and wealth
- family
- good health
- appearance
- job and career
- personal relationships
- qualifications
- type of car
- busy social life
- how your colleagues view you

Working with words | Personal qualities

1 **Read this article and answer questions 1–2.**
1 How does Howard Lawrence feel about the success of the scheme?
2 Who recommends or nominates employees for the award?

Employee of the month scheme at Elmgrove Park Hospital

The employee of the month scheme, which recognizes the work of individual staff, has been very successful. Howard Lawrence, Associate Director of the hospital trust is not surprised by this. 'At Elmgrove Park Hospital we have fantastic, **enthusiastic** staff who are highly **motivated** to ensure that each patient is relaxed and comfortable during their stay,' he says.

Nominations can be submitted either by members of staff or by patients. Since the scheme was launched in 2003, the winners have included:

James Briggs, ward assistant: April 2006. James was nominated for showing exceptional commitment to all aspects of his work and for being **flexible**, **patient**, and **helpful** at all times.

Nathan Wells, porter: March 2006. Nathan was chosen not only for being **hard-working**, **dependable**, fast, and efficient, but more importantly for his sunny personality.

Ana Suarez, clinical nurse specialist: December 2007. Her colleagues nominated Ana for being **caring**, understanding, and **dedicated**, not just to clients, their partners, and families, but also to the staff in the department.

2 Do you have a similar scheme to recognize success in your company? How else is good work rewarded (bonus / commission)? Do you think employee award schemes are a good idea? Why / why not?

3 Here are some nominations for employee of the month. Match the adjectives in **bold** in the newsletter in **1** to these descriptions. You may use more than one adjective if necessary.

'Paula is able to adapt to any changes or deal with any new situation.'

1 _____

'You never see him relaxing. He's always doing something.'

2 _____

'Samuel really wants to help customers and the people he works with.'

3 _____

'Even with difficult customers, he'll listen for as long as it takes.'

4 _____

'She's positive about any new idea. I've never heard her complain.'

5 _____

'Inga is always punctual and never off work.'

6 _____

4 Think of a colleague where you work and nominate him / her for employee of the month. Tell your partner about your employee of the month using adjectives from **1**.

5 Turn these adjectives into nouns by changing the endings of the words.

~~patient~~   dedicated   punctual   confident   flexible
creative   motivated   dependable   enthusiastic   ambitious

1 -ce: _patience_, _____
2 -ion: _____, _____, _____
3 -iasm: _____
4 -ity: _____, _____, _____, _____

6 Complete these sentences with the correct form of a word from **5**. Then work with a partner and say if the statements are true (*T*) or false (*F*) for you / your company using a different form of the word.

Example: It's not important for me to have flexible working hours.

1 It's important for me to have some _flexibility_ in my working hours. T /Ⓕ

2 I'm not a very _____ person – I always want everything to be done 'now'! T / F

3 _____ is one of my strong points – I'm never late for anything. T / F

4 I have a great deal of _____ in how my company is run and in its success. T / F

5 My company offers good incentives to ensure ongoing enthusiasm and _____ amongst the staff. T / F

6 My company is _____ to its employees and puts their needs before those of the customer. T / F

>> For more exercises, go to **Practice file 15** on page 130.

7 Write down the job titles of three people you know. Write down two qualities you think the people need for their jobs. Then, tell the class what you think. Does everyone agree?

8 Work with a partner. Talk about the qualities that are important for your job. How would you describe yourself? What happens if you do particularly well?

Example: Patience is important because I work in after-sales, and customers sometimes telephone to complain about …

ⓘ >> Interactive Workbook >> **Glossary**

Tip | *patient*

The word *patient* can have different meanings.
As a noun it means a person who is receiving medical treatment.
*He is Dr Fisher's **patient**.*
As an adjective it means being able to wait for a long time or to accept annoying behaviour without becoming angry.
*You have to be **patient** to work with Thomas. He takes a long time to do anything.*

Meetings | Appraising performance and setting objectives

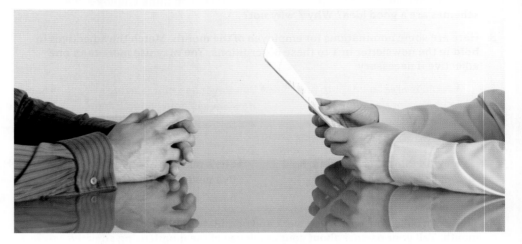

1 Chris Hately works in a factory producing shafts for cars. Chris is having his six-month performance review. Read what he has written on his form. Do you have similar forms at work?

Part A

Please answer the questions on this form and return to your line manager before your performance review.

1 Have the last six months been good / bad / satisfactory? Why?

Good. I've really learned a lot since I started here and everyone has been really helpful.

2 What do you consider are your most important achievements in the last six months?

I completed my initial training in June and was given a permanent contract.

3 Which parts of the job interest you the most? And the least?

Solving problems with machinery.

4 How could your performance be improved in your current position?

Just continue what I'm doing – by learning more.

2 62▷ Listen to the first part of Chris's performance review and add any extra information to his answers in **1**. Then compare these with a partner.

3 62▷ Match 1–7 to a–g then listen and check your answers.

1	In … ____	**a**	doing very well.
2	We're very pleased … ____	**b**	to work on.
3	You seem to be … ____	**c**	general …
4	One thing I wanted … ____	**d**	about working with other people?
5	Is it an area … ____	**e**	you'd like to develop?
6	How do you feel … ____	**f**	with your performance.
7	That's something I need … ____	**g**	to discuss was …

4 63▷ Listen to the final part of the meeting and answer questions 1–3.
1 How does Chris's manager signal that it is the end of the meeting?
2 What have they agreed to do?
3 What two questions does Chris's manager ask to check agreement?

>> For more exercises, go to **Practice file 15** on page 130.

Tip | Being less direct

You can use the past simple instead of the present simple to sound less direct, especially in sensitive situations.
One thing I wanted to discuss **was** …,
~~One thing I want to discuss~~ **is** …
Both are correct, but the first one is less direct.

5 Imagine you have a performance review. Complete this form for your job.

Part A

Please answer the questions on this form and return to your line manager before your appraisal.

1 Have the last six months been good / bad / satisfactory? Why?

2 What do you consider are your most important achievements in the last six months?

3 Which parts of the job interest you the most? And the least?

4 How could your performance be improved in your current position?

6 Now take turns to appraise your partner using the form they completed in **5**. The person leading the meeting should
- make general comments at the beginning
- give specific feedback
- discuss and ask questions about performance
- set and agree objectives at the end.

7 Work with a partner. Take turns to talk about one of the areas below. Evaluate your performance in the area you choose and say what improvements you could make. Decide with your partner on a plan of action.
- a hobby
- a sport you do
- your progress in English

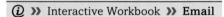 ⓘ ≫ Interactive Workbook ≫ **Email**

Unit 15 | Performance

Key expressions

Giving a formal appraisal
Overall … / In general …
I'm / We're very happy / pleased with your performance.
You seem to be doing very well.
One of your key strengths is …
Perhaps one thing to work on / consider is …
One thing I wanted to discuss was …

Encouraging self-evaluation
How do you feel about …?
How are you getting on with …?
Have you thought about …?
What do you think would help you to …?
Is this an area you'd like to develop?

Evaluating your own performance
I'm really happy with …
Something I need to work on is …
I think … is an area for improvement.

Setting objectives
So let's summarize what we've agreed.
One thing you're going to …
You intend to …
You need to think about …

Agreeing objectives
How does that sound?
Is that OK with you?
Is there anything else you'd like to add?

ⓘ ≫ Interactive Workbook
≫ **Phrasebank**

Practically speaking | How to give feedback

1 64, 65 ▷ Listen to two different versions of a conversation between Chris and his supervisor. What are the differences?

2 64 ▷ Listen to the first version again. Complete these phrases.
1 You're doing _____.
2 That's _____.
3 You've done a _____ _____.
4 _____ done.
5 _____ at it.

3 Write three jobs you have completed recently. Work with a partner. Take turns to give your partner feedback on their completed jobs using phrases in **2**.

    Example: **A** *I've just finished my report.*
               B *That's great! Well done.*

Language at work | Past perfect and past continuous

1 Read this extract from an employee's appraisal and decide if statements
1–3 below are true (*T*) or false (*F*).

Appraiser I know there had been a few problems at the other factory before you moved
here, but in the last six months, I've received lots of good reports about all your hard work.

Employee Good. That's nice to hear. I was finding it all a little difficult when I first came
to work here …

1 The employee had problems after he moved to his current factory. ____
2 The employee found it difficult for a period of time. ____
3 The employee doesn't have any difficulties now. ____

2 Match sentences a–c to uses of the past perfect / past continuous in 1–3.
1 To talk about something in progress at a particular time in the past: ____
2 To say that one event happened before another completed past event: ____
3 To give background information in the past: ____

a I knew about the meeting because I **had received** the email.
b What **were** you **working** on yesterday morning?
c Most people **were working** quietly in the office.

3 Which sentences in **2** use the past perfect and which use the past continuous?

>> For more information and exercises, go to **Practice file 15** on page 131.

4 66▷ Two people, Helena and Matthias, are describing some feedback they
received. Listen, and for each of them say
1 what feedback they received
2 why they thought their appraisals were unfair
3 what happened after their appraisals.

5 66▷ Complete these sentences with the past perfect or past continuous form of
the verbs in brackets. Then listen and check your answers.
1 I _____ (work) for a large food company which didn't employ many
women.
2 It was terrible to hear this, because I _____ (already / discuss) with
him how difficult it was to be the only woman.
3 Six months after that, I _____ (run) the factory!
4 We _____ (talk) about the usual things, but during all of this, he
answered the phone twice and even replied to an email.
5 This annoyed me because I _____ (prepare) very thoroughly.
6 I heard that he got fired, but I _____ (already / leave) by then.

6 Work with a partner. Look at this timeline for Helena with periods and key events
in her life. Make sentences about her using the past perfect and past continuous.
Example: She applied for the job while she **was studying** at university.
She'**d applied** for the job before she graduated.

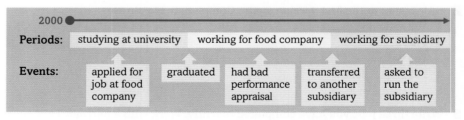

7 Make a timeline for yourself with periods of time and important events. It can be
about your studies, career, or life in general. Describe it to your partner.

ⓘ >> Interactive Workbook >> **Exercises and Tests**

Giving a successful presentation

Background

Help from the professionals

Balkan Healthfood Corp. is a successful food company in its home country of Croatia. It wants to start expanding its business into other European countries. More employees will need to go out to the market and present the company and its products to potential customers and partners. In order to do this, the company will need to retrain some of its staff and employ new staff. It has decided to start with training its existing staff in presentation skills. The company has approached Media Training Associates, an organization that gives corporate training sessions in media and presentation skills, to take charge of this project.

67▷ Listen to a trainer from Media Training Associates and read the presentation feedback form.

> **The speaker introduced the topic**
>
> very clearly   5   4   3   2   1   not very clearly
>
> Comments: _____
>
> **The phrases the speaker used to organize the content were**
>
> very helpful   5   4   3   2   1   not very helpful
>
> Comments: _____
>
> **The speaker was**
>
> very convincing   5   4   3   2   1   not very convincing
>
> Comments: _____
>
> **Other points to consider:** _____

Discussion

1   Do you agree with the tips for giving a presentation? What else would you add?

2   Work with a partner. Add more criteria to the presentation feedback form, based on your ideas in 1.

3   What do you need to think about and prepare when you give a presentation?

4   What problems might you have if you are presenting to people from other countries?

5   What are the most common mistakes people make when they give presentations?

Task

1   **68, 69▷** Two Balkan Healthfood Corp. employees are attending a presentation training session with Media Training Associates. It is the start of the day and they are asked to give a short presentation of some of their products. Listen and make notes about their performances.

2   Work in small groups. You are the trainers. Discuss the performance of the two employees in 1. Writes notes about their performances in the feedback form.

3   Work with a partner. Student A, you are the trainee in the first presentation. Student B, you are the trainee in the second presentation. Take turns to give each other feedback on your performances, based on your group discussions.

Unit 15 | Performance

Case study

95

16 | Success

Learning objectives in this unit

- Talking about achievements
- Reporting back on and evaluating research
- Generalizing
- Using contrasting language

Case study

- Acting on research

Starting point

1 Match these products to the country / region which first manufactured them or where explorers first discovered them. Check your answers in File 45 on page 146.

Products:
silk, potatoes, coffee, black pepper, chocolate, rubber

Countries / Regions:
Central and South America, Peru, India, China, Ethiopia, Mexico

2 Which countries are now the leading producers of the products in 1?

3 How important are these products in your country / company?

4 How different would the world be if they hadn't been discovered?

Working with words | Fact-finding and achievement

1 Look at the pictures in the article below. One material is used in the manufacture of these three products. Which material do you think it is?

2 Read this article and see if you were right in 1. Then answer questions 1–2.
   1 What route did the product take to get to Europe?
   2 How is it different nowadays for people to discover new products or techniques?

A perfect product

It has been an enormously important product over the ages. Its qualities of strength, light weight, and softness make it the perfect material for products such as quality clothing, parachute material, medical sutures, racing bike tyres and even a wide variety of cosmetic products like moisturizer and shampoo. But silk has not always been readily available. The Chinese jealously guarded the mysteries of silk production until (so one of the legends goes) two monks **came across** some silkworm eggs and **managed** to smuggle them out of the country, risking their lives, but taking the **know-how** with them as far as Byzantium.

The secrets of silk gradually spread through India and the Middle East, reaching Europe, where Italy was the first European country to **succeed** in establishing a successful silk manufacturing industry in the thirteenth century. France then borrowed the **expertise** of the Italian workers to create its own silk industry.

It was not easy to get the secrets of silk manufacturing out of China. But, in today's business world, it's far easier to share knowledge and skills, and to **find out** about new products or techniques. By **searching** on the Internet or even jumping on a plane to the other side of the globe, it is possible to **look for** ways of improving products, without endangering the lives of the people who make the discovery.

3 Match words or phrases in **bold** from the text in **2** to definitions 1–4.

  1 skills / knowledge: _____ , _____

  2 achieve / become able to: _____ , _____

  3 discover: _____ , _____

  4 try to find: _____ , _____

4 Work with a partner. Use words from **3** to talk about your own or your company's achievements.

    Example: My company managed to sell 10,000 units last year.
              My expertise in accounting is useful in my job, as I have to do the books
              every month.

5 70▷ Listen to three extracts about success and failure. Match them to pictures a–c.

6 70▷ Listen again. Match a word from **A** to a word from **B** to make adjective + noun phrases.

A	B
complete	disaster
absolute	flop
total	achievement
significant	breakthrough
great	triumph
amazing	waste of time
real	success

7 Which of the phrases you made in **6** deal with successes and which with failures?

8 What other adjective + noun phrases can you make from the words in **6**? Use your phrases to describe what is happening in the pictures in **5**.

>> For more exercises, go to **Practice file 16** on page 132.

9 Work with a partner. Student A, turn to File 39 on page 145. Student B, turn to File 46 on page 146. Take turns to ask each other about some events. Use phrases from **6** and **8**.

10 Work with a partner. Describe one of the following using words from **3** and **6**.

  • a training session   • a work event   • a new product

ⓘ >> Interactive Workbook >> **Glossary**

Meetings | Reporting back

1 How popular are traditional handicrafts and furnishings in your country? Where do most of them come from?

2 **71, 72▷** Trimpo is a retail chain selling traditional goods in shops across Europe. Paul O'Reilly is the chief buyer at the business's head office in Brussels. Two of his team have been on fact-finding trips abroad. Listen to Paul's conversations with Olli and Sandrine and complete this table.

	Olli	Sandrine
Destination		
Impressions and verdict		
Next step		

3 **72▷** These phrases are from the first conversation. Listen to the second conversation again and write phrases that mean the same.
1 How was your trip? _____
2 I'll fill you in on everything. _____
3 So, what were your overall impressions? _____
4 I was impressed with … _____
5 What makes you say that? _____
6 This underlines the importance of … _____
7 What we need to do now is … _____
8 We should focus on … _____

4 Choose a phrase from **3** to complete this conversation. Compare your version with a partner.
A ¹_____ in Australia?
B It could have started better!
A ²_____?
A Well, the airline lost my suitcase. Otherwise it went very well, thanks.
B So ³_____ of the operations there?
A I have to say that, on the whole, ⁴_____ everything apart from one area.
B ⁵_____.
A Well, it seems like there are real problems with cash flow.
B I suppose this ⁶_____ to find a better system of payment.
A Yes, we really ⁷_____ on improving this aspect of the business before we do anything else.

» For more exercises, go to **Practice file 16** on page 132.

5 Work with a partner. You both work for *K@ravanzerai*, a travel agency specializing in adventure activity holidays. Report back to each other on a fact-finding mission. Student A, turn to File 40 on page 145. Student B, use the information below.

> **Student B**
>
> **Situation 1**
> You are Student A's boss. Ask for a report on his / her trip. Ask him / her to justify his / her opinions. Identify action for the future.
>
> **Situation 2**
> You have been on a fact-finding trip to Brazil to find out about eco-holidays. Student A is your boss and will ask you to give a general evaluation of the trip and emphasize what you consider important. Read this information and prepare to report back on what happened.
> **Destination:** Brazil
> **Contact:** Nelson Dos Santos, Brazilian tour operator
> **Business:** Green holidays
> **Impressions:** Very well organized. Good supervision of visitors. Medical kit. Expert on the rain forest. Very good team of guides. Comfortable base-camp facilities. Difficult to get to base camp. Staff speak limited English.
> **Verdict:** A good prospect if access and language barrier can be improved.
> **Next step:** Try to convince him to join us. Send someone as guinea pig to see what the holidays are really like. Take photos for brochure.

6 Work with a partner. Think of a challenging situation you have experienced. Tell your partner what happened and what you learnt from the experience. This might have been
- a job interview
- going on a business trip
- using English on the phone.

ⓘ **»** Interactive Workbook **»** Email

Practically speaking | How to generalize

1 <u>Underline</u> the words in this list that we use to make generalizations.

> on the whole   particularly   all in all   especially   overall
> mainly   in particular   mostly   in general   generally speaking

2 73▷ Work with a partner. Take turns to make sentences with prompts 1–7 using as many of the words you underlined in **1** as you can. Listen and compare your answers.

> *Example: In general / generally speaking, I prefer to travel by train.*
> *I mainly / mostly prefer to travel by train.*

1 I / prefer / travel / by train
2 we / operate / in / the Far East
3 I / thought / it / was / an excellent presentation
4 we / don't / work / at weekends
5 it / was / a great trip
6 we / communicate / in English
7 I / was / very happy / with the way it went

3 Work with a partner. Make sentences about these ideas using words / phrases you underlined in **1**. Then compare your sentences with another group. Say how you feel about

- a trip you've been on
- travelling
- your work
- your progress in English
- your company's recent performance.

Student A, turn to File 40 on page 145.

Key expressions

Asking for feedback
How was your trip?
How did it go in / at / with …?
What were your overall impressions?
So, give me an overview.

Introducing feedback
I'll / Let me fill you in on …
I'll / Let me bring you up to date on …

Giving a general evaluation
It could have gone better.
It wasn't what I expected.
I was pleasantly surprised.
I was quite impressed with …
There were no big surprises.

Asking for a justification
What makes you say that?
Tell me more.
Why do you say that?

Emphasizing
This underlines the importance of (+ -ing)…
This highlights the need to (+ verb)…

Identifying future action
What we need to do now is …
I think the next step is to …
We need to concentrate on …
We should focus on …

ⓘ **»** Interactive Workbook **» Phrasebank**

Language at work | Contrasting language

1 Paul has concerns about working with Mr Tran, in particular about the size of Mr Tran's factory and the language barrier. Read Sandrine's email to Paul. How good is she at reassuring Paul?

Dear Paul

Thanks for your email. I can quite understand your concerns.

1 Reliability of supplies
Even though Mr Tran's factory is small, it is efficient and well organized, so he should be able to satisfy commitments.

2 Language
Despite having language problems, with a mixture of English and French, we will be able to get by. Although he may not be a great linguist, I think he is an energetic and committed businessman. I can understand that you are worried. However, if we manage to convince Mr Tran to come and see us, I think that you will be as impressed as I was. I think it will be worth it in the long run, despite the potential problems.

Best wishes

Sandrine

2 <u>Underline</u> the different contrasting words in the email in **1**.

3 What is *despite* followed by?

4 Transform this sentence using the words you underlined in the email.
   *Their head office was impressive, **but** the firm was losing money.*

>> For more information and exercises, go to **Practice file 16** on page 133.

5 Work with a partner.
   1 Your company is based in France and has regular dealings with UK customers. Your company is proposing a change of working hours from 9 a.m.–5 p.m. to 10 a.m.–6 p.m. Student B, point out the negative aspects. Student A, try to persuade your partner that it's a good idea.

Negative	Positive
Finish work later	Avoid the morning rush hour
Shorter evenings	Will be coordinated with UK colleagues
Different hours to other family members	Extra hour in bed in the morning

   2 Your company is proposing a change of logo. Student A, point out the negative aspects. Student B, try to persuade your partner that having a new logo is a good idea.

Negative	Positive
People are unfamiliar with it	More modern feel
Design process is expensive	Opportunity for new promotional campaign
New stationery needed is expensive	Easier to distance company from past disasters

6 Work in small groups. What criticisms could people make of the organization where you work? What can you say to counter these criticisms?

---

i >> Interactive Workbook >> **Exercises and Tests**

Acting on research

Background

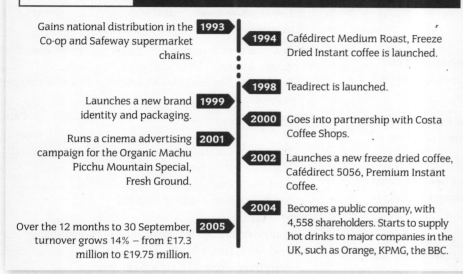

Cafédirect

Cafédirect is the UK's largest Fairtrade hot drinks company. It was founded in 1991. In 2001, it was ranked 54th on the UK's first index of fast-growing inner-city businesses, the Inner City 100. In 2002 it was ranked as the sixth-largest coffee brand in the UK. This company history shows its rise to becoming one of the most popular hot drinks companies in the UK.

1993 Gains national distribution in the Co-op and Safeway supermarket chains.

1994 Cafédirect Medium Roast, Freeze Dried Instant coffee is launched.

1998 Teadirect is launched.

1999 Launches a new brand identity and packaging.

2000 Goes into partnership with Costa Coffee Shops.

2001 Runs a cinema advertising campaign for the Organic Machu Picchu Mountain Special, Fresh Ground.

2002 Launches a new freeze dried coffee, Cafédirect 5056, Premium Instant Coffee.

2004 Becomes a public company, with 4,558 shareholders. Starts to supply hot drinks to major companies in the UK, such as Orange, KPMG, the BBC.

2005 Over the 12 months to 30 September, turnover grows 14% – from £17.3 million to £19.75 million.

The Expert View

Success depends on knowing your market and being able to respond to diverse needs. In a major global industry like tea and coffee, market conditions are very competitive. The challenge is how to meet the needs of both retail consumers (who buy their products at the supermarket) and those who buy their coffee in cafés and restaurants. These needs are very different, and vary between 'coffee cultures' (mainland Europe, North and South America) and traditional 'tea cultures' (the UK, Ireland, Poland). Only the biggest companies achieve significant presence across all markets. Others must specialize, so it's vital to know your consumers. For this reason, excellent market research is essential.

David Molian, Bettany Centre for Entrepreneurial Performance & Economics
Cranfield School of Management

Discussion

1 What has made this company so successful?

2 With more and more competitors offering similar products, what can a company like Cafédirect do to continue to be successful?

Task

You work for a British company which imports high-quality tea from India and sells it to supermarket chains and specialist retailers in the UK. Recently you have been losing sales.

1 Work in groups of up to four. Each person in your group has been given a fact-finding mission to find out the reasons for the loss of sales. Read the details of your mission and prepare for a meeting with your group. Student A, turn to File 16 on page 138. Student B, turn to File 25 on page 141. Student C, turn to File 41 on page 145. Student D, turn to File 44 on page 146.

2 Have a meeting with your group following this agenda.

Agenda

1 Report back on research and conclusions
2 Discuss concerns about others' findings
3 Decide on future action

Case study

Working with words

1 Match the adjectives in the list to comments 1–9.

fun	~~varied~~	demanding
challenging	routine	glamorous
depressing	stressful	dull
worthwhile	rewarding	

1 ❛ What I like best about my job is that no two days are the same, so I never get bored. ❜

   varied

2 ❛ One of the great things about my job is that I meet famous people and stay in some expensive hotels. ❜

   _____

3 ❛ My job keeps me fully occupied and I don't have time to think about anything else until it's time to go home. ❜

   _____

4 ❛ Sometimes I think to myself – you'll never be able to do that, but then I find a way to succeed. It really is quite satisfying. ❜

   _____

5 ❛ Every morning, I arrive at the office, switch on the photocopier, and check the phone for messages. Then I start the coffee maker and open the mail. ❜

   _____

6 ❛ I spend all day in front of a computer screen. I really don't think I can stand it much longer. It makes me feel so miserable! ❜

   _____ , _____

7 ❛ I get quite worried and anxious. So many people depend on me. Even at home, I keep thinking about work – it stops me eating. ❜

   _____

8 ❛ I really enjoy going to work. We have a fantastic time and everyone gets on so well together. It doesn't feel like work at all! ❜

   _____

9 ❛ It's not the best paid job in the world, but I know that I make a difference to people's lives. There's no greater satisfaction than seeing someone walk again after a terrible accident. ❜

   _____ , _____

Business communication skills

1 Rick Parry is a buyer for a supermarket chain. He is introducing a colleague, Marcel Grover, to Patti Kline, the representative of a key supplier. Complete their conversation with the words and phrases from the list.

so tell me	nice to meet you	sounds
~~I want you to meet~~	deal with	this is
in charge of	I'm pleased to	

Rick Come over here Marcel, [1] *I want you to meet* one of our guests. Marcel, [2]_____ Patti Kline. She works with Longridge, one of our biggest suppliers.

Marcel [3]_____, Patti.

Patti [4]_____ meet you, too. [5]_____, Marcel, what do you do?

Marcel Well, I'm [6]_____ our stores in the south of England.

Patti That [7]_____ really demanding. You know, a lot of responsibility.

Marcel Well, I don't [8]_____ everything alone. I've got a good team.

2 Put the words in *italics* in the right order to create another conversation between two guests.

Greg Good afternoon. *met / I / think / we've / don't* [1] *I don't think we've met*. I'm Greg Wilkes from the National Bank.

Jen *to / delighted / meet / I'm / you* [2]_____ _____, Mr Wilkes. My name's Jen Mills.

Greg I see you're from Research and Development.

Jen That's right. *responsible / for / We're* [3]_____ _____ product development.

Greg That sounds interesting. How long does it take to create a new product?

Jen That depends. *a / It / lot / involves / testing / of* [4]_____, so it can take several years.

Greg Really? That seems a long time. Have you got a minute? *like / introduce / to / I'd / to / you* [5]_____ my colleague – he's a scientist too.

Language at work | Present simple review | Frequency adverbs

Present simple review

Form

Positive: Add -s after the verb with he / she / it.

*I / you / we / they **work** for Ford.*

*He / she / it **works** really well.*

Negative: Use the auxiliary do / does + not + verb.

*He **doesn't work**. I **don't work**.*

Exceptions

1 The verb *be* is irregular: *I **am**, you / we / they **are**, he / she / it is, I'm not, you / we / they **aren't**, he / she / it **isn't**.*

2 Verbs ending in consonant + -y (e.g. *rely*), change the -y to an -i and add -es.

*He / she / it **relies** on financial support.*

3 Verbs ending in -ch, -o, -s, -ch, -ss, and -x (e.g. *reach*), add -es.

*He / she / it **reaches** new levels every day.*

Questions

1 With *be*, put *am / are / is* first.

***Are** you Swedish?*

2 With all other verbs, use *do / does*.

***Does** it cost a lot?*

3 With question words (*who, what, where, how*, etc.), add *do / does* to the question word.

*Where **does** he **work**? How **do** they get to **work**?*

4 If the question word is the subject, do not use *do / does*.

*Who **works** for a multinational?*

5 Indirect questions can start with expressions such as, *Can I ask …?, Do you know …?, Could you tell me …?.*

Use the same word order as for present simple statements.

***Do you know** where the report **is**?*

6 For indirect *yes / no* questions, use *if* or *whether*.

*Can I ask **if** / **whether** you **have** experience in accounting?*

Use

1 To talk about facts or things which are generally true.

*Lucia **comes** from Milan.*

*In Europe most people **work** in service industries.*

2 To talk about repeated actions or events.

*Every Monday we **have** a team meeting.*

Frequency adverbs

Use adverbs of frequency (*never, always, sometimes*, etc.) to describe how often we do something.

1 With *be*, place the adverb after the verb.

*I am **never** late for work.*

2 With all other verbs, place the adverb before the verb.

*I **often** work late.*

3 Place *occasionally, sometimes, often, usually* at the beginning of a sentence to put a stronger focus on the frequency.

***Sometimes** I work at the weekend.*

1 Complete this article with the correct form of the verbs in brackets.

Gustav Olaffson [1] *works* (work) as a geologist in the North Sea. He [2] _____ (spend) three weeks on an oil platform and then has three weeks off. While he is on the oil platform he [3] _____ (miss) his family, but he [4] _____ (try) to talk to his children as often as possible.

Interviewer Can I ask what [5] _____ (you / find) most difficult about working on the oil platform?

Gustav The long hours are hard, but I get a lot of time off between shifts.

Interviewer What [6] _____ (your job / involve) exactly?

Gustav Well, the company drills into the seabed and I analyse rock samples.

Interviewer [7] _____ (you / work) onshore as well?

Gustav No, I [8] _____ (not), but I sometimes get the opportunity to work on oil platforms in Nigeria.

Interviewer [9] _____ (you / be) happy with your job?

Gustav Yes, I [10] _____ (be), but I would like to spend more time with my family.

2 Rewrite what Julia says about her job using adverbs from the list.

| hardly ever | ~~always~~ | never |
| usually | often | occasionally |

1 Every Monday morning we have a team meeting.

We always have a team meeting on Monday morning.

2 I frequently have lunch in the staff restaurant.

_____

3 Once or twice a month I have lunch with clients.

_____

4 Most Friday afternoons, I finish work at 4.00 p.m.

_____

5 I only work on Saturdays two or three times a year.

_____

6 I don't work on Sundays – this is a personal rule of mine.

_____

Working with words

1 Put the letters in brackets in the right order to find words that match these definitions.

1 something available to exploit and use: _resources_ (ESCRORUSE)

2 timetable of activities: _____ (CSEHDLUE)

3 news on how something is progressing: _____ (UTEPAD)

4 money spending plan: _____ (BDTUGE)

5 the last day for finishing a piece of work or project: _____ (ADENDELI)

6 working together: _____ (EAWKTMRO)

7 practical abilities: _____ (LSIKLS)

2 Match 1–8 to a–h.

1 It's always difficult to allocate … _a_

2 You need to learn how to delegate … ___

3 What I like about my boss, is she always lets me get … ___

4 We're falling … ___

5 It's difficult to stay within … ___

6 If we continue like this we should meet … ___

7 Hi Melinda, it's Hanna, I need to get an … ___

8 I'm sure we'll be able to catch … ___

a resources – skilled staff are in short supply.

b behind schedule, so we all need to work this weekend.

c update on how the project is progressing.

d tasks – you can't possibly do everything yourself.

e up – there are three more weeks left.

f on with my work on my own.

g budget – we always overspend.

h the deadline without too much trouble.

3 Complete this email with the correct form of a suitable word from **2** above.

Dear Jan

I'm afraid it looks like we are not going to be able to meet the ¹_____ next Friday. We've fallen behind ²_____ because we were not ³_____ sufficient ⁴_____. We need more ⁵_____ with the appropriate skills to be put on the project immediately. Of course, this does mean that we won't be able to stay within our ⁶_____ either. I will send you an ⁷_____ after our team meeting this afternoon to let you know what is decided.

Very best wishes

Gerald

Business communication skills

1 Henry Price is organizing the official opening of a new building. He is talking his team through progress so far. Put their conversation in the right order 1–14.

___ a **Martin** You're welcome.

___ b **Ralph** Yes, leave it with me, Henry. I have some useful media contacts.

___ c **Rebecca** Yes, I'll do that. I'll ring them individually over the next two days.

___ d **Henry** Oh really? What is happening with them?

___ e **Henry** Thanks, Rebecca. Now we need someone to brief the media. Can you do that Ralph?

___ f **Henry** Good, so to recap, Melinda is dealing with the caterers, Rebecca is handling the invitations, Martin is handling the car hire firm and Ralph has volunteered to deal with the media.

_1_ g **Henry** Right, so accommodation has been organized. What's next on the list? Ah yes, before I forget, Melinda, can you contact the car hire people for the VIPs?

___ h **Melinda** I'd prefer not to if that's OK, I'm afraid I'm really busy with the caterers.

___ i **Henry** And where are we with replies to the invitations, Rebecca?

___ j **Henry** Good man Martin, thanks.

___ k **Melinda** The usual problems with menu changes – which is why I can't take anything else on.

___ l **Henry** That many? Can you check if they're coming?

___ m **Martin** As Melinda's busy, I can handle the hire firm if you want, Henry.

___ n **Rebecca** I'm dealing with them right now. We still haven't heard from 70 people though.

2 Ludo is calling a printer about some brochures. Put the words in *italics* in the right order.

Kevin Express Printers, this is Kevin speaking.

Ludo Hi Kevin, it's Ludo here. *things / going / are / How*
¹ _How are things going_ with our brochures?

Kevin *far / good / So / so* ²_____.
Basically, *according / everything / going / plan / to / is*
³_____. They're almost finished.

Ludo Great, so *track / everything / on / is* ⁴
_____ _____.

Kevin Yes, except we still *to / need / somebody* ⁵_____
_____ deliver them.

Ludo Well, *don't / why / I* ⁶_____
come and get them? Give me a call when they're ready.

Kevin OK. No problem.

Language at work | Present simple and continuous

Present simple and continuous

Form

For the present simple, see page 103.

Present continuous positive: *am / is / are* + *-ing* form
> *Delia is emailing her business partner.*

Present continuous negative: *am / is / are* + *not* + *-ing* form
> *Thomas isn't listening to me.*

Questions

For present simple questions, see page 103.

1 To make questions with the present continuous, put *am / is / are* before the subject.
> *How are you getting on?*
> *Are you making progress with the report?*

2 To give a short reply to *yes / no* questions in the present continuous, use the subject + *am / is / are.*
> *Are you making progress with the report?*
> *Yes, I am. / No, I'm not.*

Use

Use both the present simple and the present continuous to talk about the present in different situations.

Present simple	Present continuous
To talk about situations that happen regularly. *In my job I speak to customers every day on the phone.*	To talk about situations happening at or around the time of speaking. *John can't help you at the moment, he is speaking to a client.*
To talk about permanent situations or facts. *I work for DHL.*	To talk about temporary situations or activities. *Belinda works at the Manchester office, but this month she is working with her colleagues in Liverpool.*

Language tip

1 These verbs, known as state verbs, are rarely used in the present continuous, e.g. *know, believe, understand, like, love, forget, notice, remember, hate, want.*

2 Verbs like *think* or *feel* usually take the present simple but are used in the present continuous when they describe a mental activity.
> *You look angry. What are you thinking about?*

1 Complete these sentences with the present simple or the present continuous form of the verbs in brackets.

1 Carlos usually _sits_ (sit) in the main office, but today he _is working_ (work) at home.

2 What time _____ (you / have to) leave home to get to work?

3 Look at the woman over there. Why _____ (she / sit) at John's desk?

4 What _____ (you / work on) at the moment? Anything interesting?

5 What _____ (Nadia / think) about her new boss?

6 You seem quiet today. _____ (you / think) about your presentation?

7 How much _____ (a successful salesperson / earn) each year?

8 Hey, what _____ (you / do) in this room? This is for staff only.

9 Whose is this briefcase? I _____ (think) it _____ (belong) to one of our visitors.

10 They _____ (have) huge problems with the new lifts these days.

2 Match 1–8 to a–h.

1 We work every day … _c_

2 We're working every day … ___

3 What does Mark think about … ___

4 What is Mark thinking about? … ___

5 How does Jenny manage … ___

6 How is Jenny managing … ___

7 We have a problem with our distributor, … ___

8 We're having a problem with our distributor … ___

a He looks really worried.

b so we'll have to think about getting a new one.

c except Saturdays and Sundays.

d with this new project?

e because of a lorry drivers' strike.

f this month.

g the move to the Atlanta office?

h to keep everyone happy?

Working with words

1 Complete this article with verbs from the list. Some verbs can be used more than once.

take   make   ~~do~~   work

Don't worry, be happy

Employers are finally realizing that emotions have an effect on employees' performance. According to research by Pearn Kandola, a business psychology firm, 86% of employees also see a link between their moods and how well they ¹_do_ their work. Here's how to improve:

– Take control. If you want to ²_____ progress in your career, do something about it. Change your workplace or maybe even change jobs.

– If you're under too much pressure, tell somebody. Don't ³_____ late every day or be the person who always says, 'I'll ⁴_____ overtime!' See if your employer will let you ⁵_____ flexitime.

– Keep your body and mind healthy. ⁶_____ exercise and get feedback on your work. If other people appreciate you, this will make you feel more positive.

– Don't forget to ⁷_____ time for your family and friends. Make sure you ⁸_____ time off when you need it and go on holiday.

2 Choose the correct answer from the words in *italics*.

1 I'm so *excited / exciting* about this new idea for flexitime.

2 Paperwork is really *bored / boring* but often necessary.

3 He's a *relaxed / relaxing* sort of character – to the point of being lazy!

4 The most *exhilarated / exhilarating* experience in the world is parachuting.

5 It isn't physical work, but working with computers can be *tired / tiring* after a few hours.

6 Do you think he's *interested / interesting* in the vacancy?

7 This new project is so *excited / exciting*.

8 I'm too *tired / tiring* to work late tonight.

Business communication skills

1 Complete this conversation with the correct answer from the options in 1–10 below.

A Is this your first visit to Bratislava?

B Yes, it is.

A And how do you ¹__a__ it?

B Well, the people are very friendly. Two people at the train station helped me this afternoon when I arrived.

A Really? That's good.

B Then I went straight to the hotel, so I haven't really seen the city yet.

A ²_____ is your hotel?

B Fine. It's opposite the Opera House, so that's good.

A Are you keen ³_____ opera?

B No, not really, but I ⁴_____ classical music.

A Me too. I like ⁵_____ to Mozart.

B I'm also interested ⁶_____ contemporary art. I really enjoy ⁷_____ to art galleries. Are there many here?

A Yes, I think so. To be honest, I don't really like modern art, but I can ask my boss. He's ⁸_____ about that kind of thing. I can ask him now if you like.

B I ⁹_____ to go now I'm afraid, but I'll be back at the office again tomorrow.

A Oh, OK. I should ¹⁰_____ to work. See you tomorrow.

1	**a** ~~find~~	**b** know	**c** keen
2	**a** What	**b** How	**c** Where
3	**a** of	**b** about	**c** on
4	**a** hate	**b** don't like	**c** love
5	**a** listened	**b** listening	**c** listen
6	**a** in	**b** for	**c** on
7	**a** going	**b** go	**c** to go
8	**a** keen	**b** fond	**c** crazy
9	**a** want	**b** need	**c** should
10	**a** get back	**b** get on	**c** go on

2 Write these email addresses, URLs, and telephone numbers.

1 It's g, e, c at hotmail dot com.
gec@hotmail.com

2 My number's double zero, double four, three one nine, double four, oh one oh.
_____

3 My email's Lydia underscore forty-nine, at yahoo dot d for dog, t for Turkey.
_____

4 The new website is www dot, about dash, me, dot com, slash courses, underscore online.
_____

Language at work | Past simple and present perfect

Past simple and present perfect

Form

Past simple:
verb + -ed
I worked here two years ago.

Present perfect:
has / have + past participle
I have worked here for five years.

For irregular verb forms, see page 134.

Use

Use both the past simple and present perfect to talk about the past in different situations.

Past simple	Present perfect
To talk about actions or events that took place in a finished time period, e.g. *yesterday, last year, when I arrived.* She **worked** here for five years, from 1999 to 2004.	To talk about actions or events that took place in a time period that has not finished, e.g. *up to now, today, this year.* We've **manufactured** this product for over three years. How long **have** you been here?
five years 1999 2004 now	now
To talk about finished actions or events when the speaker says, asks, or knows when something happened. *I* **met** him last Saturday. When **did** he **leave**?	To talk about finished actions or events when the speaker does not say, ask, or know when it happened. We've already **discussed** this. *I* **haven't seen** him, I'm afraid.
last Saturday now	??? now
	To talk about very recently finished actions or events, with just. They've **just got** here.
Words we often use with the past simple are *yesterday, last week, last year, in 1999, three years ago.*	Words we often use with the present perfect are *for, since, yet, just, never, recently, already.*

For and *since*

Use *for* to talk about periods of time.
She's been here **for hours**.
I haven't played tennis **for ages**.

Use *since* to talk about a specific time.
This company has sold books **since 1951**.
We haven't met **since that conference in Berlin**, *have we?*

Language tip

Introduce a topic into a conversation with the present perfect, and use the past simple to ask for specific details.
A **Have** *you* **visited** *Sydney before?*
B *Yes, I have. I came here two years ago.*
A *So,* **did** *you* **visit** *the Opera House?*
B *Actually, no I didn't.*

1 Complete these sentences with the past simple or present perfect form of the verbs in brackets.

1 Anna *has worked* (work) here for ages. She still does the same job.
2 The sales office _____ (close) down over a month ago.
3 The Managing Director _____ just _____ (organize) a meeting with all line managers.
4 _____ you _____ (call) him back yet?
5 What time _____ she _____ (arrive)?
6 I don't think we _____ ever _____ (meet) before, have we?
7 We _____ (not / take) the opportunity when we had the chance.
8 Things _____ (not / improve) that much since he took over.
9 _____ you ever _____ (speak) to the CEO?
10 You know a lot about this company. How long _____ you _____ (work) here?

2 Complete these sentences with *since* or *for*.

1 They've been in business *for* ten years.
2 She's been in reception _____ eleven o'clock.
3 Michael has worked in R&D _____ over six months.
4 Have you been here _____ a long time?
5 Have you seen him _____ the last time we were here?

Working with words

1 Replace the words in *italics* with words from the list.

accurate   user-friendly   up-to-date   cost-effective
convenient   time-saving   secure   ~~customized~~
immediate   efficient   easier

1 All our cars are *changed* to suit a customer's personal needs and requirements. ___customized___

2 You'd think that keeping work in-house would be *saving us money*, but in fact outsourcing can really reduce spending. _____

3 That new café round the corner is a bit expensive, but it's really *near* for lunch. _____

4 Very few jobs are *guaranteed for life* these days. You never know when you'll be out of work. _____

5 You take a number at the bank now instead of queuing. It's really *good for reducing the long wait*. _____

6 We seem to have three people standing in one place all doing the same job. There must be a more *effective* way of using them. _____

7 This new software has made doing the monthly payroll much *less complicated*. _____

8 They've redesigned the controls to make it *easy for the operator*. _____

9 I'd like a report on the situation which is detailed and *says what's happening now*! _____

10 How *correct* are these figures? They don't appear to add up. _____

11 I'm sorry, but we can't give you an *instant* answer. We'll need a few days to discuss it first. _____

2 What are these people talking about? Match a word from the list to comments 1–4.

business class   online banking
~~consultants~~   financial adviser

1 ❛ They help the company to look at problems objectively and consider all the possibilities. ❜

___consultants___

2 ❛ Having him allows me to concentrate on earning it and not what to do with it. ❜

_____

3 ❛ It makes it so much faster than having to go to an actual building and wait behind everyone else. ❜

_____

4 ❛ I don't have to worry about turning up so early, which allows me to get a decent night's sleep before I arrive. ❜

_____

Business communication skills

1 Complete the conversation with these phrases.

~~Will it let me …?~~
What happens when …
Let me explain how it works.
You can see what happens when you …
What happens is …
One other useful feature is that …
The main thing to note is …

A So, this is the new photocopier. It should be better.

B ¹ ___Will it let me___ copy on both sides of the paper?

A Yes, of course. ² _____.
³ _____ that you have to choose the double-sided option first.
⁴ _____ the copier copies on both sides and the sheets come out here.

B I see. What else can it do?

A ⁵ _____ the photocopier can staple pages together if you want it to.

B Really? ⁶ _____
I select the double-sided and the staple option together?

A Well, basically the double-sided pages come out first, and then the copier staples them together. ⁷ _____ try it yourself.

2 Complete the sentences with the pairs of words from the list.

as well as + also   more + better   one + other
~~good + bad~~   whereas before + now
similar + different   difficult + simple
downside + plus side   benefit + drawback

1 The _good_ news is he's changing jobs, but the _bad_ news is he'll be your new line manager.

2 The body looks very _____ to the old model, but what's _____ is the engine.

3 One _____ is that the merger will expand the company, although a _____ might be that we lose our character.

4 _____ improving service to the external customer, the new network will _____ help our staff.

5 One _____ is that this machine needs two people, but on the _____ it's safer.

6 _____ we wrote it by hand, we _____ ask customers to type in their details.

7 On the _____ hand he's slow, but on the _____ hand he never makes a mistake.

8 It might seem a bit _____ to use at first but in fact it's very _____.

9 The _____ people get to know it, the _____ it will work.

Language at work | Comparative forms

Comparative forms

Form

1 Add -er to one- and some two-syllable adjectives and to adverbs with the same form as adjectives, e.g. *straight*, *fast*.

  small → **smaller**   *fast* → **faster**

  If the adjective or adverb ends in -y, change the -y to an -i and add -er.

  happy → **happier**

2 Double the consonant after a vowel at the end of short adjectives.

  hot → **hotter**   *big* → **bigger**   *thin* → **thinner**

3 Some adjectives are irregular.

  good / well → **better**   *bad / badly* → **worse**

4 Add *more* to two- or more syllable adjectives and adverbs.

  accurate → **more accurate**   *quickly* → **more quickly**

5 Add *than* after the comparative to compare two things.

  *Carole is **more sociable than** Vincent.*

Use

1 Use the comparative to compare two or more things / people.

  *This new system is **better than** the old one.*

2 To say something is the same, use *as* + adjective + *as*.

  *It's **as accurate as** the old system.*

3 To say something is different, use *not as* + adjective + *as*.

  *It is **not (isn't) as efficient as** the old system.*

4 Use *even* to make the comparative adjective more extreme and surprising. This sentence could suggest that the last boss was not very good.

  The new boss is better than the last one.

  This sentence suggests that the last boss was good and surprisingly the new one is better. Therefore the new boss must be extremely good.

  *The new boss is **even** better than the last one.*

5 Use intensifiers to emphasize the size of the comparison.

  *Sales are **a great deal** bigger this year than last year.* (big difference)

  *There were **nearly as** many customers last night as there were here at Christmas.* (small difference)

  Small difference: *slightly, nearly as … as, a little, marginally, a bit*
  Big difference: *a great deal, not anything like as … as, significantly, a lot, far, much*

  For making comparisons with nouns, see Unit 10, page 64.

---

1 Complete these guidelines on designing a website with the correct form of the words in brackets.

> To be effective, websites must always score much ¹ _higher_ (high) in what 'usability guru', Jakob Nielsen, calls 'the three Fs'.
>
> **Functional**
> First of all, a website must be as ²_____ (easy) to use as anyone else's. Badly-designed sites don't function as ³_____ (good) as their competitors' and so they lose a lot more business. Another point is that sites which are successful are continually looking at how they can be even ⁴_____ (friendly) to the user.
>
> **Fast**
> The second F is to be ⁵_____ (fast) than the rest. Customers won't want to use the website if downloading the site is ⁶_____ (slow) than with other sites.
>
> **Familiar**
> The final F is familiarity. A site which is ⁷_____ (original) than its competitors' may look good, but in the end it will be ⁸_____ (popular) if it's similar to other websites and users know how it works and what it does.

2 Adrian Sewell's company is looking for a new website designer. He is discussing the options with two members of his team. Read this information and choose the correct answer from the words in *italics*.

Name:	Fritz Neff	Maria Mendes	Jean-Noel Petit
Experience:	5 years	5 years	2 years
Salary expectation:	high	medium	medium / low
Style:	modern	traditional	experimental
Sickness record:	1 day last year	0 days last year	11 days last year

Katie Well, I think we should choose Maria. She is ¹~~significantly~~ / *more* experienced ²*as* / *than* Jean-Noel, and she didn't take any days off due to sickness last year.

Guy Yes, but I think Jean-Noel would be better ³*than* / *that* Maria. He's more dynamic and his salary expectations are also ⁴*slightly* / *as* lower than hers.

Adrian Well, I disagree with both of you. I think we should go for Fritz. His designs are ⁵*a bit* / *far* more up to date than Maria's and that's important for our image. And his sickness record is ⁶*marginally* / *much* better than Jean-Noel's and only ⁷*a bit* / *a great deal* worse than Maria's.

Katie Yes, but Maria is just ⁸*as* / *so* experienced ⁹*than* / *as* Fritz, and her salary expectations are lower.

Adrian I think we can talk to Fritz about salaries …

Working with words

1 Complete these sentences with words from the list. You may need to change the form of the words.

care   serve   require   ~~help~~   expect   satisfy

1 All your staff are very _helpful_. Whenever I have a problem, there's always someone waiting to sort it out.

2 First of all, I need to find out about your _____. What exactly do you need?

3 I'll just put you through to customer _____. They should be able to help you.

4 In this company we really _____ about our customers and we're always thinking of how we can keep them happy.

5 The results show that we're not always matching up to people's _____.

6 We regularly do market research to find out about levels of _____ with our products.

2 Choose the correct answer from the words in *italics*.

1 We usually *assess / ~~adjust~~* your progress by having tests once a month.

2 This questionnaire allows us to find out about you and *tailor / monitor* the course to your needs.

3 We *check / guarantee* complete satisfaction, or your money back.

4 Is there a way to *provide / evaluate* the success rate of the training?

5 How will you *care / ensure* the safety of the passengers?

6 To increase your heart rate while running, just *adjust / serve* the level of difficulty on the control panel.

7 We *satisfy / provide* sports equipment to the biggest names in the industry.

3 Match the words from the list to these definitions.

evaluate   guarantee   satisfy
adapt   services   care

1 something companies supply – not products: _____

2 to make sure of something: _____

3 to judge / assess something: _____

4 to change something to suit a particular need: _____

5 to look after: _____

6 to make someone feel pleased and contented: _____

Business communication skills

1 Choose the correct answer from the words in *italics*.

A I'd like to [1]*~~do~~ / fix* a date for the IT seminar.

B Didn't we [2]*attend / arrange* it for January?

A Yes we did, but not many of our people can [3]*arrive / make* it then. They say it's too soon after Christmas.

B OK. Well, the second half of February is still [4]*well / good* for me. [5]*How / What* does that [6]*suit / convenient* you?

A I [7]*prefer / 'd prefer* later in the year, actually.

2 Complete these sentences with the correct preposition.

1 Hello, I'd like to find _out_ more about your hotel.

2 We're interested _____ booking it for two nights.

3 Are conferences something you deal _____?

4 Would it be possible _____ you to stay another night?

5 Next Tuesday would be possible _____ me.

6 Sorry, I can't come _____ Thursday.

7 I'm busy next week, so can we move it _____ to the week after?

8 Instead of the afternoon, why don't we bring it _____ to the morning?

3 Match 1–8 in **2** above to a response a–h.

a Great. We have got a special offer on if you stay for longer though. ____

b Of course. No problem. So how about the Tuesday? ____

c Certainly. What would you like to know? ____

d No. I'm afraid I have to get back to the office tomorrow. ____

e That suits me too. Shall we say 10 o'clock, then? ____

f Yes, they are. How can I help you? ____

g Fine – but not too early, please, because I have a meeting at 9.00 a.m. ____

h Never mind. I'll brief you when you get back from your trip. ____

Language at work | Present simple and continuous for future use

Present simple and continuous for future use

Form

See pages 103 and 105.

Use

The present continuous and present simple can be used to talk about the future.

1 Use the present continuous to talk about a future arrangement that someone has made.

We're discussing this again at the next meeting.

2 Use the present simple to talk about scheduled or timetabled events.

The gymnasium opens at 6.30 from Monday to Friday.

3 Use the present simple after conjunctions of time, such as *after, as soon as, when, by the time.*

I'll call you back as soon as she leaves.
We can take off when everyone is on the plane.

4 We often use the present simple to talk about the future with verbs such as: *open, close, start, leave, arrive* and *depart.*

The café closes at 5.00 p.m.

Language tip

1 We usually use the present continuous for personal future arrangements and the present simple for official future arrangements.

I'm meeting James for lunch tomorrow.
The annual general meeting starts at 9.00 a.m. tomorrow.

2 We don't usually use state verbs, such as *be, believe, have* (for possession) and *need*, in continuous forms.

Do say: *I'm busy tomorrow.*
Don't say: *I'm being busy tomorrow.*

1 **Complete this phone call with the present simple or the present continuous form of the verbs in brackets.**

Enrico Hello, Sophie. It's Enrico. I'm calling to check the details for tomorrow's visit.

Sophie Hello, Enrico. Yes, everything's organized. What time [1] _does your flight arrive_ (flight / arrive)?

Enrico It [2] _____ (get in) at 9.15 a.m.

Sophie Oh yes, that's what I have written here on the schedule, and John [3] _____ (meet) you at the airport. Then he [4] _____ (bring) you back to the office.

Enrico Oh good. And [5] _____ (we all / have / lunch) together?

Sophie Yes, and then we [6] _____ (show) you around the factory.

Enrico Great. And what [7] _____ (we / do) after that?

Sophie Then we [8] _____ (have) a meal at an Italian restaurant and after that you have to go back to the airport. What time [9] _____ (your flight / leave)?

Enrico It [10] _____ (leave) at 10.30 p.m.

Sophie Oh, that's fine. We can order a taxi to pick you up at 8.00 p.m.

2 **Complete this email using the prompts in *italics*.**

Dear Maria

~~What / you / do / on / Thursday / evening?~~
1 _What are you doing on Thursday evening?_

Our team / go out / to celebrate / Torsten's birthday.
2 _____

Would you like to come?
We / meet / in reception / at 5.30 p.m.
3 _____

Then / we / have / a meal / in that new Greek restaurant.
4 _____

We could go home together afterwards.
The last train / leave / at midnight.
5 _____

Let me know if you would like to come.

All the best
Mounir

Working with words

1 Complete this review of a hotel. Use the answers to complete the puzzle and find the European city where the hotel is located.

HOTEL REVIEWS

This first-class hotel and conference centre welcomes guests from all over the world. Its ¹ _facilities_ are second to none. There are 300 ensuite rooms and five apartment suites. For business guests, they have ten meeting rooms, two of which are big enough to be used as ² _____ halls.

They also organize events for the guests – a guided ³_____ around the town centre provides popular evening ⁴_____ for those who enjoy a bit of ⁵_____. For a quieter time, they serve regional ⁶_____ every evening in their four-star restaurant. All in all, this is a top-class ⁷_____ for business or for pleasure.

```
              ¹ F A C I [L] I T I E S
         ² E              [ ]
              ³ E         [ ]
         ⁴ E              [ ]
   ⁵ S                    [ ]
   ⁶ S                    [ ]
              ⁷ V         [ ]
```

2 Replace the words in _italics_ with one of the verb phrases from the list. Add a pronoun if you need to.

go out	freshen up	eat out
pick someone up	meet up with	check in
~~drop someone off~~	show someone around	

Pedro It's difficult to park here. Can I ~~stop and leave you~~ ¹ _drop you off_ in front of the hotel?

Sabrina Sure, I'll _register_ ²_____ and then I'd like to _have a wash, and change my clothes_ ³_____.

Pedro If you like, tonight I can _give you a tour of_ ⁴_____ the old city. We could _eat in a restaurant_ ⁵_____ by the port.

Sabrina That sounds great! I'd rather _leave the hotel_ ⁶_____ than stay in my room.

Pedro I'll _collect you_ ⁷_____ at 8.30 p.m. We'll _see_ ⁸_____ Alberto and Maite in the main square.

Business communication skills

1 Raymond Roberts has an appointment with Janet Rose. He has just arrived at HBG premises. Complete their conversation with words and phrases from the list.

did you have any trouble	let me take your bag
can I get you a drink	how was your journey
It's nice to finally meet you	Likewise
let me run through	~~Welcome to HBG publishing~~
sounds great	get a chance

Raymond Good morning, I'm here to see Janet Rose.

Janet Hello, I'm Janet. ¹ _Welcome to HBG publishing_ .

Raymond ²_____ in person.

Janet ³_____. So, ⁴_____?

Raymond Well, there were traffic jams on the motorway.

Janet Ah, that must be because of the roadworks. And ⁵_____ finding us?

Raymond I must admit, I got a little bit lost in the industrial park.

Janet Don't worry. That happens to everyone. Anyway, ⁶_____ – I'll store it in my office.

Raymond I'll hang on to it if you don't mind. It's got all my stuff in it.

Janet Well, if you change your mind just tell me. And ⁷_____?

Raymond A drink ⁸_____. I'll have a cup of tea, please.

Janet So, ⁹_____ the schedule. Your first meeting is with Karen Rankin.

Raymond OK. And will I see Malcolm Briscoe?

Janet Yes, you'll ¹⁰_____ to see him this afternoon.

2 Choose the correct answer from the words in _italics_.

'Good morning everybody. I'm Sandra Wildman. On ¹_behalf / part_ of Greenblo energy, it gives me great pleasure ²_to / for_ welcome you ³_to / in_ our plant. We are going to begin ⁴_with / by_ a guided tour of the plant. Afterwards, you will have the ⁵_opportunity / availability_ to discuss Greenblo's work over a cup of coffee. I'd now like to hand you ⁶_through / over_ to Kim Akeson, who is going to look after you today. Kim will go ⁷_for / over_ the schedule and then show you around the factory. For your ⁸_self / own_ safety, can I ⁹_remember / remind_ you to stay with Kim at all times. May I ¹⁰_hope / wish_ you all an interesting visit.'

Language at work | Obligation, necessity, and prohibition

Obligation, necessity, and prohibition

Use

1 To talk about actions which are / aren't necessary, use *need to / don't need to* or *have to / don't have to*.

> We **need to / have to** watch the share price carefully.
> Back office staff **don't need to / don't have to** wear suits or ties.

2 To give an instruction that you think is important, use *must*.

> You **must** save your files before closing your computer down.

3 To talk about an absence of obligation, use *don't / doesn't have to / need to*.

> You **don't have to / need to** wear an ID badge.

4 To prohibit somebody from doing something, use *must not*.

> You **must not / mustn't** leave the designated area.

5 To say / ask if something is / isn't prohibited, use *be allowed to / not be allowed to*.

> **Are** we **allowed to** make personal calls from our workstations?
> You **aren't allowed to** bring mobile phones into the lab.

6 To remind people about rules, or to talk about rules which aren't always observed, use *be supposed to / not be supposed to*.

> I'm sorry, but you**'re not supposed to** bring drinks in here.
> We**'re supposed to** park at the back of the building (but I often park at the front).

Form

1 *Must* has no past or future form. For the past and the future use *have to*.

> He **had to** show his passport at the security desk.
> You **will have to** switch all the computers off before leaving the office.

2 *Must* is rarely used in questions – use *have to*.

> Does he **have to** lock up every day?

3 It is possible to use *need* as a modal auxiliary, especially in the negative.

> You **needn't** go to the meeting this afternoon.

Language tip

Be careful with *must*, particularly when speaking with native speakers, as this can appear rude and even aggressive. *Have to* is more commonly used.

> You **have to** work at least 35 hours each week.

---

1 **Rewrite these sentences starting with the words given. Use *must*, *have to*, *need*, etc.**

1 My job is to welcome guests and answer the phone.
I *have to welcome guests and answer the phone* .

2 It isn't necessary to bring your laptop – we have one you can use.
You don't _____ .

3 This is a no-smoking area.
We aren't _____ .

4 It is absolutely forbidden to take these documents out of the building.
You _____ .

5 In theory we're not allowed to talk in the library, but everyone does.
We're not _____ .

2 **Samantha is giving a presentation about rules and duties to some temporary members of staff at a department store in London. Read her notes and complete the presentation.**

> 'Hi everyone, I'm Samantha and I'm going to tell you some of the dos and don'ts of working here.
> You don't need to [1] *call other staff Sir, Madam, Mr, or Mrs – first names are OK* .
> You have to [2]_____ and _____ .
> You're supposed to [3]_____ and _____ .
> You mustn't [4]_____ or _____ .

---

duties
- be polite and helpful to the customers
- wear an ID badge at all times

not necessary
- call other staff Sir, Madam, Mr, Mrs – first names are OK

absolutely prohibited
- smoking in warehouse
- wearing jeans

rules which lots of people ignore
- leave bicycles at the back of the shop
- enter the shop through the main entrance

Working with words

1 Choose the correct answer from the words in *italics*.

> ### Security fears stop network administrators ¹*from / against* sleeping
>
> A new survey shows that many of the people who look after our networks can't sleep at night. Around 35% of network administrators say that monitoring the network ²*of / for* security breaches and preventing hackers ³*from / by* entering the system are major concerns. Another 24% lose sleep over how to safeguard ⁴*against / with* the latest virus.
>
> Many network administrators said they had little or no budget for training users in proper security practices on the computer. This might include learning ways to protect ⁵*for / against* hacking or checking ⁶*for / of* malicious programs.

2 Use a word from **A** and a word from **B** below to match definitions 1–8.

A	B
~~security~~	machine
unauthorized	number
security	software
CC	~~theft~~
antivirus	~~measures~~
X-ray	TV
PIN	breach
identity	access

1 actions taken to deter people like hackers or thieves:
   security measures

2 stealing people's personal information and using it:
   _____

3 without the right to look at or use something,
   e.g. personal information, on a computer:
   _____

4 a secret code used to gain access, e.g. at a cash machine:
   _____

5 it allows you to see inside bags: _____

6 when something that is usually protected, is no longer secure: _____

7 a system to allow you to watch what is happening in other parts of the building: _____

8 it protects your computer from attacks via email or the Internet: _____

Business communication skills

1 Complete the memo with the phrases from the list.

> This is because of the fact that   By entering
> I'd like to update you   As a result   We expect
> As it stands, the situation is   ~~Up to now~~

> ## Memo
>
> **To**: All staff
> **From**: Head of Administration
> **Date**: 13 October
> **Subject**: Security measures
>
> As you know, we've recently had a number of unauthorized entries to the building. ¹ _Up to now_ , no-one has had anything stolen but we need to improve our security procedures. ² _____ that you show your security passes at the main entrance, but these are never re-checked inside the building. ³ _____ we cannot employ security personnel at every door.
>
> ⁴ _____, we've decided to install a new PIN number system of security and ⁵ _____ on how this will be implemented.
>
> By 30 November, all entrances and any main internal doors will have boxes. ⁶ _____ a PIN number into the box, the door opens so that you can go through. ⁷ _____ that you will receive your personal four-digit PIN number by 3 December.

2 Put these words in the right order.

1 the / reasons / changes / what / are / for / the?
   What are the reasons for the changes?

2 how / it / I / understand / don't / works / quite.
   _____

3 it / can / tell / us / you / more / about?
   _____

4 'security breach' / do / you / mean / what / by?
   _____

5 I / will / a / understand / if / this / lot / you / correctly, / cost.
   _____

6 you / follow / not / I / I'm / sure.
   _____

Language at work | Present perfect simple and continuous | Connectors

Present perfect simple and continuous

Form

For the present perfect, see page 107.

Present perfect continuous

have / has + been + -ing form

*I **have been waiting** for you for over an hour.*

Use

1 Use the present perfect continuous for activities that began in the past and are still continuing, when you want to emphasize
- the activity itself
  *They**'ve been developing** a new product.*
- the duration of the activity into the present time.
  *I**'ve been saying** we should do this **since the project began**!*

2 Sometimes either the present perfect simple or the present perfect continuous can be used.
  *I**'ve worked** here for three years.* ✓
  *I**'ve been working** here for three years.* ✓

3 Use the present perfect simple to emphasize the result of an action, or the number of times it has occurred. Compare the following sentences.

	Emphasis
*I**'ve chaired** the team meeting three times.*	(number of times)
*I**'ve been sitting** in this meeting all day.*	(duration)
*I**'ve just finished** the report.*	(end result)
*I**'ve been working** on the report.*	(action or event)

Language tip
Do not use the present perfect continuous with state verbs, such as *be, know, understand*, etc. (See page 105 for more on state verbs and the present continuous.)

Connectors

Use

1 Use the connectors *in order that, so that, because of,* and *due to* to explain the reason for something.
  In order that / So that we can deal with your enquiry quickly, please give your reference number.
  *We need your reference number. It's **because of / due to** the security situation.*

2 Use the connectors *so, therefore, as a result,* and *consequently* to explain the result of something.
  *We need more staff to complete the job. **As a result / Therefore / Consequently**, we've employed two more people.*
  *We need more staff for this job, **so** we've employed two more people.*

Language tip
In order that / So that often come before a modal verb.
  *I tried to finish the report quickly, **so that** I could prepare for the meeting.*

1 Complete this conversation between a policeman and the owner of a small company with the present perfect simple or present perfect continuous form of the verbs in brackets.

Policeman So, how long [1] _have you been_ (be) here this morning?

Owner For about two hours. I think the alarm [2]_____ (ring) all night.

Policeman Why [3]_____ you _____ (not / switch) it off yet?

Owner Sorry, I [4]_____ (look) for the special PIN number to switch it off, but I can't find it. Anyway, I [5]_____ (just / call) the manufacturer and they [6]_____ (send) someone out. He should be here any moment.

Policeman Good. Has anything been stolen?

Owner No, I don't think so.

Policeman [7]_____ you _____ (have) any problems with the alarm recently?

Owner No, not really, but it is a bit old and we [8]_____ (talk) about changing the security system for a while.

Policeman That sounds like a good idea!

2 Choose the correct answer from the words in *italics*.

Security guidelines for airline passengers

[1]~~As a result~~ / *Due to* increased security measures at all international airports, passengers should arrive three hours before departure time.

You need to show your passport and boarding card at certain security points, [2]*so / because of* always have these documents ready.

[3]*In order to / therefore* avoid delays at security, all travellers should remove metal objects and place them in the tray.

We ask you to remove your laptop from its travel case [4]*so that / consequently* it can be X-rayed separately.

We are currently testing new body scan technology. [5]*Therefore / In order that*, certain passengers may be selected to participate in these tests.

Working with words

1 Match 1–10 to a–j.

1 In my opinion, we need to *join* … *i*

2 We have a *shared* … ____

3 They have *complementary* … ____

4 We'll need to *work* … ____

5 I think if we work together, it will be to our *mutual* … ____

6 We want someone who is a *team* … ____

7 It's time for the company to *take* … ____

8 The team isn't working well together. We need to find some *common* … ____

9 The two companies want to start a *joint* … ____

10 Telecommunications companies often try to *form* … ____

a *alliances* with web companies to enter the broadband market.

b *responsibility* for its actions.

c *goal* – together we want to become the new market leaders.

d *ground* between everyone.

e *venture* in China.

f *closely* on this project, so that nothing goes wrong.

g *skills*. Hannah is a brilliant sales person and Cindy is an excellent administrator.

h *benefit*.

i *forces* with a local partner in order to get the contract.

j *player*, not who only wants to work on their own.

2 Match the collocations in *italics* from 1 to these definitions.

1 to get together with somebody else to do something: *join forces*

2 to accept a duty to do something, or to accept blame for something: _____

3 a person who is good at working with other people: _____

4 to do something alongside someone else: _____

5 abilities that work well together: _____

6 interests and aims that you share with someone: _____

7 to make an agreement to work together to achieve something everyone involved wants: _____

8 a new business that is started by two or more companies: _____

9 a positive effect that something has on two people or two groups: _____

10 an objective that is the same as someone else's objective: _____

Business communication skills

1 Put the words in *italics* in the right order to complete this conversation between a human resources manager and a departmental manager.

Human resources manager As you know, the company is in a difficult situation at the moment. I'm afraid *is / that / likely / it* [1] *it is likely that* there will be some job losses.

Departmental manager *this / timescale / the / What's / on* [2] _____? Will people be told to leave this month?

Human resources manager Well, *plan / we / to* [3] _____ inform all affected employees by the end of the month. I'm very sorry about this. It's not something we wanted to do, but hopefully it will mean that the company's future will be more secure *long / the / run / in* [4] _____.

2 David Harper is discussing progress of his company's new website with his assistants. Complete their conversation with words and phrases from the list.

hope to have   going to tell everyone   chances are
How long will it take to   in the long term
over the next   expect   in the short term
~~what's the next step~~   this leave us   by the end of

David So, [1] *what's the next step* ? Are we still on schedule?

Ines Yes, I think so. The layout has been agreed on.

David That's good to hear. And what about the photographs?

Ines We [2] _____ a choice of the images by the end of the week.

David And how's it going with the online payment side of things, Marco?

Marco Well, as you know, [3] _____ the site will just give information, but [4] _____ it will have online payment.

David [5] _____ get this up and running?

Marco Well, we [6] _____ it ready [7] _____ November.

David So remind me, how are we [8] _____ about the new site?

Ines Well, we've printed details on our bags and wrapping paper, and all our emails have the address.

David So where does [9] _____?

Marco Well, [10] _____ few months we need to monitor the number of visitors to the site and make sure that search engines start to pick us up.

David That's great work the two of you. I think everything is on track. The [11] _____ this will give the business the boost we need.

Language at work | Talking about the future – *going to, will,* and modal verbs

going to

Form

am / is / are + *going to* + verb

I'm going to work late tonight.

Use

1 To talk about things we intend to do, or have already planned to do.

We're going to start a business together when we finish our training.

2 To make predictions based on what we can see now.

Watch out! You're going to hit your head on the door.

will

Form

will + verb

I think the new product will be successful.

Use

1 To talk about future facts.

Next year the call centre will be in Bangkok.

2 To talk about predictions.

The price of gold will continue to rise.

3 To make decisions / offers at the moment of speaking.

A Can I call for a taxi? I need to get to the airport.
B Don't do that. I'll drive you there myself.

4 To make promises.

I'll definitely finish it tomorrow.

Modal verbs: *might, could,* and *should*

Form

might / could / should + verb

The new offices should be really good when they are finished.

Use

1 Use *might* or *could* to talk about something that is possible, but not certain.

This clause in the contract might / could cause us problems later on.

2 Use *should* to talk about something that is expected to happen.

A Do you know when the next shuttle to the airport leaves?
B There should be one in a few minutes. They come every quarter of an hour.

Language tip

Be careful not to confuse the future use of *should* with *should* for advice.

You should lose weight and stop smoking.

---

1 Some guests from Russia are visiting Patrick Wilson's company. Complete the conversation with *will* or *going to*.

Angie Why are you wearing a tie today Patrick? It's not like you.

Patrick I ¹ _am going to_ meet the Russian visitors today, and I want to make a good impression.

Angie Oh, of course. I'd forgotten about that. What are your plans for today then?

Patrick Well, I ²_____ bring them to the office and show them around, but there are no plans after that, so I need some suggestions from you both.

Sasha We should probably take them out for a meal tonight.

Angie Yes, that's a good idea … I know, I ³_____ book a table at that new French restaurant.

Sasha That sounds good, and I ⁴_____ try and organize something for after the meal.

Patrick Great. Let me know when you've arranged it. Oh, look at the time! I ⁵_____ be late. I'm supposed to be at their hotel in five minutes!

Sasha Don't worry Patrick, I've got my car with me today. I ⁶_____ give you a lift.

Patrick Thanks, Sasha. That's great.

2 Choose the best answer to complete the sentences.

1 A Would you like to join us for dinner after the meeting?
  B That's kind of you, but I __c__ have an early night. I'm tired after the journey.
  a will   b could   c ~~am going to~~

2 A How do I get to your place from the airport?
  B Don't worry, I _____ be there to pick you up.
  a could   b might   c will

3 A Where's Marika?
  B She _____ be here any minute. She generally comes in at half past nine.
  a might   b could   c should

4 Guess what! My secretary _____ have another baby. She's three months' pregnant.
  a is going to   b will   c could

5 Their new product range _____ challenge our market position, there's no question of it.
  a might   b will   c should

6 You never know with Michael. These changes _____ make him angry.
  a might   b will   c are going to

Working with words

1 Complete these sentences. Use the answers to complete the crossword.

1 A French _manufacturer_ of electrical goods is outsourcing its production to China.

2 We need a more reliable _____. We can't afford to wait for spare parts.

3 We don't deal directly with shops. We let our _____ handle that.

4 Such a level of _____ costs money. We should only produce to order.

5 We need to _____ our supply chain. It has too many stages and is too inefficient.

6 We need to look at each step in the supply _____, to check that we are operating efficiently.

7 _____ is managing the supply chain, from production to the end-user.

8 We try to treat each _____ as an individual – that way they come back to us.

9 They stock their finished goods in a _____ the size of an aircraft hangar.

10 Problems with just one tiny _____ meant they had to recall 50,000 machines.

11 The chocolate factory relies on regular deliveries of _____ materials, such as cocoa and sugar, to maintain production levels.

12 Internet shopping has made life harder for the traditional _____.

```
                          3
                       2  D
                  1  2 S  4 I [ ][ ][ ][ ][ ][ ][ ]
                  M  A
                  A     5 S [ ][ ][ ][ ][ ][ ][ ]
             6 C  N
                  U  7 L [ ][ ][ ][ ][ ][ ]      8 C
                  F                               C
             9 W  A
                  C
                  T     10 C [ ][ ][ ][ ][ ][ ][ ]
                  U  11
                  R  R
             12 R E [ ][ ][ ][ ][ ]
                  R
```

2 Choose the correct answer from the words in *italics*.

1 The book is currently out of stock, but it is *on / ~~out of~~* order, so we'll have it soon.

2 We need to *stock up on / run out of* headed paper. Could you put an order in?

3 I ran *low on / out of* ink, so I couldn't print out the report.

4 We can keep *track of / on track* our order by satellite.

5 Let's stop at the next service station. We are *running low / running out* on petrol.

Business communication skills

1 Put the words in *italics* in the right order to complete this phone call between Virginie, a customer, and Kevin, a call handler.

Kevin Good afternoon, you're speaking to Kevin. How can I help you?

Virginie Hello, I am *up / ~~chasing~~ / ~~an~~ / order*
¹ _chasing up an order_ I placed three weeks ago.

Kevin *account / take / I / your / details / Can*
² _____, please?

Virginie Yes. The account number is 572638.

Kevin OK. If you bear with me a moment, I'll *into / look / it* ³ _____.
Let me see. Well, *my / to / information / according*
⁴ _____, it is still on order.

Virginie Look, I really want to know *happened / to / has / it / what* ⁵ _____.
Could *check / me / you / it / for / out* ⁶ _____?

Kevin Certainly. I'll *back / you / to / hour / within / get / the* ⁷ _____.

2 Kevin calls Virginie back. Complete their conversation with words and phrases from the list.

~~we put the order straight through to the warehouse~~
asap   charge it to
it was dispatched on   check it out
as quick as we can   something must have gone wrong

Kevin Hello, this is Kevin from DYK calling. I've got some information about your order.

Virginie Oh, thanks for calling back. So, what's happened to it?

Kevin Well, ¹*we put the order straight through to the warehouse*, and ² _____ the 25th.

Virginie But I haven't received it.

Kevin Oh, sorry about that. What was the delivery address?

Virginie We wanted it delivered to the Brussels office.

Kevin Oh, ³ _____. I'll ⁴ _____ straight away.

Virginie Look, I haven't got time for this. Could you just send them again ⁵ _____?

Kevin OK, no problem. We'll be ⁶ _____.

Virginie Thank you. And please ⁷ _____ the Brussels account, not the Paris one.

Language at work | Reported speech

Reported speech

Form

1 Use a reporting verb (*say, tell,* etc.) + your own words. If the reporting verb is in the present tense, the tense of the original statement does not change.

*'How old **is** the company?'*   He **wants to know** how old the company **is**.

2 If the reporting verb is in the past tense, you can change the tense of the original statement. The following tenses often change in this way.

Original statement	Reported speech
present simple	past simple
present continuous	past continuous
past simple	past perfect
can	*could*
will	*would*

*'How old **is** this company?'*   He **wanted to know** how old the company **was**.

*'I **can't** work this weekend.'*   John **told me** he **couldn't** work this weekend.

Use

1 Use *say* and *tell* to report statements. Use *say something (to someone)* or *tell someone something.*

'I'll find out about the order.'   He **said (to me)** he would find out about the order.
   He **told me** he would find out about the order.

2 Use *ask* and *want to know* to report questions.

3 With *wh-* questions, do not use *do / does* in the reported question. Put the verb at the end of the sentence.

'Where does it come from?'   He **wants to know** where it **comes from**.

'What is Hannah's second name?'   She **asked** what Hannah's second name **was**.

Don't say: *She **asked / wanted to know** what ~~was Hannah's second name~~.*

4 With *yes / no* questions, use *if / whether* after *ask / want to know.*

'Do you know my old boss?'   She **wanted to know if** I knew her old boss.

5 Use *ask someone to,* to report a request.

'Can you chase this up, please?'   She **asked me to** chase it up.

6 Use *tell someone to,* to report an order or instruction.

'Go and see if it has arrived.'   He **told me to** go and see if it had arrived.

---

1 **Read these extracts from conversations and complete Sylvie's explanation below.**

Monday

Sylvie Hi, Sandra, this is Sylvie from Stockwell's. Can we have our usual order as soon as possible, please?

Sandra Yes of course, Sylvie. I'll deal with it straight away.

Thursday

Sylvie I'm calling about an order I placed with Sandra. I'd like to know what has happened to it.

Assistant Oh, I'm sorry. Sandra is off sick. I'll look into it.

Friday

Sylvie Hi, Sandra. It's Silvie. Are you better now?

Sandra Actually, I wasn't off sick. My assistant said that because he didn't want anyone to know that it was his mistake. He's sent the order now. You should get it today.

Sandra Oh, I see. Better late than never, I suppose. Thanks.

Friday lunchtime

Boss Sylvie, where's that order I asked for on Monday? Why has it taken so long?

Sylvie Yes, sorry about that. I called Sandra on Monday and asked if we [1] *could have our usual order as soon as possible* . She said she [2]_____. Then, when nothing had arrived, I called back on Thursday and asked what [3]_____. The assistant said that Sandra [4]_____ and that he [5]_____. Then this morning, Sandra called me. I asked [6]_____ and she said that she [7]_____. Her assistant [8]_____ that, so no one would know it was his mistake. She told [9]_____ and we should get it this afternoon.

2 **Rewrite these sentences in reported speech starting with the words given.**

1 **Phil** 'I'm going to the bank for ten minutes.'
Phil told *me he was going to the bank for ten minutes* .

2 **Bella** 'Do you want anything from the canteen, Alan?'
Bella asked _____.

3 **Nabila** 'What is the time of next flight to Boston?'
Nabila wants _____.

4 **Richard** 'Sally, do you want to borrow *The Economist*?'
Richard asked _____.

5 **Keith** 'I'm tired of dealing with unreliable suppliers.'
Keith says _____.

6 **Jackie** 'If you can't go to the meeting, I'll go instead.'
Jackie told _____.

Working with words

1 Read these comments from people talking about their places of work. Match the compound adjectives from the list to the comments.

badly equipped	run down	~~cramped~~
spacious	well equipped	old-fashioned
state-of-the-art	well maintained	

1 ❛ I can't even stand up in here. Isn't it time we had bigger offices? ❜ _cramped_

2 ❛ The problem is, that we have more people than there are computers. ❜ _____

3 ❛ Our new factory has the most modern equipment in the world. They say the design and layout is how all production lines will be in the future. ❜ _____

4 ❛ Since we replaced the old computers with laptops, there's so much more room to work in. ❜ _____

5 ❛ They employ a lot of staff to keep the building in an excellent condition. Any repair work is done immediately. ❜ _____

6 ❛ I have everything I need in my office. A computer, a photocopier, a fax, and a coffee machine. ❜

_____

7 ❛ We have to keep calling the technicians out to fix the machinery. And when was the last time the walls were painted? ❜ _____

8 ❛ We all sit in rows and the boss sits at the front, watching us. No one is allowed to talk to anyone else unless we ask him first. ❜ _____

2 Choose the correct answer from the words in *italics*.

1 The colour isn't *exactly* / ~~*very*~~ what I had in mind.

2 That's totally out of the question. It's *fairly* / *quite* impossible.

3 Sorry, I'm *really* / *exactly* tired. Can we stop there?

4 That's *fairly* / *quite* a good idea. Shall we see what the others think?

5 The negotiations went *fairly* / *extremely* well. We didn't get everything we wanted, but neither did they. I still think we might get what we want in the end.

6 This new software is *pretty* / *not very* easy to use. I learnt all the basic functions in less than an hour.

7 We're all *not exactly* / *extremely* happy with your performance this year, so I see no need for you to make any changes.

8 She's a *very* / *pretty* effective manager who deserves the huge salary she receives.

Business communication skills

1 Rewrite these sentences starting with the words given.

1 I'm not sure it's a good idea to do this.
I have a few reservations _about doing this_.

2 How about changing the colour?
Why don't we _____?

3 Let's ask them to make a better offer.
I think we should consider _____.

4 I don't think we'll be able to convince them about our proposals.
It might prove _____.

5 Perhaps we could provide some chairs.
Couldn't _____?

6 We could always have music in the factory.
Have you thought about _____?

7 Do you mind if I don't come?
I'd rather _____.

8 I'd recommend looking at this again tomorrow morning.
I'd recommend that _____.

2 Complete the words in these responses.

A What do you think of this idea?

B Great. I [1]r_eally_ l_ike_ it.

A It seems like a bad plan to me.

B No! It's a [2]g_____ i_____.

A I think we should change the office round so that everyone shares desks.

B Sorry, but I don't think that [3]w_____ w_____.

A This new system seems slower than the old one.

B Yes, and [4]o_____ t_____ of that, it's more expensive.

A What do you think of our new TV commercial?

B Well, it isn't clear what we're selling and [5]i_____ a_____ to that, it's boring.

A Let's cancel the order for new desks.

B Yes, I like the old ones. [6]B_____, we can't afford them.

Language at work | Nouns and quantifiers

Nouns

Form

1 Nouns are either countable or uncountable. Countable nouns have a singular and plural form. Uncountable nouns have one form.
   Countable nouns: *chair (chairs)*, *employee (employees)*, *computer (computers)*
   Uncountable nouns: *time, money, information, coffee*

2 Most plural countable nouns end in *-s* but some are irregular.
   man   men   child   children

   Sometimes a speaker may make an uncountable noun countable.
   Would you like a (cup of) coffee?

Language tip

Nouns that are countable in a lot of other languages are uncountable in English.
   Do say: *accommodation*
   Don't say: ~~an accommodation, accommodations~~
   Other examples: *information, advice, equipment, furniture*

Quantifiers

Use

1 Use *some, any, a lot of* with countable AND uncountable nouns.
   There are a lot of employees in this factory.
   There's a lot of money in my bank account.

2 Use *many* and *a few* ONLY with plural countable nouns.
   How many employees are there? Only a few.

3 Use *much* and *a little* ONLY with uncountable nouns.
   How much information do you have? Only a little.

4 *Any, much,* and *many* are mostly used in questions or negative statements.
   How much money do you need?
   Do you have any problems?
   He doesn't do much work.
   There aren't many employees in this company.

5 *Some* is mostly used in questions or positive statements.
   Could you give me some help?
   I've got some work for you to do.

6 *A lot of* can be used with questions, negative statements, and positive statements.
   He gets / doesn't get a lot of support in his job.
   Do you get a lot of emails every day?

7 To make a comparison with countable or uncountable nouns you can use *more*.
   I need more time to work on this!
   We need more clients!

8 To make the comparative of *little / not much* with uncountable nouns, use *less*.
   My new boss has little time for my questions.
   My boss has less time for my questions than my old boss.

9 To make the comparative of *few / not many* with countable nouns, use *fewer*.
   The company doesn't deal with many clients.
   The company deals with fewer clients than it would like.

1 Tick (✓) the correct sentences. Change any incorrect sentences.

1 Do you have any ~~informations~~ about these people?
   information

2 How many people do you employ? _____

3 Sorry, I don't have much time. Let's be quick. _____

4 A little customers have complained about the increase. _____

5 I'm afraid we don't have many paper in stock. _____

6 There isn't much demand for this line anymore. _____

7 Give him any more time to finish this. _____

8 I've got fewer space in my new office than in my old one. _____

9 A lot of people said they preferred the taste of this one. _____

10 I'd like a little help with that, please. _____

2 Two people are checking the store cupboard at work. Complete their conversation with a suitable quantifier.

A So, how [1] *many* disks do we have in stock?

B Well, we only have a [2]_____, so we probably ought to order some more.

A How about ink cartridges? I don't think there are [3]_____ left.

B Well, there's an extra box of them here, but we'll need [4]_____ more sooner or later.

A OK. What about the coffee machine? How [5]_____ coffee is there?

B There's a [6]_____ of that, but there aren't [7]_____ packets of tea.

A Right, so that's disks, ink cartridges, and tea. Anything else?

B Well, we don't have [8]_____ at the moment, but a [9]_____ people in the office have asked me if we can have biscuits for the tea breaks.

Working with words

1 Complete these minutes of a meeting with words and phrases from the list.

majority   put forward   backing   carry out
~~hierarchy~~   brainstorming

All levels of the firm's ¹ _hierarchy_ were represented at the meeting. The meeting began with a ²_____ session in small groups, after which a spokesperson from each group ³_____ its three main proposals. A lively discussion followed, in which a large ⁴_____ supported a 'first come, first served' approach to parking. A proposal to have a new self-service canteen was less popular and only received the ⁵_____ of a third of those present. It was agreed that senior management would decide whether to ⁶_____ these decisions at their next meeting.

2 Match 1–8 to a–h.

1 He'll do anything to avoid … _f_

2 It's important to reach … ____

3 It's time for us to make up … ____

4 Have you made … ____

5 Don't bother expressing … ____

6 Rule one is never to make … ____

7 They finally reached … ____

8 She is very good at evaluating … ____

a a consensus at today's meeting.

b ideas and presenting clear summaries.

c a concession without getting something in return.

d a compromise, which pleased nobody.

e a decision about my holiday request, Paula?

f a confrontation. He hates arguments.

g our minds about which system to adopt.

h an opinion. He just expects you to agree.

3 Put the letters in brackets in the right order to find words that match these definitions.

1 to suggest an idea: _put forward_ (URPFOTWRDA)

2 general agreement between people: _____ (OENSCSNUS)

3 choices or alternatives: _____ (PIOSOTN)

4 assess / judge: _____ (EVELAUAT)

5 an argument or open conflict: _____ (AOTONROFNCNTI)

6 give / agree to something to get something: _____ (OOMCPRIESM)

Business communication skills

1 Onslow Publications has had its own staff restaurant, run by Onslow employees, for years. As a way of cutting costs, managers are having a meeting to discuss subcontracting their catering services to an outside company. Complete their discussion with words from the list.

as   face   agree   ~~personally~~   thing
absolutely   point   come   agreed   correctly

Simon ¹ _Personally_ , I think we should take this opportunity to cut our costs.

Bob I ²_____ with Simon. Let's ³_____ it, it's a luxury we can't afford.

Rupert I take your ⁴_____, but we entertain important guests in the old typesetters' room and that really impresses them.

Doris The ⁵_____ is, it's not just a question of money. ⁶_____ I see it, we should treat everybody the same. Some kitchen staff have been with us for twenty years.

Hamish ⁷_____! If they lose their jobs, they'll never find another one.

Bob ⁸_____ on, Hamish! This is a business, not an old people's home.

Simon If I understand you ⁹_____ Doris, you don't want to change anything. Is that right?

Rupert Well, we won't reach a decision today. Let's review the situation in six months. So are we all ¹⁰_____? Good. Let's move on to the next item on the agenda.

2 Correct these sentences and phrases.

1 ~~Accordingly~~ to Roger, we should open another branch. _According_

2 I'm not quiet sure about that. _____

3 Yes, I am hearing what you say. _____

4 Yes, enough fair. _____

5 As far I'm concerned … _____

6 That's fine to me. _____

Language at work | First and second conditionals

First conditional

Form

if + present simple (= condition), *will* + verb (= result)

*If we **change** our supplier, we'll **reduce** costs.*

Use

1 To talk about events that might or might not happen and their results.

*If they **close** the factory down, we'll **have** to look for another job.* (The factory might close down, but we don't know.)

2 Use the first conditional if you believe that the condition is likely or possible.

*If I **get** a pay rise, I **will buy** a house.* (You believe it is likely or possible that you will get a pay rise.)

Second conditional

Form

if + past simple (= condition), *would / might / could* + verb (= result)

*If we **changed** our supplier, we **would reduce** costs.*

Use

1 To talk about events that are less likely to happen.

*If you **wasted** less time chatting on the phone, you **would get** more work done.* (But I think you will continue to waste time.)

2 To talk about impossible or highly unlikely situations.

*If I **were** taller, people **would take** me more seriously.* (But I'll always be short.)

*If I **ran** the company, I **would make** a lot of changes.* (But I am just an eighteen-year-old office clerk.)

3 To talk about something hypothetical.

*If we **took over** their company, we **would have** access to the South American market.*

4 To be more polite, or achieve more 'social distance'.

*What **would** you **say** if I **asked** you to be Managing Director?*

Language tip

In second conditional sentences, we often use *were* instead of *was* after *if*. *Were* is more formal than *was*.

*If I **were** the manager, I **would improve** working conditions.*
*If I **was** the manager, I **would improve** working conditions.*

when, as soon as, and unless

1 We can use *unless* to mean *if not* or *except*.

*They won't let you into the restaurant **unless** you're wearing a tie.*

2 Use *when / as soon as* instead of *if*, to show you are sure that something will happen. Compare the following.

*Liz will call me **when** the client arrives.* (You are sure the client will arrive.)
*Liz will call me **as soon as** the client arrives.* (You are sure the client will arrive and when the client arrives, Liz will call you immediately.)
*Liz will call me **if** the client arrives.* (Maybe the client will arrive, but you are not sure.)

---

1 **Complete these sentences with the most appropriate form of the verbs in brackets.**

1 I know it won't ever happen, but what _would we do_ (we / do) if our restaurant suddenly _became_ (become) famous?

2 Unless you _____ (have) good financial planning, your expansion plans _____ (end) in disaster.

3 Every new recruit starts with the same opportunities. If you _____ (work) hard, _____ (you / be) promoted.

4 If I _____ (know) the answer to that question, I _____ (be) a very rich person!

5 If you _____ (have) three wishes for your career, what _____ (they / be)?

6 Unless your work _____ (improve), you _____ (have to) start looking for another job.

7 I'm not saying it's going to happen, but how _____ (you / feel) if we _____ (ask / you) to work in our Lagos office?

8 Just imagine what you _____ (do) if the firm suddenly _____ (go) bankrupt.

9 If you _____ (can) change just one thing about your working environment, what _____ (you / do)?

10 When they _____ (arrive) we _____ (be able to) start the meeting.

2 **Choose the correct answer from the words in *italics*.**

1 We will start working on the project *as soon as / ~~unless~~* the budget is agreed.

2 If we knew more about our competitor's plans, we *can / could* create a better strategy.

3 *If / Unless* you make the decision, *I'll have / I have* to make it for you.

4 *When / Unless* we improve the design, it *will look / looks* too old-fashioned.

5 She *will have to / has to* accept being unpopular *unless / if* she becomes the boss.

Working with words

1 Complete the text with the correct answer from the options in 1–9.

The teenage entrepreneur

In many ways, the company Doherty Preserves looks like your typical local food company, with a simple ¹____c____ and ²_____ customer base. It sells a ³_____ range of marmalades, jams and fruit preserves, based on old recipes, to delicatessens and local markets. And like every other food business these days, the company is aiming to reach a more health-conscious consumer, so not a ⁴_____ idea.

What is surprising, is that the company was the ⁵_____ of a 14-year-old. Now aged 16, Fraser Doherty first ⁶_____ with the idea of selling preserves when his grandmother taught him a secret recipe for marmalade. This was the 'a-ha' ⁷_____ for Fraser and within weeks he'd begun selling to the neighbours. From there he employed friends to sell door-to-door on a commission basis.

Such ⁸_____ from one so young might be put down to a good education, but Fraser says, 'It's a million miles away from what I learnt at school.' Similarly, the ⁹_____ of money has never proved a problem, 'I don't concern myself so much with profits and productivity – what's important to me is improving quality and customer satisfaction.'

1 **a** prototype	**b** catalyst	**c** ~~concept~~
2 **a** reliable	**b** dynamic	**c** original
3 **a** traditional	**b** revolutionary	**c** state-of-the-art
4 **a** revolutionary	**b** reliable	**c** simple
5 **a** facilitator	**b** brainchild	**c** invention
6 **a** came across	**b** came out	**c** came up
7 **a** time	**b** minute	**c** moment
8 **a** breakthrough	**b** innovation	**c** reliability
9 **a** obstacle	**b** prototype	**c** brainchild

2 Put the letters in brackets in the right order to find words that match these definitions.

1 something that gets in the way: __obstacle__ (OSALTBCE)
2 the first form of something new: _____ (ROPETPTOY)
3 an idea for something new: _____ (OCNEPCT)
4 something is this when you can depend on it: _____ (ELREIBLA)
5 not complicated: _____ (EMSLIP)
6 new and original: _____ (NNAIOVIVTE)
7 something is this when it can change the way things are done or thought about: _____ (AEVYROONLTUIR)

Business communication skills

1 Choose the correct answer from the words in *italics*.

1 Good morning, and thanks *for / to / at* coming.
2 I'm going to tell you *of / about / for* my new concept.
3 I'd like to begin *from / at / by* outlining the main problems.
4 I'll take questions *by / at / to* the end.
5 Let's look *at / by / from* this chart.
6 The main reason *of / for / about* this, is the drop in demand.
7 The best thing *of / for / about* this, is it's simplicity.
8 That brings me *by / at / to* the end of my presentation.
9 Can I get back to you *with / on / at* that one?
10 I totally agree *with / on / by* you.

2 Complete this introduction to a presentation with a suitable word.

1 _____ afternoon everyone.
2 I am _____ today to tell you about an exciting new way of choosing your holiday.
3 I'd like to _____ by giving you an overview of my talk.
4 _____, I'll tell you about how the concept was developed.
5 _____ we'll have a look at how it was launched.
6 And _____ we'll have a look at the website and I'll show you how it works.
7 Please feel _____ to ask questions at any time.

3 Put the final part of this presentation in the right order 1–12.

___ **a** bring immediate results. So, to
___ **b** we need to listen. Then
___ **c** for listening. Are
___ **d** see from this
___ **e** summarize, there are three
___ **f** brings me to the end of my presentation. Thanks
___ **g** ways to respond to our customers. First,
_1_ **h** So, as you can
___ **i** we need to be seen to be listening and reacting. OK, that
___ **j** there any questions?
___ **k** diagram, thinking about our customers can
___ **l** we need to act. And finally,

Language at work | Superlative forms

Superlative forms

Form

1 Add *-est* to one- and some two-syllable adjectives and to adverbs with the same forms as adjectives, e.g. *fast, straight, high.*

    small ➔ **smallest**
    fast ➔ **fastest**

2 If the adjective or adverb ends in *-y*, change the *-y* to an *-i* and add *-est.*

    early ➔ **earliest**

3 Double the consonant after a vowel at the end of short adjectives.

    hot ➔ **hottest**
    big ➔ **biggest**
    thin ➔ **thinnest**

4 Some adjectives and adverbs are irregular.

    good / well ➔ **best**   *bad / badly* ➔ **worst**

5 Add *most* to two- or more syllable adjectives and adverbs ending in *-ly* (except *early*).

    accurate ➔ **most accurate**
    quickly ➔ **most quickly**

6 Also add *most* to adjectives ending in *-ed.*

    pleased ➔ **most pleased**
    tired ➔ **most tired**

7 Don't use *most* with an *-est* superlative.

    Do say: *She is **the best** boss in the company.*
    Don't say: *She is ~~the most best~~ boss in the company.*

8 In most sentences, use *the* before the superlative.

    Do say: *This is **the fastest** car on the road.*
    Don't say: *This ~~is fastest~~ car on the road.*

Use

1 To describe the maximum or minimum.

    *This has **the largest** memory of any laptop.*

2 To place something in a position after first place.

    *We're **the second biggest** supplier in this market.*

3 Followed by the present perfect to describe our experience of something.

    *It was **the worst** food I've ever tasted.*

Language tip

Don't use *the* in certain phrases.
    Do say: *It's **best** to arrive early.*
    Don't say: *It's ~~the best~~ to arrive early.*

---

1 Correct these sentences.

1 Face-to-face communication is still the ~~most best~~ way of doing business. ___*best*___

2 I think quickest way to send it, is by courier. _____

3 Microsoft must still be the more influential company in the whole world. _____

4 It's the most beautiful place we ever visited. _____

5 Since taking this job, I'm the boredest I've ever been. _____

6 We don't want to be a second most successful. We want to be number one! _____

7 What's the biggest order you ever received? _____

8 My boss is the most busiest person in the company. _____

2 Complete this article with words from the list. If necessary, change the word to a superlative form.

    bad   good   few (x2)   flexible   second
    ~~the~~   has

Age at work

They forget things. They don't work in teams. They can't adapt to [1] ___*the*___ latest technology. These are often the reasons given for not employing older people. But new findings show that the [2]_____ workers are not necessarily the slowest and in fact slower workers often make the [3]_____ errors.

    Jutta Kray of Saarland University in Germany, who specializes in this area of research, did find that when it comes to being the most [4]_____ and quickest at decision-making, older people come [5]_____ best to their younger counterparts. In a world which demands the greatest speed of thought the business environment [6]_____ ever known, this is clearly a disadvantage. But Kray also found in other tests that the 'inflexible old' made the [7]_____ number of errors in certain tasks, so for some jobs the older employee may be the [8]_____ suited.

Working with words

1 Complete these sentences with words from the list. You will need to change the form of the words.

> fault   rely   break   ~~understand~~
> defect   damage   fail

1 Poor translation caused a major _misunderstanding_ between the parties.

2 The job advertisement was a _____. It didn't produce any suitable applicants.

3 It broke down because of a _____ contact in the electrical circuit.

4 These communication _____ between departments are becoming a real problem.

5 We can't have anyone _____ on the team. We need to depend on each other 100%.

6 The screens on all of these calculators are cracked. They were probably _____ during transportation.

7 I don't believe it! We've had yet another delivery of _____ goods from that supplier. We won't be using them again.

2 Complete this email with the correct answer from the options in 1–7.

> Dear Help Desk
>
> I really need your help. I'm trying to use a disk on my computer, but it keeps going ¹_____b_____. I think it could be that the disk is ²_____ with my computer, or maybe the CD-ROM driver is out of ³_____. It could even be a ⁴_____ in the program or a ⁵_____ on the disk. It would be great if you could fix the problem as soon as possible. I need to use the disk today because I know that the system will be ⁶_____ tomorrow for maintenance. Please don't ⁷_____ me down.
>
> Best regards
> Joe Morris

1 **a** up   **b** ~~wrong~~   **c** away
2 **a** included **b** incomplete   **c** incompatible
3 **a** touch   **b** time   **c** order
4 **a** bug   **b** rug   **c** plug
5 **a** patch   **b** spot   **c** flaw
6 **a** off   **b** down   **c** up
7 **a** let   **b** put   **c** got

Business communication skills

1 Complete this conversation with words and phrases from the list.

> do you mean by   should solve the problem   won't
> advise you to   keeps on   if I were you
> sounds as though ~~can I help~~   have you tried

Gareth Hi, Blanka. How ¹ _can I help_ ?

Blanka It's my printer. It ²_____ give me clean print-outs of anything. It just messes them up.

Gareth What exactly ³_____ 'messes them up'?

Blanka Well, it ⁴_____ missing lines and you can hardly read it.

Gareth Don't worry, it ⁵_____ it could simply be a printing-head problem. ⁶_____ cleaning them?

Blanka No. I didn't know I had to.

Gareth Yes, I'd ⁷_____ clean the heads regularly so that this doesn't happen again. I'll show you. There, that ⁸_____.

Blanka Oh, that's much better, Gareth. You've saved my life.

Gareth You're welcome. Although from now on, I'd clean the heads regularly ⁹_____.

2 Choose the correct answer from the words in *italics*.

1 It looks *like / ~~though~~* you'll have to buy a new one.

2 It's extremely annoying – she *always borrows / 's always borrowing* my calculator without asking.

3 I'm really annoyed. Ludo keeps on *taking / take* biscuits from my desk.

4 What's *matter / wrong* with it exactly?

5 There we are, that *should / must* fix it.

6 I'd *advise / say* you not to use it again – best to call the engineer first.

7 It *smells / sounds* like something must be loose – it's so noisy.

8 That should *solve / sort* the problem.

9 So what *appears / looks like* to be the problem with your computer?

10 Have you tried *put / putting* it in a different position?

Language at work | Advice and recommendation | *too* and *enough*

Advice and recommendation

Use

1 To give or ask for advice, use *should*.

*You **should** always make a backup copy of your files.*
*How do you think we **should** proceed?*

2 To introduce an option or possible course of action, use *could*.

*You **could** show them the factory first.*

3 To describe a less attractive option, use *could always*.

*We **could always** reduce our prices.*

4 To say that it would be fair or right for something to happen, use *should*.

*The company **should** dedicate more resources to quality control.*

5 To give your opinion, use *would*.

*If I were you, I **would** extend the guarantee.*

6 To criticize, use *should*.

*You **should** treat your computer more carefully.*

7 To give an instruction, use *have to*.

*You **have to** enter your password to access your emails.*

too and *enough*

Use

1 Use *too* before adjectives to say that something is more than good, more than necessary, more than is wanted, etc.

*This MP3 player is **too** expensive, customers will never buy it.*

2 Use *enough* before nouns to say that there is / isn't as much of something as necessary.

*We (don't) have **enough** time to make an intelligent decision.*

3 Use *enough* after verbs, adjectives, and adverbs to say something is sufficient / insufficient.

*She doesn't work **enough**. / It isn't warm **enough**. / He doesn't type quickly **enough**.*

4 Use *enough* as a pronoun, when a noun does not need to be repeated.

A Shall we get some more paper clips?
*B No. We've got **enough**.*

Language tip

Be careful not to confuse *very* and *too*.

*The restaurant was **very** expensive, but we enjoyed ourselves.*
*The restaurant was **too** expensive, it simply wasn't worth the money.*

---

1 A manager is discussing quality control with a visiting consultant. Choose the correct answer from the words in *italics* to complete their conversation.

Manager What [1]*would / should* you do if you were me?

Consultant Well, to begin with you [2]*have to / would* involve staff much more in improving quality during the production process. You [3]*wouldn't / shouldn't* just rely on checks at the end of the production process.

Manager OK. And how [4]*have to / should* we do this?

Consultant Well, there are different possibilities. You [5]*could / would* introduce quality circles or make people measure their performance at each stage. At the very least you [6]*would / should* have a suggestion box where people can send their suggestions.

Manager That's a good idea. I think we [7]*would / should* introduce this idea straightaway.

Consultant Yes, I [8]*could / would*, if I were you. It will show everyone you mean business.

2 Put this conversation in the right order 1–8.

____ **a** I think you should go and see him again and explain the problem.

____ **b** If I were you, I'd tell your boss that you need someone to help you.

____ **c** What if he doesn't listen again?

____ **d** But what if he says I can't have any help? What should I do then?

_1_ **e** I am really struggling to keep on top of my work load. What would you do in my position?

____ **f** I've been asking him for help for a long time – so what should I do now?

____ **g** You have to *make* him listen – you can't go on like this.

____ **h** Well you could always threaten to leave!

3 Correct these sentences.

1 Her English is ~~enough good~~ for her to go to Los Angeles.
   good enough

2 I was very tired to drive back home. _____

3 There weren't responses enough to our questionnaire to come to any conclusions. _____

4 She spoke too fast and not enough clearly for us to understand what she was saying. _____

5 The campaign was too much expensive – we didn't have enough money to finance it. _____

6 Please don't ask me to do anything else – I haven't time enough. _____

Working with words

1 Choose the correct answer from the words in *italics*.

1 All our jackets are made out ~~from~~ / of / ~~with~~ leather.

2 If you mix hydrogen *into* / *with* / *from* oxygen, you get water.

3 They pick *off* / *out* / *up* the bins about once a week and take them to the recycling centre.

4 Put your coin *at* / *through* / *in* this slot to get coffee.

5 The paper is fed *off* / *into* / *up* the printer at this end.

6 There are three main *stages* / *places* / *areas* to this procedure.

7 The *last* / *end* / *big* product is sold all over the world.

2 Put the stages of advertising on a search engine website in the right order 1–6.

____ **a** First of all, you need to say where your customers are located and what language the advertisement will be in.

_1_ **b** The basic procedure is simple – just follow the steps on the search engine's web page.

____ **c** Finally choose how you are going to pay for your ad.

____ **d** Having written it, you need to choose the keywords that describe your business.

____ **e** There are essentially four main stages.

____ **f** Then you need to write your ad.

3 Complete this text with words and phrases from the list.

> having   essentially   you're ready to   ~~basic procedure~~
> there are   once you've done   first of all

The ¹ _basic procedure_ is quite simple and ² _____ ,
³ _____ three main stages.
⁴ _____ , insert the disk. Then, the computer will automatically start to load the software. If it asks you any questions, just click 'yes' or 'next'.
⁵ _____ loaded it all, you'll probably have to restart it. ⁶ _____ all that,
⁷ _____ go online.

Business communication skills

1 Complete the emails with phrases from the list.

> we'd be delighted   I was wondering if
> ~~We would like to~~   how about

Dear Valued Customer

¹ _We would like to_ invite you to the opening of our new store on Saturday 16 August, at 10.00 a.m. As someone who regularly shopped at our previous supermarket in Waltham Street, ² _____ if you would join us for the official opening ceremony and take advantage of some very special new offers.

Dear Ralph

³ _____ you'd like to meet with us for a drink tonight at Renee's Bar. There are a few of us going from work, so
⁴ _____ coming along at around 8.00 p.m.?

---

2 Rewrite sentences 1–4 to make them informal. Use the prompts in *italics*.

1 I'm afraid I'm unable to attend.
sorry / can / come
I'm sorry, but I can't come.

2 Due to unforeseen circumstances, it won't be possible.
afraid / something / up
_____

3 I would be delighted to.
would / great
_____

4 I apologize for the inconvenience, but can we postpone it to the week after?
sorry / mess / around / but / how / the week after?
_____

3 Match a–j to 1–10.

1	Have you got … _h_	**a**	bad time?
2	Are you … ____	**b**	for a second?
3	Is this a … ____	**c**	busy?
4	Sorry to … ____	**d**	to hear that.
5	Can I interrupt you … ____	**e**	bother you …
6	Can I talk … ____	**f**	be helped.
7	These things take … ____	**g**	next time.
8	It can't … ____	**h**	a minute?
9	I'm sorry … ____	**i**	time.
10	Maybe … ____	**j**	to you for a moment?

Language at work | Passive forms

Passive forms

Form

Verbs in sentences can either be active or passive.

The passive is formed with the verb *be* + past participle of the main verb.

Tense	Passive form	Active form
Present simple	*The post **is opened** in the morning.*	*David opens the post in the morning.*
Present continuous	*The report **is being written** right now.*	*Christina is writing that report right now.*
Past simple	*I **was given** your name by a colleague.*	*Joe Langley gave me your name.*
Present perfect	*We've **been asked** to speak at the event.*	*The CEO has asked us to speak at the event.*
Modal	*It **mustn't be changed** in any way.*	*Nobody must change it in any way.*

Use

1 To talk about processes or how something is done.

   *First of all, the bottle **is washed** and sterilized. Next, **it is filled** …*

2 To emphasize the result, rather than the person or cause.

   *We **have been forced** to change our plans because …*

3 When the person who does the action is unknown, unimportant, or too obvious to mention.

   *Hello, I **was advised** to talk to you about purchasing …*

Language tip

Passive forms tend to be written down more than they are spoken. For example, we often use passives in formal business writing, such as memos and reports.

   *It **is recommended** that all staff arrange an appointment with their line managers.*

---

1 **Choose the correct answer from the words in *italics*.**

   1 The Kabul Star football ~~manufactures~~ / *is manufactured* in Afghanistan.

   2 Employees *make / are made* the footballs in a large house in Kabul.

   3 The process *starts / is started* in the garage where pieces of leather *cut and paint / are cut and painted*.

   4 The workers then *sew / are sewn* the leather pieces together to make the balls.

   5 After that the balls *wash / are washed* in the bathroom and packaged in the largest bedroom in the house.

   6 The factory only *employs / is employed* women.

   7 A charity called Humanitarian Assistance for Women *supports / is supported* the factory.

   8 The female workers *encourages and trains / are encouraged and trained* to set up their own businesses.

2 **Complete the sentences with the correct form of verbs from the list.**

need	~~know~~	choose
locate	hold	win

   1 The Tate Modern _is known_ as one of the best modern art galleries.

   2 It _____ on the banks of the River Thames in the heart of London.

   3 An old power station _____ to house the gallery.

   4 It offered the space that _____ to display the large collection of art.

   5 An international competition _____ to find a suitable proposal for transforming the power station into an art gallery.

   6 It _____ by Herzog & deMeuron, a Swiss architectural practice.

3 **Rewrite these sentences in either the passive or active form starting with the words given.**

   1 Most business these days is done over the phone.
      People _do most of their business over the phone these days_.

   2 Hans Angst set up the company twenty years ago.
      The company _____.

   3 The manager must sack employees for being late.
      Employees _____.

   4 It has been agreed to extend the hours of work.
      We _____.

   5 People in this culture regard punctuality as a sign of politeness.
      Punctuality _____.

Working with words

1 Match the adjectives in the list to comments 1–7.

confident   hard-working   enthusiastic   ~~creative~~
punctual   patient   ambitious

1 ❝ I like his original ideas and new ways of approaching things. ❞
creative

2 ❝ She doesn't seem to have any doubts about her abilities. ❞
_____

3 ❝ I think they'll both do anything to get to the top. ❞
_____

4 ❝ It's important, as a manager, to spend time listening to your employees and not expect them to always get things right the first time round. ❞
_____

5 ❝ He's always the first one in and the last one out, at work. You never see him resting. ❞
_____

6 ❝ Whatever the plan, she's always smiling and ready to try it out. ❞
_____

7 ❝ Workers in this country are never late for work. It's considered very bad. ❞
_____

2 Complete these sentences by finishing the words.

1 People like doctors and nurses must be so dedicat_ed_ to their work.

2 I'm not convinced about the depend_____ of this machinery. It's very old.

3 We're a car_____ company, where the customer is number one.

4 You need a lot of motivat_____ when you're self-employed.

5 May I say how help_____ all your staff have been today. Thank you very much.

6 They say that women are able to do more than one job at a time and are more flexib_____ than men.

7 He's young and has lots of enthusias_____, so we should probably spend time and money on training him.

Business communication skills

1 Complete this conversation with suitable words or phrases.

A In [1] _general_, we're very [2]_____ with your performance. You seem to be doing very well since you started. How do you [3]_____ about the last six months?

B I'm really [4]_____ with my work and the staff seem to like me.

A Yes, one of your key [5]_____ is motivating your team. You [6]_____ to be doing very well. However, one [7]_____ I also wanted to discuss was a complaint we had from one employee.

2 Choose the correct answer from the words in *italics*.

A How are you getting [1]*on / off / ~~out~~* with these late orders?

B I think we've dealt with most of them.

A That's great. Have you thought [2]*with / about / for* how we can avoid delays like this in the future?

B Personally, I think communication between purchasing and the warehouse is an area [3]*at / with / for* improvement.

A You might be right. I think we should have another meeting next week. Is that OK [4]*to / from / with* you?

3 Complete this conversation with verbs from the list.

~~summarize~~   intend   add   do   sound

A So let's [1] _summarize_ what we've agreed. One thing you're going to [2]_____ is talk to your line manager about your idea for a new system. And you also [3]_____ to join the English classes at lunchtime. How does that [4]_____?

B Fine.

A Is there anything else you'd like to [5]_____?

Language at work | Past perfect and past continuous

Past perfect

Form

had + past participle

Use

1 To say that one event happened before another completed past event.

   *The meeting **had ended** when he arrived.*

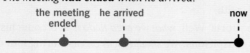

the meeting   he arrived   now
ended

2 The past perfect often appears in sentences with conjunctions, such as *when, by the time, because, so.* The other verb in the sentence is often in the past simple.

Other rules

Words often used with the present perfect are also often used with the past perfect. They are *for, since, yet, just, never, recently, already.*

   *The email had **already** been sent when John noticed the mistake.*

Past continuous

Form

was / were + *-ing* form

Use

1 To talk about something in progress at a particular time in the past. It often appears with the past simple in the same sentence.

   *We **were talking** when he arrived.*

Note that the past action might happen whilst the continuous action is in progress (a), or it might interrupt and stop the continuous action (b).

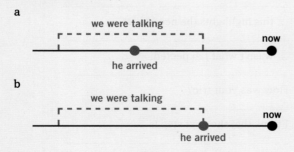

a

we were talking
                                          now
he arrived

b

we were talking
                                          now
he arrived

2 To give background information in the past.
   *We **were phoning** customers all day.*

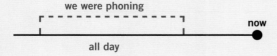

we were phoning
                                          now
all day

---

1 Choose the correct answer from the words in *italics*.

'Several years ago, I ¹*have worked* / *was working* as the quality technician with a computer manufacturer. Well, I ²*hadn't been* / *wasn't* there many weeks when, one day, we ³*were all finishing* / *all finished* off – it was around 5.00 p.m. – and the supervisor came by. He ⁴*was saying* / *said* he was going round the factory and asking everyone for feedback on a new idea of his to improve a process on the production floor. He ⁵*was asking* / *hadn't asked* me up to this point, but everyone else wanted to go home, so I said I'd have a look. But while I ⁶*was suggesting* / *had suggested* reversing a couple of steps in the process, he suddenly ⁷*stopped* / *had stopped* me and explained why my suggestions weren't possible and walked off. Anyway, six months later I was reading my annual appraisal report from the same supervisor, when I ⁸*was coming* / *came* across this line, "He is unable to accept other people's opinions." He obviously ⁹*wasn't liking* / *hadn't liked* the feedback on his idea six months before, and he ¹⁰*has waited* / *had waited* all that time to criticize me!'

2 Complete this interview with the past perfect or the past continuous form of the verbs in brackets.

Journalist You opened your first clothes shop in 1998, Mary. So, did your interest in fashion begin there or ¹ *had you always been* (be) interested?

Mary Yes, I suppose so. I ²_____ (have) a number of jobs in the Hong Kong fashion industry long before I opened my own shop. And that was all at the time when clothes with a Chinese look ³_____ quickly _____ (become) very fashionable around the world. Although, even as a child, while I ⁴_____ (grow) up in America, I knew that was something I wanted to do.

Journalist So why didn't you stay in the USA, where there was already an established industry?

Mary Well, when my boyfriend, now my husband, was offered a job in Hong Kong, I ⁵_____ just _____ (graduate), so I was free to go anywhere.

Journalist And was it while you ⁶_____ (run) your own shop that Tiger Retro approached you?

Mary That's right. Actually, they ⁷_____ (ask) me once before.

Journalist So why ⁸_____ you _____ (not take) the job previously?

Mary At the time, my own business ⁹_____ (do) really well and I wanted to see how far we could go with that …

Working with words

1 Choose the correct answer from the options to complete these sentences.

1 Can you help me _____*b*_____ my briefcase? I don't remember where I put it.
   a look into   **b** ~~look for~~   **c** find out

2 We _____ to finish the report by working all night.
   a could   **b** succeeded   **c** managed

3 It was totally unexpected – we _____ some documents about the founding of the company.
   a came across   **b** found out   **c** looked for

4 Scientists have _____ in producing a substitute for natural rubber.
   a succeeded   **b** managed   **c** been able

5 They are still _____ for new energy sources.
   a searching   **b** finding out   **c** coming across

6 We need to find someone with management _____ to run the training session.
   a expertise   **b** skill   **c** achievement

2 Match a word from A to a word from B and complete sentences 1–5.

A	B
~~absolute~~	success
amazing	breakthrough
significant	~~flop~~
great	achievement
complete	waste of time

1 The conference was an *absolute flop*. Only five people came to my presentation.

2 The trip was a _____. I spent three days there and found out nothing.

3 There has been a _____ in negotiations for the new site.

4 The sugar-free version has been a _____. Sales have doubled in three months.

5 Salesperson of the year three years running! What an _____! Nobody has ever managed it before.

Business communication skills

1 Boris has just come back from Madrid, where he was discussing the takeover of a family-run business. He is now having a conversation with his boss, Ingrid. Put their conversation in the right order 1–10.

____ **a** Boris Well, I have to say, the first day *could have gone better*.

____ **b** Ingrid Oh dear, *this underlines the importance of* finding out everything about who we are dealing with.

____ **c** Boris Well, *what we need to do is* overcome his suspicions. *We should focus on* reassuring him that he has nothing to fear.

_1_ **d** Ingrid Welcome back, Boris. So, *how did it go*?

____ **e** Ingrid Oh, really? *Tell me more.*

____ **f** Ingrid So where does this leave us?

____ **g** Boris Yes, but there is a limit to how much research we can do.

____ **h** Ingrid No time like the present. *So give me an overview*, then.

____ **i** Boris Well, if you've got a couple of minutes, *I'll fill you in* on everything.

____ **j** Boris Well, *I was impressed with* the sister, but her brother gave me a cold reception. He feels threatened by the plans.

2 Match the words and phrases in *italics* from **1** above to 1–9.

1 I was pleasantly surprised by …
   I was impressed with …

2 Let me bring you up to date.
   _____

3 So, what were your overall impressions?
   _____

4 … this highlights the need to …
   _____

5 … wasn't what I expected.
   _____

6 How was your trip?
   _____

7 I think that the next step is …
   _____

8 What makes you say that?
   _____

9 We need to concentrate on …
   _____

Language at work | Contrasting language

Contrasting language

Form

1 Place *although* and *even though* at the beginning of the sentence or between the two contrasting parts of the sentence.

Although *the conference was a waste of time, we made some useful contacts.*

We made some useful contacts, **even though** *the conference was a waste of time.*

2 Put a comma before *but* and place it between the two contrasting parts of the sentence.

The conference was a waste of time, **but** *we made some useful contacts.*

3 Break the two contrasting parts into two sentences when you use *however*.

The conference was a waste of time. **However***, we made some useful contacts.*

4 *Despite* is either followed by a noun, the *-ing* form, or noun + *-ing* form. It can also be followed by *the fact that* if you do not want to use the *-ing* form.

Despite the terrible weather*, the business trip to India was a great success.*

Despite the weather being terrible*, the business trip to India was a great success.*

Despite the fact that the weather was terrible*, the business trip to India was a great success.*

Use

1 Use *but* to show a contrast between two parts of a sentence.

We need more staff, **but** *we can't afford to employ anyone else.*

2 *Although, even though, despite,* and *however* can also be used to show contrast.

Despite the fact that *it is a Swedish company, the staff communicate in English.*

It is a Swedish company. **However***, the staff communicate in English.*

Even though *it is a Swedish company, the staff communicate in English.*

Language tip

Even though gives more emphasis than *although*.

Although *they had given plenty of notice, their boss wasn't happy.*

Even though *they had given plenty of notice, their boss wasn't happy.*

---

1 Rewrite these sentences using the words in brackets.

1 Although your last order was late, we are prepared to give you another chance. (*however*)

   Your last order was late. However, we are prepared to give you another chance.

2 She is our best salesperson. However, she is bad at paperwork. (*even though*)

   _____

3 They only have two products. It is an extremely successful business. (*despite* + verb + *-ing*)

   _____

4 They went ahead with the project, even though the research was unfavourable. (*despite* + *the fact that*)

   _____

5 The meeting went on and on but we made some useful decisions. (*although*)

   _____

6 Although he didn't know that the company was for sale, he did have an idea of how much it was worth. (*however*)

   _____

2 Correct these sentences. Sometimes more than one answer is possible.

1 Although the meeting was a great success, we felt really happy.

   Although the meeting was a great success, we felt really depressed. / Although the meeting was a total disaster, we felt really happy.

2 However the seminar was a waste of time, we enjoyed meeting our new colleagues.

   _____

3 But he was miserable, he earned a lot of money.

   _____

4 Despite we forgot our notes, we managed to give the presentation.

   _____

5 But the office was big, there wasn't enough space for all the desks.

   _____

Verb	Past simple	Past participle	Verb	Past simple	Past participle
be	was / were	been	lie	lay	lain
bear	bore	born	light	lit	lit
beat	beat	beaten	lose	lost	lost
become	became	become	make	made	made
begin	began	begun	mean	meant	meant
blow	blew	blown	meet	met	met
break	broke	broken	pay	paid	paid
bring	brought	brought	put	put	put
build	built	built	read	read	read
burn	burnt / burned	burnt / burned	ride	rode	ridden
buy	bought	bought	ring	rang	rung
catch	caught	caught	rise	rose	risen
choose	chose	chosen	run	ran	run
come	came	come	say	said	said
cost	cost	cost	see	saw	seen
cut	cut	cut	seek	sought	sought
deal	dealt	dealt	sell	sold	sold
do	did	done	send	sent	sent
draw	drew	drawn	set	set	set
dream	dreamt / dreamed	dreamt / dreamed	shine	shone	shone
drink	drank	drunk	show	showed	shown
drive	drove	driven	shrink	shrank	shrunk
eat	ate	eaten	shut	shut	shut
fall	fell	fallen	sing	sang	sung
feed	fed	fed	sink	sank	sunk
feel	felt	felt	sit	sat	sat
fight	fought	fought	sleep	slept	slept
find	found	found	speak	spoke	spoken
fly	flew	flown	spell	spelt / spelled	spelt / spelled
forbid	forbade	forbidden	spend	spent	spent
forget	forgot	forgotten	split	split	split
forgive	forgave	forgiven	spoil	spoilt / spoiled	spoilt / spoiled
freeze	froze	frozen	spread	spread	spread
get	got	got	stand	stood	stood
give	gave	given	steal	stole	stolen
go	went	gone / been	stick	stuck	stuck
grow	grew	grown	strike	struck	struck
have	had	had	swim	swam	swum
hear	heard	heard	take	took	taken
hide	hid	hidden	teach	taught	taught
hit	hit	hit	tear	tore	torn
hold	held	held	tell	told	told
keep	kept	kept	think	thought	thought
know	knew	known	throw	threw	thrown
lay	laid	laid	understand	understood	understood
lead	led	led	wake	woke	woken
learn	learnt / learned	learnt / learned	wear	wore	worn
leave	left	left	win	won	won
lend	lent	lent	wind	wound	wound
let	let	let	write	wrote	written

File 01 | Unit 1

Case study, Task, Exercise 1, page 11

Job Property developer
Company EBI (Elite Building International) – builds and sells property in the UK, France, Italy, and Spain.

Reasons for attending networking event
Professional: Look for business partners. Want to find a printer for your brochures and promotional literature.
Personal: Would like to arrange a study tour for your daughter.

Interests Collecting modern art, golf

Job Event organizer
Company Instant Events – organizes conferences and hospitality events (venue, catering, photographers, printed invitations).

Reasons for attending networking event
Professional: Make contacts and find potential customers. Find partners who can offer exciting events and motivational prizes.
Personal: Would like to organize your next holiday.

Interests Extreme sports, languages, travel

Job Travel agent
Company Romano Travel – specializes in exciting and unusual holidays, e.g. sledging with dogs in the north of Canada, eco-tourism in the Brazilian rainforest.

Reasons for attending networking event
Professional: Sell your holidays. Find new partners.
Personal: Make friends. Improve your social life.

Interests Sport, travel, cooking

Job Cook and caterer
Company EPG – specializes in international cuisine. Has cookery schools for young people in Florence and Lyon.

Reasons for attending networking event
Professional: Would like to expand the business into gastro-tourism. Look for partners in the travel industry and people who can take care of promotional material and packages.
Personal: Would like to find people who share your hobbies.

Interests Languages, sport, exotic travel

Job Hot-air balloon pilot
Company Hot Air Experiences – offers flights over castles, forests, and famous landmarks across Europe. Also arranges trips to African game parks. Great as incentives and prizes to customers and sales staff.

Reason for attending networking event
Professional: Find new partners. Find a sponsor for your next expedition.
Personal: Meet some interesting people.

Interests Photography, music

Job Marketing manager
Company Speakeasy, a chain of language schools with centres in all the major European capitals. Also runs holiday courses for young people in different countries.

Reasons for attending networking event
Professional: Find new partners and customers.
Personal: Would like to buy a property in Spain.

Interests Eating out, travel, walking, cycling

Job Customer services manager
Company Paper Solutions – hi-tech printers specializing in promotional literature and company prospectuses for prestigious organizations.

Reasons for attending networking event
Professional: Make new business contacts.
Personal: Meet some interesting people.

Interests Golf, tennis, travel

File 02 | Unit 3

Working with words, Exercise 2, page 18

Work-life balance quiz

What your score means

0-4 Your life is out of balance. Put less emphasis on your job and give more time to family, friends, and leisure pursuits.

5-9 Your work-life balance is OK but be careful. You need to spend more time relaxing.

10+ Your work-life balance is good. It's about 50:50. Don't change it!

File 03 | Unit 2

Business communication skills, Exercise 8, page 15

Student A

You went to the Project 1 meeting. Your partner went to the Project 2 meeting. Call your partner to find out what's happening with Project 2. Then, tell your partner about Project 1. These are the things you need to know.

Project 1 – organizing a training day for staff
- Venue for training session – room booked
- Hotel for trainers – Victoria Hotel has available rooms, trying to negotiate discount
- Lunch – nothing so far. Need someone to book caterers and negotiate payment.
- Information pack for trainees – need to ask trainers to send schedule and summary of training day
- Transport between hotel and office for trainers – need to book taxis

Project 2 – raising money for a local children's charity
- Posters and leaflets?
- 10 km sponsored run?
- Charity sale?
- Other?

File 04 | Unit 2

Case study, Task, Exercise 2, page 17

Group A

You are working on the venue and all the equipment.
Your responsibilities:
- Organizing the installation of the dance floor, the sound system, the toilets, and the kitchen equipment.
- Painting and decorating the whole building.
- Buying plants and furniture for the relaxation zone.

Your progress: All the equipment has been ordered. The energy-generating dance floor is ready to install, and the kitchen and toilets have been installed.

Problems: You need a specialist electrician to complete the work on the dance floor and link it up to the sound system and the lights. The company you booked has pulled out and you need to find a replacement.

File 05 | Unit 4

Case study, Task, Exercise 2, page 29

Student A

Summarize these results for your partner. Do not read out the figures, but compare the results of last year and this year.

> **Example:** *The number of staff using public transport is a great deal lower than …*

	Last year	This year
% of staff using public transport	59	36
% of staff walking or cycling to work	22	21
% of staff sharing a car to work	11	23

File 06 | Unit 5

Business communication skills, Exercise 3, page 32

Student A

You are the facilities manager for a chain of hotels in Singapore and Thailand. Call your partner to ask about the services they offer. Ask if a visit is possible. Give this information to your partner.
- A chain of exclusively 5-star hotels.
- Some of the hotels have gym facilities that are eight years old.
- There are twelve hotels in total. Two have no gym faciities.
- You are speaking to your finance manager about the budget next week.

File 07 | Unit 5

Case study, Task, Exercise 1, page 35

Student A

1 You are the hotel manager. Read some more reviews from recent customers.

> ### Customer feedback
>
> 'The customer service is a well-deserved 1 star!!'
>
> 'When we eventually arrived at the hotel after bad directions, the Duty Manager was really rude to my wife as I was parking the car.'
>
> 'The TV stopped working on the first day and although they promised to fix it, nothing happened.'
>
> 'The staff, on the whole, I am sorry to say, were very abrupt and were most definitely not trained in customer service.'

2 Call Student B who works for a business consultancy.
   - Explain that you are calling to ask for some help. You want to improve your customer reviews.
   - You would like the hotel to have an image that would attract business people wanting to relax and take a break from their busy lives.
   - This is high season and staff are all very busy, but you usually have some time free on Monday mornings and you have a half day off on Wednesday afternoons.

File 08 | Unit 7

Business communication skills, Exercise 5, page 45

Student A

Read this email, make notes, then update your partner.

> To: All administrators
> From: Head of Administration
> Subject: New security measures
>
> As many of you are aware, we've recently been having a number of problems with the underground car park. In one case, an employee had her bag stolen from her car. As a result, we've decided to install CCTV in all parts of the car park and in the corridors around the offices.
> By the end of the month, you will see these cameras around the building. The cameras are connected to TV screens at reception.

File 09 | Unit 12

Starting point, Exercise 1, page 72

1 / 2 vacuum cleaner (1901)   4 photocopier (1938)
1 / 2 instant coffee (1901)   5 Velcro (1948)
3 parking meter (1935)   6 handheld calculator (1966)

File 10 | Unit 6

Case study, Task, Exercise 1, page 41

Student A

You are the Human Resources Director of a Swedish company that is working closely with an Indian company on a joint venture in India. Many of your staff are now based in India. You are meeting with your Indian colleague. You have both received complaints from your own employees working on the project in India.

1 Read through the information below before you begin.
2 Take turns to exchange information. Tell your partner about a problem below that your Swedish employees are having. Your partner will try to explain why. Then your partner will tell you a problem his / her Indian employees are having. Use the 'Business etiquette' information below to explain the possible reasons for the problems.

Problems reported by Swedish employees

'My local Indian team members are always late for meetings. It's such a waste of my time having to wait so long for our meetings to start.'

'No wonder we are missing deadlines – my Indian colleagues take really long lunches – I hardly leave my desk all day! And I start work earlier.'

'My colleague never finishes a job when she says she will – I'm finding it really hard to plan my own workload.'

'The managers that report to me never consult me – they often just ask their staff to do things that are not in the best interests of the project.'

> ### Sweden – Business etiquette
>
> **The working day:** The working day often starts early, at 8.00 a.m. or earlier, and lunch is often only a half-hour break at around midday.
>
> **Concept of time:** Arriving at meetings on time and starting them promptly are very important. If you are going to be late for any reason you must phone and let someone know. Being late is seen as poor etiquette.
>
> **Communication styles:** Swedish communication style is direct and open – people say what they think. This can seem rude but is not meant to be so.
>
> **Status and hierarchy:** Equality is an important social value in Sweden. Swedes like to establish relationships on an informal level and at work they usually address everyone by his / her first name.

File 11 | Unit 2

Case study, Task, Exercise 2, page 17

Group B

You are working on the launch party event.

Your responsibilities:

- Booking the DJs and other acts.
- Organizing the special events, such as ethical clothing and make-up displays.
- Ordering all the food and drink for the event.
- Hiring and training staff.

Your progress: You have started booking people and so far the response is good. You have found local suppliers for most of the food and drink. You have advertised for staff and have a number of candidates. You need to interview candidates, hire them, and set up a training day.

Problems: The famous DJ you booked is no longer available. You have found a replacement but he is asking a lot of money which will take you over budget. You still need to find a supplier of organic beer.

File 12 | Unit 4

Case study, Task, Exercise 2, page 29

Student B

Summarize these results for your partner. Do not read out the figures, but compare the results of last year and this year.

> *Example:* *The number of staff arriving late is a great deal higher than …*

	Last year	This year
% of staff arriving late	53	87
% of staff doing flexitime	33	55
% of staff unable to find alternative parking (within walking distance of the company)	43	44

File 13 | Unit 5

Case study, Task, Exercise 1, page 35

Student B

You work for a business consultancy. Student A calls you. Ask for more information.

- What sort of reviews has the hotel received? What are the main problems?
- What sort of image does the hotel want to project?
- Arrange to visit the hotel. You are free on Thursday and Friday this week or Tuesday and Wednesday next week.

File 14 | Unit 5

Business communication skills, Exercise 3, page 32

Student B

You are the facilities manager for a chain of hotels in Croatia. Call your partner to ask about the services they offer. Ask if a visit is possible. Give this information to your partner.

- A chain of 3-star and 4-star hotels near the beach.
- One of the 3-star hotels has a fitness gym which is fifteen years old. You want to update that one and have new gym facilities in your other hotels.
- You have one 4-star hotel and three 3-star hotels.
- You have a comfortable amount set aside for installing these facilities.

File 15 | Unit 6

Case study, Task, Exercise 3, page 41

1 Have a film made showing day-to-day business and the lives of employees in the Swedish company and day-to-day business and lives of employees in the Indian company. It would include interviews with staff describing what they do and how they go about their jobs. Show this to all employees.

2 Set up a virtual chat room so that colleagues can communicate anonymously with each other to air their problems, find out what the reasons might be, and to share thoughts about their own cultures.

3 Get an external trainer to run a training course for Swedish and Indian managers about how to raise intercultural awareness. The course includes role-plays and language training.

4 Have a 'culture sharing meal / day' where Swedish and Indian colleagues spend a part of the day sharing their cultural background with each other over Indian and Swedish food.

5 Bring Indian managers to Sweden for a visit to observe how Swedish employees go about their day-to-day business. These managers would then report their observations to their Indian employees.

File 16 | Unit 16

Case study, Task, Exercise 1, page 101

Student A

Mission: Face-to-face market research in local supermarket. Get customers to taste the tea.

Result: Not good because

- some customers don't ever drink tea
- other customers like the taste but think the price is too high
- many customers have never seen this brand in the supermarket before.

Conclusion: Need to persuade supermarkets to make tea more prominent on the shelves. Offer special deals.

File 17 | Unit 6

Case study, Task, Exercise 1, page 41

Student B

You are the Human Resources Director of an Indian company that is working closely with a Swedish company on a joint venture in India. Many of your staff are now managed by Swedish managers. You have received this file of comments from your Indian employees. You are meeting with your Swedish colleague who has also received comments from their Swedish employees.

1 Read through the information below before you begin.
2 Take turns to exchange information. Your partner will tell you about a problem his / her Swedish employees are having. Use the 'Business etiquette' information below to explain the possible reasons for the problems. Tell your partner about a problem that your Indian employees are having. Your partner will try to explain why.

Problems reported by Indian employees

'My manager is very rude at the start of meetings – we don't get an opportunity to greet our colleagues properly and make small talk.'

'My Swedish colleagues would rather work than join us for lunch.'

'My Swedish colleagues are rude sometimes – they say things like: "This is not as good as your last report."'

'My Swedish colleagues address me by my first name in front of my Indian team who I have been managing for many years. This is terrible.'

India – Business etiquette

The working day: Breakfast meetings are not common. The working day usually begins around 9.30 – 10.00 a.m. Business lunches are often quite long – 90 minutes is not uncommon.

Concept of time: Levels of speed, efficiency and punctuality will be different from those in the West: if someone promises to meet you in ten minutes, expect arrival in twenty.

Communication styles: Indians often over-promise because they want to please: admitting a job is difficult to get done is often considered rude or weak.

Status and hierarchy: Managers are expected to 'manage'. This includes making key decisions, often with little or no consultation, and telling subordinates what to do.

File 18 | Unit 7

Business communication skills, Exercise 5, page 45

Student B

Read this email, make notes, then update your partner.

To: All administrators
From: Head of Administration
Subject: New security measures

As many of you are aware, we've recently been having a number of problems with virus programs on the network. In one case, a hacker logged on and tried to read private employee information. As a result, we've decided to install a new software program and to start a new system of passwords.

By the end of the month, the new software will automatically scan your computer when you open it. You will also receive a new password every month to log on to your computer. Your department manager will give you this password on the 1st of every month. Please do not pass this on to anyone else in or outside of the company.

File 19 | Unit 8

Business communication skills, Exercise 6, page 51

Student A

You are responsible for the organization of office space. This is a difficult topic because
• more people are working in less space
• there are fewer individual offices.

Your plans are to
• hold a meeting with staff in existing departments
• explain the situation and ask for their views.
By the end of the month: hope to have a lot of recommendations
Next month: brief office fitters and choose furniture
In two months' time: be ready for move

1 Tell your partner what you are working on, how you expect it to go, and describe your plans.
2 Your partner will describe his / her plans for the project he / she is working on.

File 20 | Unit 2

Case study, Task, Exercise 2, page 17

Group C

You are working on publicity for the club and the launch party.

Your responsibilities:

- Advertising the launch party with leaflets and posters.
- Issuing special invitations for local business people.
- Recording a commercial for the local radio station.
- Setting up a website and making sure it is up to date.

Your progress: The leaflets and posters are ready. You are still waiting for the invitations. The website has been designed and is working well. The radio commercial has been recorded and needs to be approved by the team.

Problems: You need help to distribute the leaflets and posters. The website needs to be updated more frequently and expert help is expensive.

File 21 | Unit 8

Case study, Task, Exercise 2, page 53

Group A

Read these advantages of virtual working and share them with Group B.

- **More efficient use of time** – a team that stays in close contact and keeps an accurate record of its own progress is more likely to get something done on time and under budget.
- **Efficient use of training budget** – organizations that already have the necessary technology and skills for online communication have reported big savings on airfare, hotel and restaurant costs, and other expenses associated with face-to-face training.
- **Increased productivity** – too often organizations rely so much on meetings that a decline in overall productivity is experienced. Team members don't waste time walking down corridors, talking in the doorways along the way, and waiting for others to arrive.
- **Greater participation** – virtual team members can decide when and where they will participate and as a result they might feel able to participate more fully than they otherwise would.
- **Better use of individual time** – twelve minutes into a meeting, your reason for attending may be over. You could leave, then return later to 'listen in' and perhaps add something more.
- **Greater equality** – when you can't see the other people involved in the meeting, the organizational hierarchy doesn't completely disappear, but it does fade further into the background, allowing individuals to express their position more fully and easily.
- **Less air pollution** – when team members are able to work from home or the office, and avoid travelling for meetings, they lower their impact on the environment.

File 22 | Unit 9

Business communication skills, Exercise 5, page 57

Student A

Situation 1

Conversation 1

You are the customer. You work for an oil company. You want to order two drill pieces from S1 Engineering.

You have an account with the company. It is HK568.

Call S1 Engineering.

Conversation 2

You urgently need the pieces you ordered five days ago.

Call the company and find out about your order.

Situation 2

Conversation 1

You are a call handler for Haddows Trading, a fashion distributor. A customer calls you to place an order.

Give this order reference: HTGS899.

Conversation 2

You receive another call from the customer.

There has been a problem with the order. Find out what the problem is and invent an excuse / explanation.

Promise to take immediate action. (You can send a delivery van today – no extra charge.)

File 23 | Unit 10

Case study, Task, Exercise 1, page 65

Student A

Read this information on visitor numbers at last year's event. Decide what attractions and facilities were popular, and make recommendations for this year's events to the rest of the committee.

Total number of visitors: 358 (adults)

Numbers of visitors (approximately) that

- watched a promotional video about the work of the charity: 27
- rode on the Tour de France simulator: 152
- had lunch at the outdoor barbecue: 289
- took the guided tour of the factory: 95
- completed the quiz about the company: 43
- tried out the bikes on a special course: 235
- bought a lottery ticket for the charity (bicycles as prizes): 117
- had children who used the children's play area: 145
- used the outdoor café: 231

File 24 | Unit 9

Case study, Discussion, Exercise 5, page 59

Maersk Logistics' solution for Castorama Polska

1 Created an 'integrated logistics environment' which
- handles the supply and distribution process as a whole, rather than separate stages
- operates an information system based on purchase orders (a computer system that has information on all customer orders and purchases and automatically orders any products that Castorama are / will be running low on)
- takes care of the negotiations with suppliers and all the documentation.
2 Improved the online tracking system for products and information as follows.
- Castorama staff can log on to the system and find out where a customer's order is at any time.
- Staff can keep track of every order – when it was dispatched, how long before delivery, any changes in schedule, etc.
3 Reduced lead times and transportation costs by
- handling all the sourcing from European and Polish suppliers, including transportation
- controlling transportation costs
- channelling orders through one distribution centre in Central Poland – orders are repacked on to trucks and distributed to different stores throughout Poland
- keeping the supply of key products up to date at central warehouse.

Results
- information is better
- efficiency has improved
- client satisfaction has increased
- sales are increasing
- confidence in Castorama's capabilities has improved – among customers and suppliers

File 25 | Unit 16

Case study, Task, Exercise 1, page 101

Student B

Mission: Research sales and marketing history. Find company data and analyse it.
Result: Surprising because
- sales decreased after company started exporting to mainland Europe – these consumers prefer coffee and herbal teas
- weak marketing campaign two years ago – expensive with bad results – concentrated so much on continental Europe that the key UK market was forgotten and sales dropped.

Conclusion: Continental Europe is potentially big market. Need to launch new campaign there, but not forget importance of UK market.

File 26 | Unit 13

Case study, Task, Exercise 1, page 83

Student C

You work in logistics. Read these complaints you have received from customers.

Two months ago I placed an order for some wooden toys for my grandchildren. When I contacted you three weeks ago to say they hadn't arrived, you kindly sent me the order. Now not only do I have the order you re-sent, but this morning the original order finally arrived! What should I do with the extra order?

The Bohemian glassware you sent me is lovely. But one of the glasses is broken. They were inadequately wrapped. There just wasn't enough packaging for a long-distance order.

I am very upset because an item I ordered took over three weeks to reach me. I don't know if it is the postal service in my country, or the service in yours which is unreliable, but if you can't keep the two weeks promise then you shouldn't make it. I don't have much confidence in national postal services – have you considered UPS or DHL?

File 27 | Unit 14

Case study, Task, Exercise 1, page 89

Student A

Read the information about the check-in procedure and present it to your group.

Self check-in machines at the airport

1 passenger puts credit card in machine or enters flight number on touch screen

2 passenger booking details are retrieved

3 security questions are answered on screen

4 boarding pass is printed out (and luggage tags if needed)

5 luggage to be checked in is taken to 'bag drop' area

6 passport check is carried out at departure gate

Advantages
- will reduce costs because fewer check-in employees will be needed
- will reduce waiting times, leading to improved customer satisfaction
- passengers with only hand luggage can check in more quickly (e.g. business customers)

File 28 | Unit 8

Case study, Task, Exercise 2, page 53

Group B

Read these disadvantages of virtual working and share them with Group A.

- **Over-reliance on email** – communication can take up to four times as long as one face-to-face meeting, especially as non-verbal communication transfers 63% of meaning.
- **Failure to respond to messages** – employees might have to wait for responses before they can continue their work. This means that their workflow is affected and they might waste a lot of time.
- **No socializing** – socializing with team members helps to improve relationships and often makes teamwork more effective. Face-to-face contact is also essential in building trust. Without trust, relationships can break down.
- **More time needed** – multicultural teams can take up to seventeen weeks to become as effective as teams of the same culture, and without face-to-face contact this can take even longer.
- **Working over different time zones** – it is difficult to schedule meetings so that everyone can be involved.
- **Intercultural communication issues** – travelling to other countries increases awareness and understanding of cultural differences and this leads to improved communication. Without business travel, misunderstandings due to cultural differences are more likely.
- **Cost issues** – although virtual working means that less money will be spent on travel, the problems connected with developing effective virtual teams might actually cost the company more money in the long term.

File 29 | Unit 10

Language at work, Exercise 8, page 64

File 30 | Unit 9

Business communication skills, Exercise 5, page 57

Student B

Situation 1

Conversation 1

You are a call handler for S1 Engineering, a company which provides spare parts for the oil industry.

A customer calls you to place an order.

Give this order reference: 965/LQ.

Conversation 2

Five days later you receive another call from the customer. Check the caller's account details and find out what the problem is.

Give the following explanation:

Explain that the order was delayed by two days because of a strike. The customer will receive the order later this afternoon.

Situation 2

Conversation 1

You are a customer from the fashion trade. You want to order fifteen green skirts from Haddows Trading, a fashion distributor. Your account number is VX890. Call Haddows Trading.

Conversation 2

You have just received the order from Haddows Trading. Unfortunately it contained fifty green shirts. You are very unhappy. Call and complain. Ask for a solution.

File 31 | Unit 10

Case study, Task, Exercise 1, page 65

Student B

Read this visitors' feedback from last year's event. Decide what attractions were popular, and make recommendations for this year's events to the rest of the committee.

Comments and suggestions

'The Tour de France simulator was really amazing! Where can I buy one? I had a great day. Why don't you have more activities for children next year? And maybe a bicycle race?'

'We really enjoyed trying out the bikes on the special course. How about some cycle training next year?'

'The factory was very interesting and everyone was extremely friendly. The only thing was that there were a lot of people waiting for the Tour de France simulator, so we couldn't try it. Perhaps we can next year!'

'I liked seeing the factory, but my kids thought it was rather boring. What about having more family entertainment in the park outside? What about a display of extreme cycling?'

'We bought two bikes for our kids. The prices were very good and it was great to know we were helping the charity in their work at the same time.'

File 32 | Unit 9

Case study, Task, Exercise 1, page 59

Student A

You interviewed some people who used to be regular Toyztime customers. Your partner has interviewed Toyztime employees at one of the main stores. You asked the customers this question: 'Why have you stopped shopping at Toyztime?'.

1 Read the comments carefully.
2 Take turns to report what you heard to your partner. Listen to what your partner says and find a corresponding comment from a customer.

Example: **A** *One customer told me that they went to a Toyztime store to buy …*
B *Right. It sounds like they do have problem there. An employee I spoke to said that their deliveries are often late because …*

Toyztime customers' comments

a 'I wanted to buy a particular toy at Toyztime for my grandson's birthday but they were out of stock. They told me they were expecting a delivery that Friday morning and said they'd keep one aside for me to pick up in the afternoon. When I went in at 3.00 p.m. on the Friday I was told that the delivery hadn't arrived yet. What a waste of my time! I won't be shopping there again.'

b 'I was told by a sales assistant that a product I ordered would take about ten working days to arrive at the store for collection. I called after ten days to check if it had arrived. It hadn't and the person I spoke to couldn't even tell me when I might expect it to arrive! I couldn't wait any longer so got it from a different company.'

c 'When I asked why the product I was interested in was cheaper at a competitor's store, the manager just told me they had had to put their prices up. As long as I know I am getting the products cheaper elsewhere, I won't be going back to Toyztime.'

d 'I called to check if my local store had a certain toy I wanted in stock. The man I spoke to looked it up on the system and told me there were three in stock. When I got to the store though, there were none. It was the second time something like that has happened, so I've decided to buy toys elsewhere.'

e 'Several times I've been into Toyztime to buy a toy and been told it's out of stock as it's such a popular item. Often it takes up to two weeks for them to get it in again. At some other shops they can get the item in for you the next day – I prefer to use shops that can do that for their customers.'

f 'On two occasions now, I've seen new toys advertised on TV and expected Toyztime to sell them. When I went in to my local store, however, I was told that as the product was fairly new, it hadn't been ordered yet. Luckily I found what I wanted at another chain of toy shops the same day!'

File 33 | Unit 13

Language at work, Exercise 6, page 82

Student A

Situation 1
You are working in a new team. The problem is that most of your team work on the other side of the building. You need to talk to them face-to-face regularly, and you are wasting time by going to see them all the time.

1 Explain your problem to your partner.
2 Ask for advice.

Situation 2
Listen to your partner's problem. Here are some possible solutions to give.

- Get the company to buy desk fans.
- Change your working hours so you aren't working at the hottest time of the day.
- Work from home.
- Refuse to work until it's fixed.

File 34 | Unit 13

Case study, Task, Exercise 1, page 83

Student A

You are in charge of the website. Read these complaints you have received from customers.

> Urgent
>
> I ordered some goods from you two weeks ago. I have had a communication from my bank saying that there has been an attack on my account. Fortunately they have been able to protect my account, but can you assure me that your payment system is 100% trustworthy?

> I want to buy something from your site, but I keep getting a message saying that there is an incompatible algorithm. What does that mean? Is there another way of paying?

> Dear One World Bazaar,
>
> It is very slow to download your site. Where we are we don't have broadband. I really want to order stuff from you but this is too frustrating.
> PS Do you really need all the animations on your website? I don't see what they bring to it. It takes a lot of time to import the plug-ins.

File 35 | Unit 10

Case study, Task, Exercise 1, page 65

Student C

Read this costing for the attractions and facilities for last year's event. Last year you went over budget on the event so make sure you don't this year. You have a total budget of €15,000. Decide what you think you can afford and make recommendations for this year's events to the rest of the committee.

- Promotional video about the work of the charity: no cost
- Tour de France simulator: €550
- Catering for outdoor barbecue: €3,000
- Guided tour of the factory: €195
- Quiz about the company: no cost
- Building a special course for bike trials: €1,200
- Charity contribution on sales of bicycles and / or clothing: €5,400
- Lottery tickets for the charity (bicycles as prizes): €500
- Public event insurance: €1,000
- Portable toilets: €450
- Children's play area: €550
- Overtime payments for staff: €2,000

File 36 | Unit 14

Case study, Task, Exercise 1, page 89

Student B

Read the information about the check-in procedure and present it to your group.

Online check-in

1 passenger goes to airline website and enters name and flight booking number

2 flight details are confirmed

3 passenger prints out their own boarding card

4 passenger arrives at airport

5 luggage to be checked in is taken to 'bag drop' area

6 boarding pass is scanned electronically at departure gate

Advantages

- will reduce costs because fewer check-in employees will be needed
- passengers will check in before arriving at the airport so there will be no waiting in queues – increased customer satisfaction
- business customers can check in at home or at work and will be more relaxed at the airport

File 37 | Unit 13

Language at work, Exercise 6, page 82

Student B

Situation 1

Listen to your partner's problem. Here are some possible solutions to give.

- Ask to move desks to be nearer your team.
- Arrange just one daily meeting at a halfway point in the building.
- Alternate days when you go to them and they come to you.

Situation 2

The air conditioning has broken in your building. It is summer and very difficult to work in these high temperatures.

1 Explain your problem to your partner.
2 Ask for advice.

File 38 | Unit 13

Case study, Task, Exercise 1, page 83

Student B

You work in sourcing and marketing the products. Read these complaints you have received from customers.

Hi,
I have just received the hat I ordered. Unfortunately it's too big. It goes over my ears and I can't see anything! I think there's a problem with the way you describe your sizes.
Normally I take size 56, but this is huge. Can I send it back for a smaller size?
Carlo

Hi
I ordered an amber ring from you to give to my mother for her birthday. It arrived yesterday and I have noticed that there is a dead insect inside the amber. Personally I find this quite interesting, but I'm afraid that my mother will not appreciate it. Could I send the ring back and get a replacement in time for her birthday? It's in two weeks.
Darren

I ordered one of your beautiful Swazi dresses, but when I tried it on it was much too tight. I am normally a large – but with these sizes I imagine I would need extra large!! Can you be clearer about the sizes?
PS I gave the dress to my niece – she looks lovely in it.

File 39 | Unit 16

Working with words, Exercise 9, page 97

Student A

1 Ask your partner about these events. For each question ask *How did … go?*

   Example: *How did sales of the air-conditioning unit go?*
   - sales of the air-conditioning unit
   - the trip to Argentina
   - the launch of the new organic beauty products
   - the presentation on the company mission statement

2 Read this information, then answer your partner's questions about the success of each event.

> **Product: hand-knitted sweaters**
> - Projected sales: 5,000 units
> - Actual sales: 2,000 units
>
> **Trip abroad: fact-finding trip to India**
> - People: lots of important people, masses of knowledge
> - Result: established partnership with top expert
>
> **Launch of new product: white wine**
> - Details: wine buyers invited to taste new wine
> - Result: problem with bottling process – wine tastes bad – buyers not interested
>
> **Presentation: company's position in the market**
> - Details: not enough research done on competition
> - Result: colleagues bored and managers unimpressed

File 40 | Unit 16

Business communication skills, Exercise 5, page 99

Student A

Situation 1

You have been on a fact-finding trip to Nepal to find out about climbing holidays. Student B is your boss and will ask you to give a general evaluation of the trip and emphasize what you consider important. Read this information and prepare to report back on what happened.

Destination: Nepal

Contact: Magnus O'Neill, New Zealander – famous amateur climber, friendly and lively

Business: Climbing holidays

Impressions: Too wild and independent. OK for very fit, experienced mountaineers, but too much for beginners.

Verdict: Needs to do more on safety. Improve comfort of base-camp facilities.

Next step: Too much work to do. If we carry on with this type of project, we need a more reliable team, better comfort, and much better safety. Recommend not working with him.

Situation 2

You are Student B's boss. Ask for a report on his / her trip. Ask him / her to justify his / her opinions. Identify action for the future.

File 41 | Unit 16

Case study, Task, Exercise 1, page 101

Student C

Mission: Research into activity of competitors. Visit tea trade fair.

Result: Useful because
   - competitors offer wider range of products, including popular fruit teas
   - other competitors are successful with Fairtrade products.

Conclusion: To be competitive, need to evolve, create new products, appeal to the serious tea drinker.

File 42 | Unit 9

Case study, Task, Exercise 1, page 59

Student B

You interviewed Toyztime employees at one of the main stores. You asked them this question: 'What problems are you having with stock?'.

1 Read the comments carefully.
2 Take turns to report what you heard to your partner. Listen to what your partner says and find a corresponding comment from an employee.

Example: A *One customer told me that they went to a Toyztime store to buy …*

   B *Right. It sounds like they do have a problem there. An employee I spoke to said that their deliveries are often late because …*

Toyztime employees' comments

a 'I'm responsible for dealing with our suppliers but I don't have time to do this, keep on top of all the documentation, and run the store too. This means I sometimes don't get around to ordering low-stock items or new products that we should be stocking. I'm sure the other store managers have the same problem. And, if we don't have items in stock, we lose our customers.'

b 'When we run out of stock on popular products it takes ages to get more from our suppliers.'

c 'Very often our deliveries are late because the drivers can't find us or because the traffic is heavy in the rush hour. It is quite tricky as, like some other Toyztime stores, we are in the back streets of the city – but it shouldn't happen as often as it does.'

d 'When customers call to ask about deliveries and when certain items will be in stock, we have no way of checking if stock has been dispatched and when it's likely to arrive in store.'

e 'Our stock control system sometimes shows that we have more items in stock than we actually do. I do try to remember to update it when a product is purchased but sometimes I forget.'

f 'I've had to put our prices up to cover the rise in transportation costs. Our pricing is not very competitive any more.'

File 43 | Unit 14

Case study, Task, Exercise 1, page 89

Student C

Read the information about the check-in procedure and present it to your group.

Biometric check-in

1 passengers register their passport information, and face- and eye-recognition datanumber

2 passport information is put on a card with a microchip that passengers can carry with them

3 at check-in, the card is read and the passenger's face is scanned to confirm that the passenger matches the data stored in the chip

4 boarding pass is printed out (and luggage tags if needed)

5 luggage to be checked in is taken to 'bag drop' area

6 passenger goes to a security gate where the card is read and their face is scanned again

Advantages
- simpler and faster airport check-in process
- increased security

File 44 | Unit 16

Case study, Task, Exercise 1, page 101

Student D

Mission: Focus group. Tea experts invited to discuss ways of improving product.
Result: Very helpful because
- better quality tea leaves needed to justify high price
- experts recommended selling weaker tea in mainland Europe – these consumers don't normally add milk.

Conclusion: Need to find new suppliers to cater for different tastes. Have two different ranges – one cheaper one for mass market, one more expensive, high-quality for specialist market.

File 45 | Unit 16

Starting point, Exercise 1, page 96

India black pepper
Mexico chocolate
China silk
Peru potatoes
Central and South America rubber
Ethiopia coffee

File 46 | Unit 16

Working with words, Exercise 9, page 97

Student B

1 Read this information, then answer your partner's questions about the success of each event.

Product: air-conditioning unit for the home
- Projected sales: $400,000
- Actual sales: $600,000

Trip abroad: fact-finding trip to Argentina
- People: trade fair not well publicized – not many people there
- Result: two weeks there – no useful contacts made

Launch of new product: organic beauty products
- Details: supermarket shoppers given free trials
- Result: positive response to free trials – shoppers buy additional products

Presentation: company mission statement for the coming year
- Details: lots of information, excellent use of PowerPoint, innovative mission statement
- Result: colleagues impressed and motivated

2 Now ask your partner about these events. For each question ask *How did … go?*

   Example: How did sales of the hand-knitted sweaters go?
- sales of hand-knitted sweaters
- the trip to India
- the launch of the new white wine
- the presentation on the company's position in the market

CD 1

Unit 1

01

Ingrid I'm a project coordinator for a charity. We provide aid to Africa and I usually spend about four months a year in the field. My job involves managing our field teams and communicating our aims to government officials. I sometimes find this depressing, because there's just so much bureaucracy – and corruption too. But then, when I return to Africa and I see the results of our work, like new clinics, hospitals, and schools, I think it's all worthwhile and I have a real sense of achievement.

02

Mansour OK, well, I'm an air traffic controller. This means I'm in charge of a section of airspace and keeping in contact with pilots in that zone. It's a challenging job – our most difficult time of the year is the holiday season when planes are taking off and landing every couple of minutes – it takes total concentration, all the time. I usually work a six-hour shift, and by the end I feel exhausted. But it's rewarding to know that I've enabled thousands of passengers to travel safely.

03

Conversation 1

Hannah Hi, Luc. I want you to meet Jo Johansson. Jo is from the Langley Foundation. Jo, this is Luc Akele, one of our area managers.

Jo Nice to meet you, Luc.

Luc Yes, you too. So, what do you do at the Langley Foundation?

Jo Well, I deal with fund applications.

Luc Fund applications? That sounds challenging.

Jo Yes, well, sometimes we have to make difficult choices. And what do you do, Luc?

Luc Well, I'm in charge of our sub-Saharan Africa operations.

Jo Sub-Saharan Africa?

Luc Yes. I oversee projects and make sure that the money is well spent. Then I have to report to our main sponsors.

Jo I see. So how much time do you spend in the field?

Luc Well, I usually do five or six trips a year, sometimes more.

Jo That's a lot of time away from home.

Conversation 2

Hitoshi Good evening. I don't think we've met. I'm Hitoshi Watanabe from Head Office.

Dr Mayer I'm delighted to meet you, Ms Watanabe. My name's Dr Walter Mayer.

Hitoshi I'm very pleased to meet you too, Dr Mayer. I see from your badge that you are with FPR Pharmaceuticals.

Dr Mayer Yes, that's right. I'm responsible for their medical donations programme. I handle all the inter-governmental work.

Hitoshi That sounds very rewarding, knowing that you are helping so many people.

Dr Mayer Yes, it is, although it involves a lot of negotiation, which can be quite slow.

Hitoshi Yes, I can imagine that.

Dr Mayer So which part of Japan are you from, Ms Watanabe?

Hitoshi Actually, I'm from Brazil. I am third-generation Brazilian.

Dr Mayer Oh, I'm sorry. I thought … well …

Hitoshi Please don't apologize. I am proud of my Japanese heritage. Do you have a minute? I would like to introduce you to someone.

04

1 Well, I deal with fund applications.
2 Well, I'm in charge of our sub-Saharan Africa operations.
3 I oversee projects and make sure that the money is well spent.
4 I'm responsible for their medical donations programme.
5 I handle all the inter-governmental work.
6 It involves a lot of negotiation.

05

A I'm a recruitment consultant.
B A recruitment consultant?
A Yes. I oversee recruitment for ten of our key accounts.
B That sounds really demanding.
A It can be at times. So tell me, what exactly does your job involve?
B Well, I'm responsible for the department's spending.
A Oh right. Do you enjoy your job?
B I love it. It's great to be in a such a position of responsibility.
A Really? I think I'd find it stressful.

Unit 2

06

So this is my project – a centre for senior citizens. We have to finish by the end of the week, and I think we'll meet the deadline. We fell behind schedule because of the Thanksgiving holiday, but we managed to catch up last week and we're back on track now – we may even finish ahead of schedule.

…

It was hard at first, knowing how to allocate resources – you know – who does what, when, how much it will cost, stuff like that. I have managed to stay within budget, but only just!

…

I think the key thing I've learnt is the importance of delegation. I try as much as possible to delegate tasks and trust people to get on with them. If I tried to do everything myself, we'd never finish on time. Teamwork is essential and I get updates from people every two days, so that I don't lose control of the project.

…

I'm very happy with the project – so far, things are going according to plan. So, fingers crossed for the last few days.

07

Samira Hello. Samira speaking.

Jamie Hi, Samira. It's Jamie. How are you?

Samira Oh hi, Jamie. I'm fine, thanks. What can I do for you?

Jamie I'm just calling for an update on the centre. How are things going over there?

Samira Well, so far so good. Everything's back on track.

Jamie Great. So what's happening with the decorating?

Samira We're still painting the ceiling – it'll take another day or so.

Jamie OK. And where are we with the lighting?

Samira We've finished that – it looks great.

Jamie Good – that was fast.

Samira Yes, but we're still waiting for the carpets.

Jamie Oh. OK, I'll call the suppliers and find out where they are. So, to recap, the painting's nearly done, the lighting's finished, and we're just waiting for the carpets?

Samira That's right.

Jamie Great. So it's all going according to plan. Listen, I'm coming over to the centre tomorrow. How about we get the team together to allocate tasks for the final stages? And I'll give you an update on the carpets then.

Samira Sure. No problem.

Jamie Good. Well, I'll let you get back to work. See you tomorrow.

Samira Yes, see you tomorrow. Nice talking to you. Bye.

Jamie Bye.

08

Jamie Hi, everyone. Oh, I'm not interrupting, am I?

Samira Oh, hello, Jamie. No, not at all. It's just me, Bruno, and Josie at the moment.

Bruno Hi.

Josie Hello.

Jamie Hi. Good to see you again. Oh, this all looks great.

Samira Thanks. There are a few things still to be done, though. Oh, did you call the carpet people?

Jamie Yes. They said they would bring it tomorrow, before eight o'clock.

Samira So, we need somebody to be here then to open up. Bruno, can you do it? You live near here.

Bruno Yeah, sure, no problem. Leave it with me.

Samira Thanks. Now, the other thing is we're going to need more paint from that cheap wholesaler on the other side of town.

Jamie Well, I can go there this afternoon if you want, and bring the paint in tomorrow.

Samira Mm. Thanks, but we'll need it sooner if the carpet is arriving tomorrow.

Josie Listen. I have my car. Why don't I go there now, get the paint, and we can finish the ceiling this afternoon?

Samira Good idea. Do you know where it is?

Josie Er … not really.

Samira OK. Bruno, can you go with her?

Bruno I'd prefer not to if that's OK. I really want to finish the back room.

Samira Well, I'll come with you, then. Oh, Bruno, you can carry on with the rest of this paint, and then the three of us can finish it together this afternoon.

Bruno I'm sorry, I have an appointment this afternoon.

Samira Oh, of course, I forgot. OK, Josie and I will finish the painting this afternoon.

Jamie So, you two are going to get the paint, and Bruno is going to meet the carpet people tomorrow. What else do we need to do at the moment?

Samira Well, I'm sure we could find something if you really wanted to help out …

09

Volunteer … Clubbing isn't normally a very environmentally friendly activity.

Interviewer Really?

Volunteer No, definitely not. It uses large amounts of energy for heating and cooling the room, for lighting … It uses a lot of water in the toilets and washrooms, every night. Plus all the glass and the plastic bottles – huge amounts of waste. And besides this, you know, clubs, they need to be refurbished quite often – new floors, new paint, new equipment. It uses a lot of materials, a lot of resources.

Interviewer Yeah, I can see that. So how is this club different?

Volunteer OK, well we're planning to have a lot of sustainable features. The best one is the energy-generating dance floor.

Interviewer How does that work?

Volunteer Oh, it's great. It's made of a special material that takes the energy of the dancers and uses it to power the music and the lights – low-energy lighting of course. Then we're putting in a system where the toilets will use rain water. There's a system that controls the temperature – and the walls change colour as the temperature changes. What else …? Oh, well, we're having a rooftop garden for relaxation, like a kind of chillout zone …

Interviewer It sounds great. And you're having a launch party soon?

Volunteer Yeah, that's right. Really soon, actually. We're expecting about twelve hundred people. We're having a lot of different music, really good DJs, visual projections by Urbi and Orbi … We're planning to have free organic beer. And there'll be ethical clothing companies like Kuyichi doing consultations …

Interviewer Sounds like a lot of work.

Volunteer A lot of work, yeah, but it's fun. It all needs very careful planning. We're making good progress, and we're on schedule, but there's still a lot to do …

Unit 3

10

Nina Hi, Florin.

Florin Oh, hi, Nina. How are you? How was last night?

Nina We made some progress but the meeting lasted three hours.

Florin You're kidding.

Nina No, I got home at about midnight. I'm really tired.

Florin So, why are you in so early?

Nina I have to present my findings at eleven o'clock.

Florin I think Anton would have waited for the results.

Nina I know, but I don't have time. I've still got five days' holiday left from last year and I'm taking the kids camping tomorrow. They're so excited.

Florin That'll be nice.

Nina What about you? Did you go out again last night?

Florin No. My girlfriend had to work late too. So I made dinner and watched a boring documentary about plants. She wants to take me somewhere this Saturday, but I've already told Anton that I'll join him and the sales team from Kyoto for golf.

Nina Maybe you should take some holiday too.

Florin I don't have any left. Remember – I used it all for my walking tour in Morocco.

Nina Oh, that's right. I should give you some of mine!

11

1 I got home at about midnight. I'm really tired.

2 I'm taking the kids camping tomorrow. They're so excited.

3 I made dinner and watched a boring documentary about plants.

12

Leif … So how was your first week? Do you like working in HR?

Mirella Yes, it's great. I'm really interested in Human Resources now. And I really enjoy working with Kris. He has so much experience.

Leif Good. Do you want to stay with him or spend some time with Marketing next week?

Mirella I don't mind.

Leif I know Marketing have a conference coming up in Copenhagen and I thought you could go with them.

Mirella Great.

Leif You can see what they do and of course you get to see Copenhagen.

Mirella Sounds good.

Leif Is this your first time in Europe?

Mirella Yes, it's my first time out of Brazil.

Leif Really? I'm very fond of Brazil.

Mirella Have you been there?

Leif A number of times, actually. Mainly to Rio on business. Anyway, we need to make sure you have plenty of time for travel while you're here.

Mirella Kris is taking me to the country this weekend.

Leif Good. What sort of things do you like doing?

Mirella Hm, I really like just walking around a city to get to know it a bit. And I need to do some shopping as well.

Leif Oh, there are plenty of shops in the city if you like that.

Mirella Actually, I'm not crazy about shopping but I need a few things for my room.

Leif There are also some really interesting museums if you like that kind of thing.

Mirella Um, actually I'm not keen on museums either, but I like going to art galleries.

Leif That's good, because there are lots of galleries too. How is the accommodation? How do you find the family?

Mirella It's fine and the family has been very nice.

Leif That's good.

Mirella They're very quiet compared to mine! I have four sisters.

Leif Really? ... Oh, look, before I forget ...

13

Leif Really? ... Oh, look, before I forget. Next week, you'll have a desk to work from. I'm sorry you didn't have a place this week.

Mirella Oh, it's no problem.

Leif And you have a phone and your own email address.

Mirella Wonderful. Let me write it down.

Leif Your extension is three five one. Press nine for an outside line.

Mirella What's the company number?

Leif Double zero, four six is the international code for Sweden. And then 096 745 6745. And your email is mirella underscore two, at dipris dot S E.

Mirella Is that S for sugar, E for egg?

Leif That's right. OK, well, I need to go, I'm afraid.

Mirella Me too.

Leif Can I give you a lift?

14

Conversation 1

A ... we can sort that out this afternoon if you like.

B Yes OK. Anyway, I'd better get on.

A Yes, me too.

B So, see you later.

A See you later.

Conversation 2

A ... but if you need anything else, just let me know.

B OK.

A Well, I should get back to work.

B OK. Thanks for your help.

A No problem. See you tomorrow.

B Yes, see you.

Conversation 3

A ... yes, Thursday is fine.

B Great. Well, I need to go now, I'm afraid.

A OK. Thanks for calling.

B Speak to you soon.

A Yes, OK. Bye.

15

Leif Hi, Mirella. Sorry I'm late. Have you been here long?

Mirella No, I've only just arrived.

Leif How was your weekend?

Mirella Good, thanks.

Leif Did you go to the gallery on Saturday?

Mirella Yes, I did. It was fascinating. Have you ever been there?

Leif Yes, a couple of times. Oh, Miriam ...

Miriam Hi, Leif.

Leif Miriam, have you met Mirella?

Miriam No, I haven't. Hi, Mirella.

Mirella Hello.

Leif Miriam is the person we need to see about working in Marketing this week.

Miriam It's all arranged and I've just organized a desk for you to work from. It's next to mine. Oh, Leif! I still haven't asked you about your tennis match.

Leif Don't worry. I lost.

Miriam That's good.

Mirella I don't understand.

Miriam Leif played tennis at the weekend with a really important client.

Leif It's good for marketing if the customer wins. So I had to lose the match for Miriam.

Mirella I see.

Leif Actually, I haven't played for ages, and he was much better than me! Anyway, shall we go to your office?

Miriam Sure. Let's go.

Unit 4

16

1 The problem with all these sites is that you have to book everything separately and it takes such a long time. It's also difficult to get exactly what you want because you can't see all the options. I can never seem to get a cheap deal.

2 I don't like using the cash machines outside because people walk past all the time. But if I go to a cashier, it takes so long to get information about my account because of the queues. And they're only open when I'm working, so I have to go during my lunchtime.

3 We really need to access all the latest news that is relevant to our business. The problem is, it takes so long to find what we want on all the different websites. And some of their search options are ... are really difficult to use.

17

1 They provide an excellent service. We can rely on them to deliver orders on time and that allows us to maintain excellent relationships with all our customers.

2 Being up to date with what's happening in the world is really important to me. And this also lets me know what's happening in the money markets, wherever I am. It also makes it easier to make quick decisions about what to buy and sell.

3 It's so much faster than going there and I don't have to worry if it is open or if there are a lot of other people. I just log on any time, and all I do is choose the products I want and give my credit card number. It really helps me to manage my time better.

4 I was so happy when it opened. It lets me work full-time and still have time with my child in the middle of the day.

18

Presenter Thanks for coming today. As you know, we have a new customer database.

Staff Hurray!

Manager Well, nothing could be as slow as the old system!

Presenter Yes, well. As I say, the good news is we have a new database. But the bad news is that it will take a few weeks before we can use it in all our hotels. Now, it might seem a bit difficult to use at first, but in fact it's very simple. Your staff will need some training on how to use it. So the purpose of today is for you to start to become familiar with it.

Now, up on the screen you can see what happens when you open the program. It looks very similar to the old database. But what's different, is this bottom half. As soon as you type in the details, it starts to suggest what kind of room the customer might like and what rooms are free. In other words, as well as giving the customer more of what they want, it also makes it quicker to process a booking for a regular customer and give them their favourite room.

Manager Will it let me make notes on the client?

Presenter Yes, you can type notes into this section for future reference. For example, if you want to advertise a special promotion to male customers over the age of forty, then it'll tell you who they are.

Manager How does it know what to match?

Presenter It has these drop-down menus, which allow you to categorize the information when the booking is taken. The more detailed the information, the better the match. So, on the one hand, it'll take you more time to get the information, but on the other hand, we think it'll save time later on.

Manager So what happens when the customer doesn't want to tell you their age, for example?

Presenter Well, obviously one downside is that you can't demand the information. But on the plus side, the customer can book online now, and hopefully they'll give us the extra information then. In other words, the more they tell us, the quicker the booking is next time they call …

19

1 As you know, we have a new customer database.

2 So the purpose of today is for you to start to become familiar with it.

3 As I say, the good news is …

4 Now, up on the screen you can see …

5 In other words, as well as giving the customer more of what they want …

Unit 5

20

Elena … Anyway, I'm calling for some information. I'd like to find out about your services for hotels.

Sergio OK. Can you tell me a little more? What type of hotels?

Elena Well, I represent a chain of four- and five-star hotels. We're based in Switzerland, but on your website you don't have an operator in Switzerland, so I thought Italy was the nearest.

Sergio That's right, yes.

Elena Good. Well, we're interested in updating our current fitness rooms for guests. Is that something you deal with?

Sergio Yes, certainly. How old are your current facilities?

Elena About ten years old. They're rather out of date and our customers often comment on this.

Sergio OK. How many hotels are we talking about?

Elena We currently have eight hotels with health and fitness facilities, and three others that need them.

Sergio And what budget do you have for this?

Elena That's difficult to say, really. Would it be possible for someone to come and see our facilities?

Sergio Yes, of course. Actually, we're coming to Switzerland next month.

Elena Really?

Sergio Yes, we already have another client in Zurich. Is that near you?

Elena Not too far. I'm in Bern. It's only a couple of hours away.

Sergio Fine. Can we arrange a meeting then?

Elena Sure.

Sergio Let's see. Well, my trip begins on the 30th of January. That's a Monday …

21

Sergio Yes, of course. Actually, we're coming to Switzerland next month.

Elena Really?

Sergio Yes, we already have another client in Zurich. Is that near you?

Elena Not too far. I'm in Bern. It's only a couple of hours away.

Sergio Fine. Can we arrange a meeting then?

Elena Sure.

Sergio Let's see. Well, my trip begins on the 30th of January. That's a Monday. How about Tuesday the 31st?

Elena I'd prefer the Wednesday.

Sergio The 1st of February? Yes, that suits me.

22

Elena Hello. Elena Schenker speaking.

Sergio Hello, Elena. This is Sergio Lanese from Technogym.

Elena Hello. Nice to hear from you again.

Sergio How are things?

Elena Fine, thanks.

Sergio Sorry for calling so late in the day.

Elena That's OK. I've only just got back to the office.

Sergio Is this a busy time for you?

Elena Yes, the ski season is our busiest time of year.

Sergio Of course. Is there plenty of snow? What's the weather like?

Elena There's a lot of snow, which is good. It's snowing right now, actually.

Sergio Good. I'm actually calling about my visit. I'm afraid I've just realized I can't make the Wednesday. Can we move the meeting back to Thursday?

Elena OK … yes, the afternoon is free.

Sergio Great – there's a train that arrives at 12.30. So after lunch? At 2.00?

Elena OK. Two o'clock then.

Sergio Thank you. Sorry about that, I have an extra meeting on the Wednesday.

Elena No problem. See you then.

Sergio OK, thanks. Bye.

Elena Bye.

23

Conversation 1

A Sorry for calling so late.

B Don't worry – I don't usually finish before 7.00.

Conversation 2

A How are things?

B Everything's going fine, thanks.

Conversation 3

A Is this a busy time for you?

B No, I'm not too busy at the moment.

Conversation 4

A What's the weather like?

B It's really beautiful and clear.

Conversation 5

A Hello, Anna. This is James.

B Hello. How are you?

24

1 We're coming to Switzerland next month.

2 Customers often comment on this.

3 I'm calling for some information.

4 My trip begins on the 30th of January.

Unit 6

25

Interviewer Can I ask why you have come to Seville?

Traveller 1 Actually, I'm on a research trip. I'm looking for somewhere to hold our next European conference.

Interviewer Oh, really? So, what does that involve?

Traveller 1 Well, visiting different venues, you know, hotels and exhibition centres that could host a big event, and looking at their facilities. I also need to find out about the entertainment a city like Seville can offer – opportunities for sightseeing, the nightlife …

Interviewer Oh, the nightlife is very good – there are lots of restaurants and bars. And where are you staying?

Traveller 1 At the Patio. It's a small family hotel in the centre, opposite the cathedral.

Interviewer Yes, I know it, it's a very nice place. It's very well known for its hospitality.

Traveller 1 That's good.

Interviewer So, is it all business, or will there be time for pleasure?

Traveller 1 Well, a little bit of both, I hope. If I have time, I'll maybe go on an excursion to Cordoba. I'd also like to try some local specialities in the restaurants, and to do some shopping and buy a few souvenirs too.

26

Interviewer Excuse me, can I ask you, is this your first time in Seville?

Traveller 2 Yes, it is.

Interviewer And are you here on business or for pleasure?

Traveller 2 Well, I'm here for a trade exhibition, but I hope to have some time to look around, you know, enjoy the sights.

Interviewer Can I ask where you are staying?

Traveller 2 At the Hotel Doña María.

Interviewer Oh, that's very nice, very central. How are you getting there?

Traveller 2 I'm waiting for a colleague to pick me up in his car. He's going to drop me off at my hotel on his way to the exhibition centre.

Interviewer Do you have any plans for the evening?

Traveller 2 Well, I'd like to go to the hotel first and check in.

Interviewer Of course … You've had a long journey?

Traveller 2 Yes, I want to freshen up, have a drink, then probably go out for a meal.

Interviewer Do you have somewhere in mind, or …?

Traveller 2 Well, I'm meeting up with a couple of Spanish colleagues. They're going to show me around the old town. And after that, I guess we'll eat out somewhere … Oh, this looks like my ride.

Interviewer Well, have a good time.

Traveller 2 Thank you, I will. Nice talking to you.

27

Marvin Hello, I'm Marvin Bernstein. I have an appointment with Jacinta Ross.

Jacinta Hi, I'm Jacinta. Welcome to our new facility.

Marvin Thank you. It's nice to be here.

Jacinta It's nice to finally meet you in person.

Marvin Likewise.

Jacinta So how was your journey?

Marvin It was fine, there was quite a lot of traffic.

Jacinta Ah. And did you have any trouble finding us?

Marvin No, not at all, your directions were excellent.

Jacinta I'm glad to hear it. Here, let me take your coat.

Marvin Uh, that's OK. I'll hang on to it if you don't mind.

Jacinta Of course not. Uh, can I get you a coffee, or would you like to freshen up a bit?

Marvin A coffee sounds nice.

Jacinta OK. Come this way and I'll run through today's programme. Here you are. Have a seat.

Marvin Thanks.

Jacinta So, first of all, I thought you could join a tour of the facility this morning. Aruna Singh is showing some people around. Then, we'll catch up again at lunchtime, and after that, I'll introduce you to the team.

Marvin And will I be seeing Dilip Patel today?

Jacinta He's introducing the tour this morning, but you'll get a chance to meet up with him over lunch.

Marvin Great.

Jacinta Now, remember, you'll need this ID card to get around the site. Make sure you keep it on you at all times.

Marvin No problem. And what about my car? Am I allowed to leave it in the staff car park?

Jacinta Yes. Don't worry about that. I'll clear it with Facilities. What's your registration number?

Marvin It's …

28

Dilip Good morning everyone. My name is Dilip Patel, and I am the Head of Public Relations. On behalf of JJP Electronics, it gives me great pleasure to welcome you to our facility. We're going to begin with a guided tour. Afterwards, you will have the opportunity to meet our engineers over lunch. I'd now like to introduce you to Aruna Singh who is going to show you around the plant. Before I hand you over to Aruna, can I remind you that this is a working factory. So for your own safety, please be sure to stay with her at all times. May I wish you all an enjoyable and instructive visit.

Aruna Thank you, Dilip. Good morning, everyone. If you'd like to follow me, we'll begin the tour.

29

Conversation 1

A Would you like a drink?

B No thanks, I'm fine.

Conversation 2

A Do you fancy a drink?

B That would be great, thanks.

Conversation 3

A Would you like a drink?

B Yes, please. A coffee would be nice.

Conversation 4

A Can I get you a drink?

B A drink sounds good.

Conversation 5

A Do you fancy a drink?

B I'd love one.

Conversation 6

A Do you want a drink?

B I'm afraid I don't have time.

30

Aruna We're now standing outside the clean room. This is where we assemble the units. It's called a clean room because it has to be completely dust-free – dust is our biggest enemy. If dust gets into a unit, it can destroy the unit.

Visitor 1 Are we allowed to go inside?

Aruna Yes, of course. Everyone entering the clean room has to wear one of these special overalls made of synthetic materials – we call this a bunny suit. You also have to wear a helmet and an air-filter mask.

Visitor 1 Is it dangerous?

Aruna No, you don't need to worry. This is to protect the units from you.

Visitor 2 Do we have to get undressed?

Aruna No, you don't have to undress. You wear the bunny suit over your street clothes. You mustn't wear any natural fibres because of the particles they produce.

Visitor 2 So no wool or cotton?

Aruna That's right. You're not supposed to wear jewellery or watches either. We need to follow a very strict procedure for putting on the bunny suits. So, if you'd like to come this way …

Unit 7

31

Extract 1

A OK, everyone. What I want to do today, is to explain the new security procedures. I'll talk about the background to the situation, then I'll run through the principal changes. As you know, we've recently been having a few problems with people just walking in off the street. Up to now, no one has stolen anything, but we obviously need to safeguard against that happening. Er, because of this, we've decided to upgrade the system. So, first I'd like to update you on the plans for changes to security procedures around the building …

Extract 2

A … So, as a result, we've been installing these electronic boxes on all the entrances around the building over the last few weeks. These are for a new swipe card system that will come into operation at the end of the month.

B Sorry, but what's the reason for changing the current system? How long has Security been having a problem with the system of badges?

A For quite a while, I'm afraid. We've had three incidents reported since the beginning of the month. It's because security can't always check everyone's badge when they come in. By swiping these cards through these electronic readers on every door, we can check a person's identity anywhere in the building.

C Sorry, but I don't quite understand how they work. Can you tell us more about them?

A Mm. When you come to a door, you just swipe the card through this box at the side, and it opens.

B Do you mean that we have to swipe every time we want to go through a door?

A I'm afraid so, but the current situation, as it stands, simply doesn't prevent people from entering your office. By checking for identity at all the main doors, we hope to solve the problem, or at least make it safer.

32

Conversation 1

A Have you heard the news?

B No. What's happened?

A John has been fired.

B You're kidding!

Conversation 2

A I've just heard something really interesting.

B What?

A Apparently we're all getting a bonus this year.

Conversation 3

A You shouldn't go on the Internet too much. The IT Department monitors our PC use.

B Really? I've never heard that before.

A Oh, yeah, they check how much time we spend on it.

B How long have you known about that?

A Since I started here.

Conversation 4

A Guess what I've just seen?

B What?

A They're advertising for a new Accounts Manager.

B That's great. Why don't you apply for it?

Unit 8

33

Harriet OK, so this is Geri. Let's have a look at her responses.

Conrad OK, then. Statement one. She disagrees with that. That's good, isn't it? I mean, we want someone who takes responsibility for their own work.

Harriet Mm, yeah, absolutely. And two. She put 'agree'. That's rather worrying – we want someone who's a team player, and who can work closely with other people.

Conrad Yes, but even team players have to work on their own.

Harriet Yes, but she will have to join forces with other people quite regularly. I just wonder if she'll cope with that. Anyway, what about three? She put 'agree'. For me that's a good answer – she recognizes the importance of people having complementary skills.

Conrad Yes, I agree with you. Number four? Oh, 'agree' again. That's not so good.

Harriet No, not good at all – especially as our department is about finding common ground between people and forming alliances. It's definitely not about one side winning.

Conrad Do you think she wants to show us she's competitive? I mean, everyone knows that for a joint venture to work well it has to be of mutual benefit.

Harriet Um, so they can achieve their shared goals. Yes, maybe. Let's look at the last two, shall we? So, five, she agrees with that, that's good.

Conrad So she's open to suggestions.

Harriet And six? She put 'agree'. Maybe she has problems trusting her colleagues. I'm not too happy about that.

Conrad Um, me neither. I think we should address this point in the interview …

34

Carmen Now our aim is to make the move as smooth as possible. What's happening with the office space, Erica?

Erica Well, everything is going according to plan. We expect to be ready on schedule.

Carmen That's great. Where are we with the revised department structure?

Dieter That's under control too. We just need to put in the finishing touches.

Carmen Fantastic. Great work, everyone. Now, Nikos, tell us about your plans.

Nikos Thanks, Carmen. Well, as we know, a lot of mergers are unsuccessful because of a 'two-camps' mentality. .

Dieter To a certain extent this is inevitable.

Nikos Yes, but we hope to reduce problems to a minimum.

Carmen I agree. So where does this leave us?

Nikos Well, over the next few weeks, I plan to hold a series of small meetings, say over coffee, where people can meet informally and develop a relationship.

Erica That's a good idea. They'll get to know each other before working together. How long will it take to involve all the staff?

Nikos Well, I intend to have seven or eight sessions.

Carmen What's the timescale on this?

Nikos To involve everyone? By the end of next month.

Carmen Mm. So, what's the next step?

Nikos Well, before I can finalize the arrangements, I need a list of Buckler's key people.

Erica I'll prepare a list this afternoon.

Nikos Great. Then we can liaise, and we should have a schedule by Tuesday.

Carmen Good. We're also going to organize a big event for everybody. I'd like it to be fun, so if anyone has any ideas, I would be extremely grateful.

Dieter Perhaps Nikos and I could work on this together.

Carmen That's an excellent idea. Anyway, let's not forget that it is likely that there'll be a few problems in the short term, but the chances are there

won't be too many personality clashes in the long run. I'm confident that with careful handling the process will be pretty smooth.

35

1

I had a look at your report. It's very well written – well done.

2

A What do think of this design?

B Hmm, it's a start. What do the other team members think?

3

That's pretty much finished now. Great work, everyone.

4

A How about if we freelance this out? It'll give us more time.

B That's an excellent idea. Do you want to try and find a freelancer?

5

A I have an idea – we could join forces with the Antwerp team.

B That has potential. I'd like to look at other options first, though.

CD 2

Unit 9

36

Interviewer You're an independent computer manufacturer. That's right, isn't it?

Steve Yes, that's right. We make up machines to our customers' specifications.

Interviewer So you're a bit like Dell, then?

Steve If only! We're tiny by comparison. But we believe that customers like the personal touch. We can spend a lot of time discussing their needs and the type of machine they need. And if there's a problem, they don't have to send the machine away, they just come to the shop. Of course, we don't have Dell's advantages – that is, in terms of their suppliers – so we have to keep a lot of components in stock.

Interviewer How do you make sure that you don't run out?

Steve Well, everything has its own bar code which shows up on the database.

It tells us what we have left, if it's on order, and so on – see?

Interviewer Right. Obviously you never want to run out of basic items.

Steve That's right – it's really not good to be out of stock.

Interviewer So, does the database automatically place an order if you're running low on something?

Steve No, it just warns us we're low on stock. You don't want to stock up on components which are going to become obsolete.

Interviewer OK. Now, a lot of your components come from Asia, don't they?

Steve That's right. We generally have them sent by an international courier.

Interviewer So, do you take advantage of the tracking facility?

Steve It depends, really. I mean, if something's not particularly urgent, then I don't bother. But if there's an essential package, I keep track of it very closely.

37

Linda Composource. Linda speaking. How can I help?

Gisele Good morning. My name is Gisele Kern from Abracomp in Germany. I'm following up an order I placed two weeks ago. I'd like to find out what has happened to it.

Linda I see. Can I take your account details?

Gisele Yes, the account reference is PG 278.

Linda I'm sorry, was that BJ?

Gisele No, P for Peter, G for George.

Linda OK, thanks. If you'll bear with me a moment, I'll call up your details. Let me see … So, when did you place the order?

Gisele On the 11th of February.

Linda Right, I've got it here. It was a repeat order for 2,000 motherboards. We put it straight through to our warehouse. According to my information, it was dispatched that afternoon.

Gisele Something must have gone wrong, because we haven't received them. I'm not happy about this at all. Could you check it out for me?

Linda Certainly, I'll look into it immediately. Would you like me to call you back, or will you hold while I contact the warehouse?

Gisele I think I'd better hold, because this is a real problem for me. I need this to be sorted out as soon as possible.

Linda I'll be as quick as I can.

Gisele Thanks. I really want to know what's happened to it.

38

1 This is the Human Resources Department. I'm afraid we are unable to answer the phone at the moment, but please leave your message and a contact number, and we will call you back.

2 The office is closed from 6 p.m. until 8 a.m. Please call back during office hours.

3 All our lines are busy at the moment. Please hold and we will try to connect you as soon as possible.

39

Hi, this is María José Fernández. It's four o'clock on Monday the 12th. I was just calling about your order. I have a few questions to ask you. Could you please call me back? You can reach me on 07892 159753. Thanks.

40

Linda Hello, Ms Kern?

Gisele Yes. Still here.

Linda Sorry about the delay.

Gisele That's OK. So, have you found out about my order?

Linda Yes, I asked the warehouse to check what had happened to it. They told me it had gone two weeks ago.

Gisele Two weeks ago? Wait a moment, how did they send it?

Linda They said they'd sent it by sea.

Gisele By sea! But I always get my orders by international courier. I'm sure I told them to send it by courier when I placed the order.

Linda Let me look. Well you said asap, which I guess is by courier.

Gisele So where is it now?

Linda Well, I asked if they knew where it was. They said in a container in the ocean somewhere.

Gisele OK ... Well, in that case, can you send me four hundred by courier? I need them urgently.

Linda Yes, of course. I'll deal with it immediately and get back to you within the hour. I'm very sorry about this.

41

Gisele You are through to Gisele Kern's voicemail. I'm not at my desk right now, so please leave a message after the beep.

Linda Ms Kern. It's Linda from Composource, calling at 3.30. I'm calling about the details of your order. We have sent four hundred motherboards by courier today, the 26th of February. I told the courier to mark it top priority. They should be with you in two days. The reference number is HA 9872367, so you'll be able to track the parcel's progress. Once again, I'm very sorry for the problem with the original order. If you have any further problems, please don't hesitate to call me.

Unit 10

42

1 I can't believe it. Your new offices are really amazing. In your old headquarters you couldn't move for people and furniture, but this is great. It's all very well-designed.

2 Wow, I can see what you mean about this factory. All the machines are fairly old, and the building looks like it's going to fall down. Everyone is extremely motivated, though.

3 It's not exactly state-of-the-art and the offices are not very modern, but this is a pretty successful company, so they must be doing something right.

43

Manager OK. So that's the plan for the main offices. I really like it. Now, there's just one other thing. What about the idea of a crèche and relaxation area?

Architect Well, it might prove difficult to have both. I'm afraid there isn't much space for both of them.

Manager OK. Well, I think we should consider having the crèche first. Besides, I have a few reservations about having an 'Anarchy Zone'!

Architect You might be better off without it if employees spend too long in there!

Manager Exactly. I'd rather not have it.

Architect Well, just say the architect said it wasn't possible.

Manager Good idea. So where can we put the crèche? We thought about ... here, next to the canteen.

Architect Sorry, but I don't think that would work. I'd recommend putting it here – in this area behind reception. Then employees can leave their children as they arrive. And also, it's quite a long way from the factory area, which is good for health and safety.

Manager Great!

44

1 There isn't much space in them to put personal belongings. And when I get changed, they don't hold any clothes. Perhaps if we had a few shelves, it might help.

2 It would be a great idea to have some running machines, or perhaps even a sauna? I suppose the only problem is that a lot of employees only have a little time after work for exercise so it might not be worth it.

3 There aren't many places in the factory to relax. There are a few chairs in that room, but only a few people use it because it's always so hot, and so messy. Why not turn it into a room with a TV or music?

Unit 11

45

Interviewer What's your company like, Franz?

Franz Well, it's a large company. We're a major car manufacturer.

Interviewer And how are decisions made?

Franz Well, in a traditional way, I would say. Senior managers make decisions and expect everyone else to follow.

Interviewer With no consultation?

Franz Not really. Not what I would call consultation.

Interviewer So what happens if the workforce doesn't agree?

Franz Well, the union is quite strong, so it can give the workers' point of view.

Interviewer And does this lead to strikes?

Franz No, not very often. Generally, everyone tries to avoid confrontation. Both sides make concessions and they reach some kind of compromise, you know, a consensus which is more or less acceptable to everyone.

46

Interviewer So, Stella, how are decisions made?

Stella Well, we're organized on democratic principles – no one's in charge and there's no hierarchy. We have regular meetings where we brainstorm ideas. You know, we work together and generate lots of different ideas and suggestions – everybody has the right to put forward ideas and proposals. Then we examine the options in detail and decide which one should get our backing.

Interviewer So if the majority's in favour of it, then it goes ahead?

Stella Not exactly. We'll only go for something if there's a two-thirds majority.

Interviewer And is it successful?

Stella We like it, it works for us. I'm always happier carrying out a decision in which I've had some sort of say.

47

Aidan Basically, a lot more people are involved in the decision-making process. It usually starts with middle managers who put forward an idea for something.

Interviewer What, like a change they'd like to introduce?

Aidan Yes. And, what they do is they produce a document which goes to everyone who might have a say. As the document is passed around, people express their opinions, or make suggestions until they reach a consensus.

Interviewer Right.

Aidan And eventually it moves up the management spiral to senior managers who carefully evaluate the ideas in the document before making a final decision.

Interviewer So, it's quite a long process.

Aidan True, it does take a lot of time, but the big advantage is that we can carry out major decisions and avoid confrontation at the same time. We also avoid a lot of the problems which happen when you make up your mind too quickly.

48

Extract 1

Stefan Personally, I think we should look seriously at this opportunity. We need to think about expanding.

Ilse Yeah, I agree with you, Stefan. If we move out of town, we'll have room to expand, and parking will be easier.

Patrick Yes, but come on, Ilse, most of our customers are students. They won't be able to get to the shopping centre unless they have a car.

Stefan I hear what you're saying, Patrick. All the same, don't forget the others who do drive. Let's face it, parking is impossible around here …

Extract 2

Stefan … Well, here's an idea. What if we kept the shop here and opened up in the shopping centre? We could have the best of both worlds.

Ilse Yes, that's a nice idea, but we don't have the financial resources to do both.

Stefan The thing is, if we wait too long, the best locations in the centre will be taken.

Patrick I'm not convinced. As far as I'm concerned, it's far too risky. I think we should wait and see who else is moving there.

Ilse OK, Patrick, I take your point. But you know, according to newspaper reports, the new centre will be like a magnet for big retailers, so we need to make up our minds quickly …

Extract 3

Stefan … OK, so if I've understood you correctly, Patrick, you think we should just wait and see. So, where do we go from here?

Ilse Well, to be honest, I don't think we can reach a decision today. I think we need to talk to a consultant and get some expert advice. Why don't we contact Jeff Arnold?

Patrick Yes, that's a good idea. Mind you, I don't think he's ever played a computer game in his life.

Stefan You're right. There again, he does have years of experience … So are we all agreed, then? We contact Jeff?

Ilse Yeah, that's fine with me.

Patrick Me too.

49

1 Yes, but come on, Ilse, most of our customers are students.

2 Let's face it, parking is impossible around here …

3 The thing is, if we wait too long, the best locations in the centre will be taken.

4 Well, to be honest, I don't think we can reach a decision today.

Unit 12

50

Conversation 1

A I have a good job with a good income, and my employer is fine – a bit traditional, but they've always been very reliable. But I really need a change. I want a job that's … well, more exciting and more dynamic.

B Maybe you need to come at this differently.

A How do you mean?

B Well, why not try to make the company you work for a bit more up to date? Make it the kind of place you really want to work in …

Conversation 2

A Hello. Sorry, what's your name? I can't read your badge.

B It's William.

A Hi, William. What's your question?

B Well, I've come up with a revolutionary idea for cleaning the house, but I want to know how I can sell it.

A That's interesting. I'm in the sales business. What's your product?

B Well, it's a prototype at the moment. But it's a sophisticated piece of technology that allows you to monitor the level of dirt in the home. It all came about when I was cleaning the carpets one day …

Conversation 3

A Well, I've always wanted to start my own business, but I always come to the conclusion that I can't do it.

B What kind of business were you thinking of?

A Well, I had this idea the other day when I came across an article in the paper. It's simple really – and not very original – but this person had started a home-catering company from their own kitchen – you know, cooking for dinner parties or preparing buffets at weddings. That kind of thing. The article said there's a lot of money in it.

B It's funny, but I think I read the same thing. I even said to my husband I should do something like that.

A Really?

51

PR Manager Good morning, everyone, and thanks for coming. We have a lot to do, so let's start. I'd like to begin by explaining the basic concept behind the meeting this morning. First, I'm going to talk for a few minutes about where this company is. Then, we'll try to define how we want our customers, clients, and even our competitors to view Bertran RL. And finally, after coffee, we'll try to come up with a mission statement. OK? Great. Oh, and please feel free to ask questions whenever you want.

52

PR Manager Right. First of all, let's look at this slide. As you can see, it has a number of words that describe our company. These are answers from some of our oldest and newest customers to the question, 'What words describe Bertran RL?'. You'll notice that some words are in blue and some are in red. So, which words do you think represent the views of our oldest customers? Which ones are the most satisfied with our products?

53

PR Manager OK. That's everything I want to say for the moment. Thank you all for listening. Now it's your turn to do some talking. The main reason for this meeting is to try and create a new, innovative company mission statement. But before I ask you to brainstorm for a while in small groups, are there any questions? Yes, Rudi.

Rudi Sorry, but do you think that a mission statement is very useful? I know lots of companies with a mission statement saying how innovative they are – the employees even have them on notices around the offices. But no one can tell you what it is or even what it means.

PR Manager Good question, and I know what you mean. But we think it's a good idea because Bertran RL isn't just a small family business any more – we're enjoying the fastest growth we've ever known. We are now the second biggest technology company in the region, which is great, but it also means we need everyone in the company and all our new customers to know who we are and what we represent.

54

A So that brings me to the end of my presentation. Are there any questions?

B Yes. You gave us some projections for the next five years, but what about the figures for after that?

A Can I get back to you on that one? I'll need to check the data when I'm back in my office. I'll email you, if that's OK. Any other questions?

C Don't you think our customers might disappear in the next few years, because of the current situation?

A Sorry, I don't think I follow you. What situation are you talking about?

C The environmental situation. Surely we'll lose a lot of our customer base because we aren't in line with environmental guidelines.

A Yes, I know what you mean, but this is why we are trying to deal with this problem now.

Unit 13

55

Conversation 1

Ruth Hi, Magda. What's the matter?

Magda It's this report. I just can't do it.

Ruth Why? Is it too difficult?

Magda No, it's not that. I just don't have enough time. My boss keeps on giving me extra work and I don't know when I'll be able to do it all.

Ruth What do you mean by 'extra work'?

Magda Well, she gives me things to do on top of my normal workload, and I can't manage it all. What shall I do?

Ruth Well, it looks like you have a communication problem to me. Have you tried talking to her? She might not even know that you're too busy.

Madga No I haven't.

Ruth Well, I'd ask to speak to her if I were you. She needs to know you feel overworked.

Magda OK. But in the meantime, what about this report?

Ruth Well, if you really don't have enough time, I think you should ask for an extension on the deadline. That should sort it out temporarily. But you have to get it approved by management first. It's easy enough to do – there's a simple form to fill out. I'll email it to you.

Magda Thanks, Ruth.

Conversation 2

Help desk Good afternoon. How can I help?

Customer It's my laptop. It keeps on going wrong all the time.

Help desk OK. What's wrong with it exactly?

Customer Well, it's always crashing and it won't remember the time or the date. It's so frustrating. Until now it's been completely reliable.

Help desk When you say 'it's always crashing', do you mean it actually switches off, or does it freeze?

Customer It switches off after about twenty minutes.

Help desk Well, it sounds as though it could be a battery problem. How old is the laptop?

Customer I've had it about three and a half years.

Help desk Well, basically, you could just use the electrical lead, but the best thing would be to buy a new battery. That should fix it.

Customer OK. How much would that cost?

56

Conversation 1

A Communication has become a nightmare. Do you know what I mean? It just isn't working.

B Absolutely. It's a real problem. We'll have to discuss this seriously at the next meeting.

Conversation 2

A … Then, all you have to do is fill in this form and pass it to Joanna. Then she'll report the incident and you just have to wait for further instructions. Does that make sense?

B Kind of, but could you explain the first part again?

Conversation 3

A It sounds as though you've got a mains problem. You'll need to switch everything off, then reboot remotely, before you try to perform the function again. Is that clear?

B I don't get why I have to switch everything off.

Conversation 4

A I think the best thing would be to speak to the manager. It sounds as though this won't get solved on its own. If you tell management, at least they'll be aware of the problem, do you see?

B Yes, I see what you mean. I just don't feel comfortable doing that.

Unit 14

57

Karl … So, that's all I want to say for the moment. Thank you very much for listening. Are there any questions?

Participant Yes. I understand that you can make the biodiesel fuel out of the jatropha plant but can you explain the exact process? I mean, is it very complex?

Karl OK, thanks for your question. Actually, the basic procedure is fairly simple and has been possible for some time, but it's only in recent years that it's become economical. Essentially, there are two main stages: growing and processing. First of all, jatropha plants can be grown in hot climates and on poor land, so they are easier and cheaper to grow than many other types of vegetable biodiesel crops. When you are ready to harvest them, trucks pick up the seeds. Having brought the seeds to the refinery, you feed them into a grinder. Essentially, conversion to biodiesel is a one-stage process. Once the oil is taken out of the seeds – extracted – you're ready to mix it and heat it with methanol. Finally, you have a very good quality fuel and you can put it into any transport vehicle. And you also have a diesel engine which produces about half the CO_2 emissions of a normal diesel engine.

58

Anton Excuse me. Can I interrupt you for a second?

Karl Of course.

Anton I enjoyed your talk. It was very interesting.

Karl Thank you. I'm glad you could come.

Anton In fact, I represent a group of investors who are very interested in your proposal for a new refinery. I'd like to invite you to Moscow.

Karl That would be great.

Anton My name is Anton Golovkov. Would you like to join me for a drink?

Karl I'd love to, but I'm afraid I have another appointment right now. Do you have a card? How about if I call you next week?

Anton Yes. Here you are – you have my number on the card. And in the meantime, I'll talk to my colleagues about jatropha seeds.

59

Anton Hello. Anton Golovkov speaking.

Karl Hello, Mr Golovkov. This is Karl Kirstler speaking. You came to my presentation last week.

Anton Yes, of course. I haven't forgotten.

Karl Is this a good time to call?

Anton Yes. Go ahead.

Karl Well, I was wondering if you were still interested in my company's proposals?

Anton Yes, I am, and I know I invited you to come and meet us, but there's been a slight change of plan which means we might have to wait for a while.

Karl Oh, I'm sorry to hear that. But you're still interested?

Anton Er, well, some of my colleagues want to wait because they are also interested in other types of biofuels. As a result, we won't be able to give you a date at this stage.

Karl I understand. These things happen, but it's a shame that we can't meet soon because the project has received a lot of interest from a number of other investors …

60

Good morning, and thanks for coming. Today, I'd like to talk about how business is really done. Well, for most of us, business is done through networking and meeting people. That means we tend to do business with people we like and trust. So the next time you attend a conference or you're going out to dinner with a new client, it's important to remember that a contract, or a job, can be won or lost on first impressions and clever networking. One important thing is to find out in advance about other people. If you've been invited out to a business dinner, you need to know who else is going and what they do. Also, think of things to say and ways to start the conversation. So a phrase like, 'Hello, I was given your name by a colleague' is a useful opening because it means you have a connection – you can talk about the person you both know and this will lead on to other areas of interest. If there's someone you really want to meet, then try to be introduced by someone else, rather than meeting them 'cold'. Something else to remember is …

61

1 Business is done through networking and meeting people.
2 A contract, or a job, can be won or lost on first impressions.
3 If you've been invited out to a business dinner, …
4 Hello, I was given your name by a colleague …
5 Try to be introduced by someone else.

Unit 15

62

Appraiser Come in, Chris. Take a seat. Coffee?

Chris No, I'm OK, thanks.

Appraiser OK. Now, I have the forms you filled in here. Thanks for getting them in on time. As you know, the main aim of this meeting is to appraise your performance and set some goals for the next six months. So, we'll begin by discussing your comments and then we'll start setting some objectives. I'll also be adding a few notes on the form. OK?

Chris Sure.

Appraiser I would like to say before we begin that in general, we're very pleased with your performance. You seem to be doing very well.

Chris Well, that's good to know.

Appraiser I know there had been a few problems at the other factory before you moved here, but in the last six months, I've received lots of good reports about all your hard work.

Chris Oh, good. That's nice to hear. I was finding it all a little difficult when I first came to work here, but it's easier now.

Appraiser Great. Now, one thing I wanted to discuss was this on your form. You mention solving problems with machinery. Is this something you like or dislike, and is it an area you'd like to develop?

Chris Yes, it's something I like. I like challenges.

Appraiser OK, good. So, is there anything you don't like about the job?

Chris No, not really.

Appraiser No?

Chris Well, I think maybe we have too many meetings. And I like it when I'm given a job and can get on with it.

Appraiser How do you feel about working with other people?

Chris It's OK, but I think I'm someone who likes working alone. I think maybe that's something I need to work on.

Appraiser Right, now …

63

Appraiser … So, let's summarize what we've agreed. You're interested in more technical training, so one thing I'm going to do is speak to the Head of Engineering about the possibilities.

Chris That sounds good.

Appraiser And one thing you're going to do is look at the questionnaire I've given you on teams and team working. Is that OK with you?

Chris Yes. Fine.

Appraiser Now, is there anything else you'd like to add? We've still got five minutes.

Chris No, I don't think so …

64

Supervisor Hi, Chris. You're doing well.

Chris Oh, thanks. I'm about halfway through.

Supervisor And how are you getting on with the new type of shaft?

Chris Not bad. I had to adjust the machines a little, but they're fine.

Supervisor Oh, that's great. You've done a good job.

Chris Just one thing. I found a fault in one of the shafts.

Supervisor Really?

Chris Look. Just here.

Supervisor This could be serious. I'd better send this over to R&D. Well done for spotting it.

Chris Do you want me to continue?

Supervisor Sure. Keep at it for the moment and I'll let you know what they say.

65

Supervisor Chris. Have you finished yet?

Chris I'm about halfway through.

Supervisor Only halfway?

Chris Well, I had to adjust the machines for this new type of shaft.

Supervisor Oh, I see.

Chris Sorry, there's one other thing. I found a fault in one of the shafts.

Supervisor Where?

Chris Look. Just here.

Supervisor Why didn't you tell me straight away? This is really serious. I'd better send this over to R&D.

Chris Do you want me to continue?

Supervisor No. Stop. Don't touch anything.

66

1

Helena I was working for a large food company which didn't employ many women. At my first performance appraisal the Production Manager told me that if I didn't work as part of a team, I'd never get on in the company. It was terrible to hear this, because I had already discussed with him how difficult it was to be the only woman. Anyway, as it turned out, he was wrong, because six months later, I was transferred to another subsidiary and six months after that, I was running the factory!

2

Matthias One reason I left my last company was because of a performance review I'd had with our HR Manager. We were talking about the usual things, but during all of this, he answered the phone twice and even replied to an email. This annoyed me because I had prepared very thoroughly for this appraisal. Then at the end, he handed me a typed review and asked me to sign it. I asked if I could take it out of the office to read it and he said 'No'. Anyway, I quickly read it and it didn't match our discussion. One thing was that he'd said I was doing really well, but the review said I would only get a three per cent raise. Some weeks later, I heard that he got fired, but I'd already left by then.

67

Media Training Associates was founded in 2000, and since then, we have helped improve the presentation skills of representatives from more than a hundred companies, including many in the FTSE-100.

There are many elements to an interesting presentation but if you can get these three right, then you're well on the way to making a good impression.

Firstly, know your audience. Don't just think about what you want to say – put yourself in their shoes and think about what they'll be interested in hearing. Don't assume knowledge – if the group is mixed, try to bring everyone up to speed by including a mixture of old and new facts. Anticipate any areas of conflict or disagreement and try to ensure you have dealt with these.

Secondly, have a clear structure. Three key points to illustrate your theme is ideal, with a strong beginning and ending. Give the audience a map – explain the point of your presentation, give them indications to where you are going and how you are going to get there.

And lastly, visual aids. Visual aids sometimes hinder instead of help. Slides should be kept simple, not packed with information, complicated diagrams, and bullet points. It's amazing how often people's words don't match the infomation on the slides. The audience ends up confused, and doesn't remember any of it.

68

Er … good morning and … er thanks … er … for coming. I'm going to tell … um … I'm going to tell you about some of our products. Er … this is the first one. Er … Croatian olive oil. As you know, it's … er … better than olive oil from other countries. And … er … we think it will be popular in the rest of Europe because … er … it's healthy. Oh … er … feel free to ask questions if you want. And I think families will buy it … er … for cooking. Er … and also we have paprenjak cakes … which um … are nice too. Thanks for listening. Are there any questions?

69

Good afternoon. It's very nice to be here and to have this opportunity to present some of our traditional Croatian food products to you. I will be talking briefly about our olive oil, and then I will present a Croatian speciality – paprenjak cakes. At the end of my presentation you will get a chance to try the products and I will be glad to take any questions.

…

So this is our olive oil. We all know about the health benefits of olive oil and this olive oil tastes fantastic. The quality is excellent because of the Croatian soil conditions and climate. We can also offer a competitive price, so I'm sure it will do well in Europe.

…

Now let me present a product that you might not know about. These are paprenjak cakes and they're traditional in Croatia. They're made using honey, walnuts and pepper. The combination of sweetness and pepper is delicious and it will definitely be something new and different for people to try.

…

So those are two of our most popular products. Some samples will be coming round now for you to taste. Are there any questions?

Unit 16

70

1 I suppose I feel a bit sorry for him. I'm sure he didn't expect it to be such an absolute flop. Everything went wrong from start to finish – it really was a total disaster. I didn't learn anything new and it was just so boring! I wish I hadn't gone. It was a complete waste of time.

2 They've worked really hard on this and finally it looks like they've made a significant breakthrough. Everyone is very excited about it and we are sure it's going to be a great success in the not-too-distant future.

3 What an amazing achievement! Nobody thought they'd be able to do it. It's hard to believe they managed to complete such a huge project in only six months. It's a real triumph.

71

Paul Welcome back, Olli. How was your trip to India?

Olli Oh, it could have gone better. If you have a few minutes, I'll fill you in on everything.

Paul Sure. So what were your overall impressions?

Olli Well, on the whole, I was impressed with the welcome Mr Rahman gave me, but I think we're wasting our time with them.

Paul Oh, really? What makes you say that?

Olli Well, their factory is incredibly chaotic and old-fashioned – they're still using equipment from twenty years ago. They really need to modernize.

Paul It's difficult to believe – they certainly don't give that impression. But at least there are no problems with communication.

Olli True, but that doesn't make up for everything else, believe me.

Paul I see. This underlines the importance of seeing the operation in place. And did you find out what the problems were with the last consignment?

Olli Yes, I managed to pinpoint some problems with the paperwork.

Paul So, what's your verdict? Should we continue with them?

Olli To tell you the truth, I think we should let the current contract run, and then look for someone else.

Paul Well, he won't be happy. What we need to do now is make sure that the rest of the orders are completed.

Olli We should focus on improving their systems.

Paul Yes, and perhaps review the situation in a couple of months if things improve.

72

Paul Hi Sandrine. Nice to see you back. How did it go in Vietnam?

Sandrine Fine. If you can spare me some time later today, I'll bring you up to date.

Paul I'm meeting some of our shop managers this afternoon, but I'm free at the moment – let's talk about it over coffee.

Sandrine Sounds great.

Paul So, give me an overview.

Sandrine Well, I was pleasantly surprised. I think that Mr Tran is an extremely good prospect.

Paul I'm glad to hear it. Tell me more.

Sandrine Well, the factory is small, but the business is really dynamic and efficient. They use modern equipment and skilled craftsmen – the furniture is of excellent quality. I'm sure that if we gave him the right kind of support, he could become even better.

Paul That's good to hear. Any communication problems?

Sandrine Well, a few. But with a mixture of French and English we succeeded in understanding each other.

Paul Hmm. OK, then. And did you make any other useful contacts?

Sandrine Yes. While I was travelling around, I came across some beautiful handicrafts. I made contact with a wholesaler and I've brought back some samples.

Paul Good, I look forward to seeing them. This highlights the need to build in time to have a look round.

Sandrine I agree. So where does this leave us with Mr Tran?

Paul Well, I think the next step is to get him over to visit us and show him our operation.

Sandrine Great. I'm going to speak to him in the next few days. I'll invite him then.

Paul Good. We need to concentrate particularly on developing our relationship and finding out more about him. Let's invite him over as soon as possible.

73

1 In general, I prefer to travel by train.

2 We mostly operate in the Far East.

3 I thought it was an excellent presentation overall.

4 Generally speaking, we don't work at weekends.

5 On the whole, it was a great trip.

6 We mainly communicate in English.

7 All in all, I was very happy with the way it went.

OXFORD

UNIVERSITY PRESS

Great Clarendon Street, Oxford OX2 6DP

Oxford University Press is a department of the University of Oxford.
It furthers the University's objective of excellence in research, scholarship,
and education by publishing worldwide in

Oxford New York

Auckland Cape Town Dar es Salaam Hong Kong Karachi
Kuala Lumpur Madrid Melbourne Mexico City Nairobi
New Delhi Shanghai Taipei Toronto

With offices in

Argentina Austria Brazil Chile Czech Republic France Greece
Guatemala Hungary Italy Japan Poland Portugal Singapore
South Korea Switzerland Thailand Turkey Ukraine Vietnam

OXFORD and OXFORD ENGLISH are registered trade marks of
Oxford University Press in the UK and in certain other countries

© Oxford University Press 2007

The moral rights of the author have been asserted

Database right Oxford University Press (maker)

First published 2007
2016 2015 2014 2013 2012
20 19 18 17 16 15 14 13

ISBN: 978 0 19 476801 6   (Book)
ISBN: 978 0 19 473939 9   (Pack)

Printed in China

This book is printed on paper from certified and well-managed sources.

ACKNOWLEDGEMENTS

*The authors and publisher are grateful to those who have given permission to reproduce
the following extracts and adaptations of copyright material:*pp95, 158 Based on
information from www.mediatrainingassociates.co.uk. Reproduced by kind
permission of Media Training Associates.

Although every effort has been made to trace and contact copyright holders
before publication, this has not been possible in some cases. We apologize for
any apparent infringement of copyright and if notified, the publisher will be
pleased to rectify any errors or omissions at the earliest opportunity.

Illustrations by: Jasmin Chin/ Inkshed p 64, 142; Melvyn Evans p 66; Ned
Jolliffe p 55, 79, 82, 97; Willie Ryan/ Illustration pp 13, 37, 85

*We would also like to thank the following for permission to reproduce the following
photographs and copyright material:* Alamy pp 7 (supermarket checkout/David
Hancock), 19 (art gallery/Jeff Morgan/The Arts), 24 (laptop/graficart.net),
25 (music download/vario images GmbH & Co.KG), (mobile TV/David
Hancock), (online purchase/Steve Hamblin), (creche/Picture Partners), 42
(security guard/J.R. Bale), (credit card/Konstantin Sutyagin), 44 (swipe card/
mediacolor's), 61 (Fallows Court/Mark Boulton), (High Towers/Bilderbox),
(Watson's Wharf/Jon Arnold Images), 63 (open plan office/Chris Gascoigne/
VIEW Pictures Ltd), (separate offices/Jan Caudron /Anaklasis), 65 (cyclist/
Photofusion Picture Library), 78 (milk/Agripicture Images), 95 (olive oil/
A Room With Views), 96 (ties/David Trevor), 101 (tea picking/David Pearson);
Axiom Photographic Agency pp 6 (underground entrance/Alberto Arzoz),
72 (domes/Jon Spaull); Corbis pp 12 (scaffolding/Construction Photography),
(volunteers/C. Devan/zefa), 17 (Disc jockey/Harry Vorsteher/zefa), 19 (climber/
Eric Perlman), 20 (Shine Pictures/zefa), 24 (warehouse/Roger Ball), 47
(laptop/B. Pepone/zefa), 48 (operating theatre/Bernardo Bucci), (sailing/Henrik
Trygg), 54 (port/Jürgen Effner/dpa), (Dell assembly/Ed Kashi), 59 (warehouse/
Walter Hodges), 78 (pipeline repair/Karen Kasmauski), 83 (weaver/Diego
Lezama Orezzoli), 125 (LWA-Dann Tardif); Getty Images pp 6 (Ed Lu/Alexander
Nemenov/AFP), 7 (pilot/David Frazier), 8 (Romilly Lockyer), 18 (swimming/
Bryce Duffy), (office at night/Seth Joel), 19 (cyclist/John Terence Turner), 25
(courier/Kai-Uwe Knoth/AFP), 36 (Miguel Medina/AFP), 38 (Hitoshi Nishimura),
41 (Axiom Photographic Agency/Giles Caldicott), 44 (key/Peter Dazeley),
48 (Red Cross/Scott Peterson), 71 (call centre/William Thomas Cain), 72
(Breakthrough cafe/Romilly Lockyer), 80 (Allison Michael Orenstein), 84
(Lester Lefkowitz), 89 (check-in/Daly & Newton), 96 (David Hecker/AFP), (tyre/
David Paul Morris), (shampoo/Vincent Besnault), 136 (Macduff Everton); PA
Photos p 60 (table football/John Cogill/AP); Photolibrary.com pp 78 (toaster/
Charlie Abad), 98 (Rene Mattes); Punchstock pp 6 (International Space
Station/The Stocktrek Corp/Jupiter Images/Brand X), 7 (Ingrid/Louis Fox/
Digital Vision), (Mansour/Jon Feingersh/Blend Images), (teacher/George
Doyle/Stockbyte), 11 (pixland), 14 (image100), 23 (Image Source Pink), 25
(canteen/Digital Vision), 26 (pixland), 29 (cyclist/Digital Vision), 30 (tailor/
Blend Images), 32 (Corbis Premium Collection), 35 (Blend Images), 36
(Digital Vision), 42 (CCTV/Digital Vision), 44 (ID badge check /Beathan), 44
(Push-button door/James Lauritz/Digital Vision), 48 (chef/Banana Stock), 50
(ImageShop), 53 (meeting/Jupiter Images/Comstock Premium), 56 (Corbis
RF), 62 (O'Brien Productions), 66 (mountaineer/Digital Vision), 68 (Comstock),
74 (Tony Weller/Photodisc), 78 (shirts/Corbis Collection), 86 (moodboard),
90 (Brooke Fasani), 92 (Digital Vision), 106 (Tim Pannell); Reuters pp 77
(Alessandro Bianchi), 90 (National Ballet of Cuba/Claudia Daut); Rex Features
pp 30 (Technogym/Chris Gascoigne / View Pictures), 60 (VW factory/Sipa
Press); Science Photo Library p 84 (Colin Cuthbert); Still Pictures p 84 (Joerg
Boethling).

Images sourced by: Pictureresearch.co.uk

Cover photo by: Chris King

Photos on p5 courtesy of Cranfield School of Management

*The authors and publisher would also like to thank the following individuals for their
advice and assistance in developing the material for this course:* Lucy Adam, Pat
Allan, Kate Baade, Hannah Blanning, Jo Brook, Jayne Chivers, Allison Dupuis,
John Ferris, Joanne Fessler, Christopher Holloway, Zsofia Kocsardi, Alastair
Lane, David Massey, Susannah McKee, Penny McLarty, Jill Prewett, Paulina
Scheenberg, John Sydes, Susan Tesar.

The publisher would also like to thank the faculty, course participants, and
alumni of Cranfield School of Management who contributed so much to the
development of the course. Particular thanks are due to David Simmons,
Director of International Development, whose enthusiasm, generosity, and
persistence really have made all the difference.

Special thanks to Gail Pasque